Connie Mack's '29 Triumph

Connie Mack's '29 Triumph

The Rise and Fall of the Philadelphia Athletics Dynasty

by

WILLIAM C. KASHATUS

Foreword by Dave Kindred
Afterword by Ted Taylor

McFarland & Company, Inc., Publishers
Jefferson, North Carolina, and London

For Ken Farshtey,
an inspirational teacher-coach, old friend,
and Yankee diehard

Frontispiece: **Connie Mack and the 1929 Philadelphia Athletics (courtesy of the National Baseball Hall of Fame).**

British Library Cataloguing-in-Publication data are available

Library of Congress Cataloguing-in-Publication data are available

Library of Congress Catalog Card Number: 98-89555

ISBN 0-7864-0585-6 (case binding : 50# alkaline paper) ∞

Printed in the United States of America

McFarland & Company, Inc., Publishers
  Box 611, Jefferson, North Carolina 28640

ACKNOWLEDGMENTS

Writing about a team that dominated the national pastime thirty years before I was born was quite a challenge. None of the players were still alive when I began the enterprise. Thus, this book represents a collective effort. Ted Taylor, the president of the Philadelphia Athletics' Historical Society, and Dave Kindred of *The Sporting News* were willing to take the time to read and comment upon my work, as well as to contribute to it. Without their support, guidance, and constructive criticism, this book would never have been written. I am deeply obligated to both of them. Bruce Kuklick of the University of Pennsylvania also gave me the benefit of his knowledge of the old A's during the research phase of this project and, later, read and critiqued the manuscript, reminding me of my responsibilities as an historian.

I also relied on the children, grandchildren, friends and future teammates of the 1929–31 A's for their personal insight. To these people, I owe a tremendous debt of gratitude. They are Wayne Ambler, Rudolph Baizley, Joseph Barrett, Ruth Clark, Eddie Collins, Jr., Frank Cunningham, George Earnshaw, Jr., the Reverend John Evans, Carl Goldberg, Joe Hauser, Kathy Keim, Senator Connie Mack, James McAndrew, Rube Oldring, Jr., Shirley Povich, the Reverend Jerome Romanowski, and Louis Verna.

The staff of the National Baseball Library at Cooperstown, New

York, provided prompt, courteous, and indispensable assistance, especially Timothy Wiles and Milo Stewart. My thanks also go to the staffs of the Free Library of Philadelphia and Temple University's Urban Archives.

Special thanks are due to: Mike Leary and John Timpane of the *Philadelphia Inquirer*; Michael O'Malley of *Pennsylvania Heritage*; and the editors of *American History*, all of whom have allowed me to share my knowledge of the Philadelphia Athletics with their readership.

A more personal debt of gratitude is owed to the late James Michener, who served as a role model and provided a special insight that allowed me to write a fitting conclusion for the book. No less inspirational have been my students at the William Penn Charter School where I taught during the years I was working on this project.

Above all, I am indebted to my wife, Jacqueline Butler; our two sons, Timothy and Peter; and my parents, William and Balbina, who have always given me their steadfast support and unconditional love. Few men ever admit to having heroes, but I am unabashedly grateful for being married and born to mine.

CONTENTS

FOREWORD

C uriously, for a man born during the Civil War, Connie Mack's name came up often during the 1997 World Series. Such was Mack's impact on baseball in the 19th and 20th centuries that he is relevant near the 21st. His name was invoked in connection with the dismantling of the world champion Florida Marlins, usually by baseball writers who began their sentences, "Not since Connie Mack dismantled his great Philadelphia A's teams..."

The Marlins' owner, billionaire H. Wayne Huizenga, invested almost $300 million in the five years of his team's existence. Then, after the Marlins won the '97 World Series, Huizenga put the team up for sale and ordered the player payroll cut from $53 million to under $20 million. The stars who had won the Series were soon gone, traded away for youngsters with low salaries.

So dramatic was Huizenga's fire sale of a championship team that the only precedent was, in fact, the work of Connie Mack. Not once but twice, Mack created Philadelphia A's dynasties—his teams won five World Series—and then presided over sales and trades that transformed those champions into mediocrities.

Mack's first downsizing of the A's came in 1915; the second began in 1933. They were as ruthless as anything Huizenga had in mind in 1997. So, on that issue, today's baseball pundits were correct in connecting Mack and Huizenga. But on the more important issue—did the owners' business decisions hurt the game?—the pundits failed to recognize a clear distinction between Mack and Huizenga.

Mack was a baseball lifer: first a player, then a manager, and last an owner-manager. He sold and traded his stars, yes. But he did it for the purest of motives. He wanted to stay in the game he loved. Only by reducing costs could he do that.

In contrast, Huizenga, a corporate tycoon with no baseball experience, bought into the Marlins to make money. As it became clear he would lose money, he decided to sell out. Before selling, though, he needed to trim the payroll to make the franchise more attractive to a buyer; in short, he didn't care about the game of baseball, he simply wanted out of the business.

There is a difference. For Mack, baseball was first a game. For Huizenga, who once described a fly ball as "a transaction," baseball was first a business.

William Kashatus' *Connie Mack's '29 Triumph: The Rise and Fall of the Philadelphia Athletics Dynasty* is a timely antidote to the Huizenga-like infection that has corrupted baseball today. Kashatus writes of a golden era in baseball when the game became the national pastime. For a nation of rough-and-tumble immigrants, baseball became the very symbol of the American Dream, a game of infinite possibilities dependent on a man's skill and courage—but always a game and only tangentially a business.

Having fun even as he teaches us lessons of Philadelphia's urban and ethnic history, Kashatus uses his book to provoke an argument that any baseball fan will love: "Who do you like, the '27 Yankees or the '29 A's?" Only a scholar with a passion for baseball could have written so persuasively in support of an idea that, I dare say, has occurred to few people outside the Philadelphia city limits.

Kashatus believes that the 1929 Philadelphia Athletics should be considered the best baseball team ever. You may be able to read the book and still believe that the 1927 Yankees of Babe Ruth and Lou Gehrig were the greatest. But here's a guarantee: Read this book and you will come to appreciate, maybe for the first time, as I certainly did, the talent and ferocity of the '29 A's.

Such an appreciation is important to any sports fan because we spend so much time in happy arguments trying to answer the question, "Who's best?" Unanswerable though the questions are, fans come up with impassioned answers, often substituting volume of voice for what is lacking in logic.

Was Muhammad Ali or Joe Louis the greatest heavyweight boxer ever? Who do you like, the Packers of the 1990s or the Packers of the 1960s? Could Secretariat have left Man o' War up the stretch? Starting a basketball team from scratch, do you take Michael Jordan or Wilt Chamberlain?

First in 1944 and again in 1988, *The Sporting News* conducted surveys of baseball writers asking them to vote on baseball's best team. Both surveys came back as expected—in overwhelming support of the '27 Yankees. To be certain, those Yankees long since have moved from reality to myth, all but universally acclaimed as the best their game has produced. Lesser mortals are left to argue, "Who's second best?"

To his readers' profit and pleasure, Kashatus argues against that premise. The delight of his book is that Kashatus, while admitting he is a fan bringing a fan's biases to the argument, also is a scholar practicing a certain detachment. He gives the Yankees an edge in hitting, though an edge so slight as to be invisible. The rest he gives to the A's. He says they were the better team defensively, had better pitching and had a better bench.

And not only were the A's a better team, Kashatus says, they well might have been a more colorful team. He brings to life heroes we know only by lifeless names. We meet Mickey Cochrane, the catcher described by a teammate as "the fiercest, scrappiest, cryingest" player he's ever known. The great hitter Al Simmons is a "vicious" competitor. Pitcher Lefty Grove trashes the clubhouse in defeat. The mighty slugger Jimmie Foxx, known as "The Beast," is a physical phenomenon who at age 10 presented himself to the U.S. Army recruiters and was nearly accepted for duty.

Unlike today's multimillionaires out of touch with the common man, the A's of Philadelphia were working men who were part of their city. Kashatus even gives us their addresses, usually within walking distance of the ballpark. There, in a young and rambunctious metropolis of ethnically diverse neighborhoods, lived immigrants with little in common other than their shared passion for independence and baseball.

Connie Mack's '29 Triumph takes us into that fabulous urban milieu when this nation was shaping the 20th century. We meet bootleggers and ballplayers; we read of home runs and murders. We live through the Roaring Twenties and the Depression. We meet the inventor Thomas Edison and the clueless Shoeless Joe Jackson. When the old pitcher Lefty Gomez sees an astronaut heft a moon rock in 1969, we hear him say, "So there's the ball Foxx hit off me in '29."

All of this Kashatus gives us, a bonus of sorts in his homage to the 1929 Philadelphia Athletics. No longer can these A's be called "forgotten."

> Dave Kindred
> *The Sporting News*
> Fall 1998

Introduction

THE LEGEND OF CONNIE MACK

B aseball historians consider Connie Mack the paragon of managers. His exceptional knowledge of the game, impeccable
professional disposition, and extraordinary ability to manage
players captured the attention of the baseball world at a time when
the game was riddled with scandal, intemperance and rowdyism. He
won nine pennants and five World Series and built two championship
dynasties during his fifty years as manager of the Philadelphia Athletics. But the career of the Tall Tactician was *not* a string of successes.

The truth is that Connie Mack managed only two kinds of teams
during his half-century in the City of Brotherly Love—unbeatable
and lousy. His nine pennants were balanced with 17 last-place
finishes. Mack's 3,776 victories as a manager were only exceeded
by the 4,025 defeats he suffered, still a record for most losses by a
single manager.[1] And his careful nurturing of two championship
dynasties was only matched by his ruthless dismantling of two of
the greatest teams of all-time, first in 1915 and again in 1933. What's
more, Mack's own life reflected the changing currents of the national
pastime itself.

Born December 23, 1862, at East Brookfield, Massachusetts,
Cornelius McGillicuddy was the son of Irish immigrants. He worked

in a shoe factory and played baseball for the local team until 1886, when at age 24 he entered professional baseball as a catcher.[2] Changing his name to "Connie Mack," he began his career at a time when professional ballplayers were considered even less prestigious than vaudeville actors. Prior to the late 1860s the game had been regarded strictly as a form of exercise for young men. The pitcher threw underhanded from 45 feet away, the batter requested either a low or high ball and the only player on the field who wore a glove was the catcher.[3] The introduction of a payment system in the late 1860s and the establishment of the National League in the 1870s changed the game forever. In the public's eyes, this "professionalization of baseball was degrading to our great national game, making it a business."[4] Detractors considered the owners of the professional clubs to be the "real culprits," and those who played for money, "accomplices in a great conspiracy that would eventually destroy the game."[5]

As a player, Mack could hardly be accused of destroying baseball. He embodied the more colorful nature of the game. Never a great hitter, compiling a batting average of .249 during an 11-year career, Mack was better known for his excellent skills as a catcher. Often he would rag an opposing hitter or call for a quick pitch, and he was even known to "tip the bat" on occasion. It is questionable, however, whether Mack resorted to these tactics to win ball games or simply to survive. At 6'1" and 160 pounds, there wasn't much of an alternative.

As a manager, Connie Mack sought to bring integrity to the game and to attract wider public interest in it. He began managing in 1896 with the Pittsburgh club of the National League, but quickly became disgruntled with ownership over the administration of the franchise.[6] Three years later, Mack left to establish a new league on the condition that he be given absolute freedom in running his own team. Together with two enterprising businessmen, Ban Johnson and Charles Comisky, Mack organized the Western League and managed his own franchise in Milwaukee. A year later the Western League became the American League and entered professional baseball as the rival to the National League.[7] The timing of the venture could not have been better.

By 1900, the National League suffered as teams were losing

money at the gate and owners had divided into two warring camps over the issues of players' salaries and other administrative expenditures. For its economic survival, the National League was forced to drop four teams from its organization, teams that were quickly assumed by the new American League. The Philadelphia Athletics went to Connie Mack.[8]

Almost from the moment he set foot in Philadelphia, Mack created controversy. He frequently said that the purpose of the American League was "to protect the players," unlike the National League, which sought to "protect the magnates," earning him the wrath of the league's owners.[9] But Mack was quick to support his statement with action, and in his first full year as the Athletics manager, he offered sizable pay increases to attract some National League stars to his team. He caused even more controversy when his greatest catches came from the rival league's Philadelphia Phillies. Not only did Mack land a pitching staff for his Athletics by signing former Phils Chick Fraser, Bill Bernhard and Wiley Piatt, but he captured a real prize when Phillies' second baseman Napoleon Lajoie defected to the A's. When Phillies president John Rogers discovered Mack's conspiracy, he obtained injunctions against his former players, forcing them to move onto other teams after the 1901 season. For two years afterwards, Fraser, Bernhard, Piatt and Lajoie were unable to play when their teams appeared in Philadelphia.[10]

John McGraw, the feisty manager of the National League champion New York Giants, was so enraged by Mack's efforts he spited the A's by predicting they would turn out to be a money loser, the "White Elephants" of the new league.[11] Mack found the remark so amusing that he adopted an elephant as the team's mascot. Not only did a likeness of the creature adorn the A's uniform, but Mack actually purchased an elephant for the enjoyment of the fans. Four years later, Mack, with elephant in tow, met McGraw's Giants at Shibe Park for the 1905 World Series. Though he didn't capture the championship that year, Connie got the last laugh when his A's defeated the Giants twice, first in 1911 and again in 1913.

Mack's real genius, however, came from his unique ability to discover and harness the talent of collegians and dim-witted roustabouts alike, molding them into a productive team. At the same time, his keen eye for talent sometimes made him blind to their personal shortcomings. To his credit, he was the first to use college ball as a proving ground for the majors at a time when other managers scouted the sandlots for talent. His discoveries included three of the game's all-time hurlers—Eddie Plank from Gettysburg, Charles Albert "Chief" Bender from the Carlisle Indian Institute, and Jack Coombs from Colby—as well as exceptional infielders Eddie Collins (second base) from Columbia University and Jack Barry (shortstop) from Holy Cross. All of these players were good, clean-living citizens. At the other end of the spectrum were some of the most incorrigible, foul-mouthed players in the game, including "Shoeless" Joe Jackson and George "Rube" Waddell.

Jackson came from a South Carolina mill town. Along with his six brothers, he worked in the mill and played ball for the town's team. At age 19, he was hired to play for a semiprofessional club in Greenville, South Carolina. When he arrived in Philadelphia in 1908, he had already acquired the moniker "Shoeless Joe" for having played one game in his stocking feet, the result of poorly fitting new spikes.[12]

During his first week in Philadelphia, Jackson missed his family so much that he hopped a train to Greenville without Mack's permission. When Mack discovered the young outfielder missing, he ordered one of his coaches to "go down to Greenville and get this fellow's brothers and sisters and whole family to come with you if necessary, but bring him back!"[13] Later that season, Jackson—on his way to the ball park for a game—was "seized," as he put it, with a "gripping desire to go to the theater." Letting his desire get the best of him, he forfeited the game to spend the afternoon at a burlesque house.[14]

Taken by his great hitting ability, Connie Mack stayed with Jackson, even though he was disheartened by his behavior. Playing the role of mentor, Mack offered to pay for a tutor to help the illiterate Jackson learn to read and write. Jackson stubbornly refused the help. Unfortunately for Shoeless Joe, the fans, aware of his illiteracy, took every opportunity to tease him about it. During one game in Detroit, Jackson was standing on third base after hitting a triple and a raucous fan jeered at him: "Hey Jackson, can you spell cat?" As the crowd laughed, Jackson glared at the offending spectator, spit out a stream of tobacco juice and retorted, "Hey mister, can you spell shit?"[15]

Jackson would become the greatest natural hitter in the history of baseball. Unfortunately, he would earn that reputation in an abbreviated career that ended in disgrace. After leaving Philadelphia in 1911, Shoeless Joe played for the Cleveland Indians and later for the Chicago White Sox. In 1919, Jackson and seven of his Chicago teammates were accused of throwing the World Series in a conspiracy that has gone down in history as the Black Sox Scandal. By the age of 31, Connie Mack's one-time prospect had been banished forever from baseball.

George Waddell was another of Mack's eccentric players. Mack had heard of Waddell, a young left-hander who was playing semi-pro ball in Pennsylvania, as early as 1899. He was a very attractive prospect, able to throw a burning fastball and a sharply breaking curve, and was said to have more natural throwing ability than any pitcher in the Keystone State at the time. Despite rumors of Waddell's intemperance and promiscuity, Mack offered the southpaw a job by telegramming him daily for two weeks. Finally, Waddell agreed to play for Mack on the condition that the enterprising manager pay for his debts and rescue his belongings from a pawn shop. Mack agreed to these conditions but also laid down some rules of his own. Waddell would have to report daily to a guardian hired by Mack who would be sure that the young pitcher's wife received half of his $2,400 salary.[16]

Waddell came to the Athletics in 1902 and won more than 20 games in each of the following four years. Although the A's slipped from second to fifth place in 1904, Waddell was one of the team's more consistent players, posting a 26–11 record in a season he began with 10 consecutive victories. In 1907, the left-hander won 19 games and led the American League in strikeouts for the sixth year in a row. During his five years in Philadelphia, George Waddell provided the Athletics with two pennants, more than 150 victories, and carved a name for himself in the annals of baseball folklore.

The uninhibited Waddell fit the part of a classic country yokel. His walk, a farm boy's gait with an accompanying swaying from the shoulders, won over Philadelphia's fans. When he walked to the mound they would yell, "Hey, Rube!" and he would bow from the waist. Once he called in all three of his outfielders and all the infielders, except the first baseman, and made them stand by the mound while he struck out the side.[17] On another occasion, while pitching against the St. Louis Browns, Waddell stormed into the stands and assaulted a gambler who had been jeering at him, returned to the field to strike out a batter, and then hit the double that gave him the victory![18] Perhaps his most remarkable feat, though, was pitching both ends of a doubleheader, winning the first game in 14 innings and then returning to pitch another complete nine-inning game. Rube was so thrilled with his achievement that he turned cartwheels all the way to the clubhouse.[19]

Years after he had retired from the game, Rube Waddell was accused of throwing the 1905 World Series by feigning an injury and refusing to pitch even one game. The Athletics, favored in the Series because of their strong pitching corps of Waddell, Plank, and Bender, lost the championship in five games to the New York Giants. When he died in 1914, *The Literary Digest* delivered what was perhaps the most fitting eulogy for Rube Waddell: "He was one of those characters, at once the most enviable and the saddest in the world, who are too great at heart for the civilization in which they live."[20]

Not all of Connie Mack's ballplayers were as colorful as Waddell or as incorrigible as Jackson, but they did possess some of the greatest talent in the game. Mack built his first 1910–1914 championship dynasty, for example, around the famed "$100,000 Infield," a term that captured the financial value of the four players who composed it. Second baseman Eddie Collins and third baseman Frank "Home Run" Baker were future Hall of Famers. Collins played more seasons in the majors than any other player in the 20th century. Eight of those seasons were spent in an Athletics uniform. When he debuted with the A's in 1906, the 19-year-old Collins used the pseudonym "Sullivan" because he had a year to complete at Columbia University.

Collins' aggressive, confident manner earned him the nickname "Cocky," and, to be sure, he had much to be cocky about.[21] For ten seasons he batted better than .340. An extraordinary baserunner, he led the American League in stolen bases four times, his highest season totaling 81 in 1910. What's more, Collins had a way of getting on base. He served as Mack's number two hitter in the lineup and drew 60 to 199 walks a year, giving him an exceptional on-base percentage of .400 in his eight seasons with the A's.

While Collins provided speed on the basepaths and contact hitting, Baker lent his power to the lineup. The premier power hitter of the so-called "Dead Ball Era," Baker earned the nickname "Home Run" for his two dramatic blasts in the 1911 World Series.[22] He led the American League in homers for four consecutive seasons, from 1911 through 1914. Swinging a 52 ounce bat, Baker hit 93 home runs in his 13-year career, an exceptional total considering the heavier weight of the baseball during that era. He also led the American League in RBIs in 1912 with 133, and in 1913 with 126, and was still able to compile a .307 career average, unusual for a hitter who swings for the fences.[23]

The other two members of that famous $100,000 infield were shortstop Jack Barry and first baseman Stuffy McInnis, both considered to be among the best defensive players of the era at their respective positions. Barry was adept at turning the double play, while McInnis has been credited as the inventor of the "knee reach," the first player to do a full, ground level split in reaching for a throw.

The pitching for that championship dynasty was dominated by Eddie Plank and Charles Albert "Chief" Bender. Plank, who held the dubious honor of having two nicknames—"Gettysburg Eddie" (for his central Pennsylvania hometown) and "Fidgety One" (because of his delaying tactics on the mound)—pitched the team to six pennants. Joining the Athletics is 1901, Plank won 17 games in his rookie year and went on to win 20 or more during each of the next four seasons. Unfortunately, Gettysburg Eddie had hard luck in World Series competition, posting a 2–5 record during his years in Philadelphia.

It was Chief Bender who proved to be the ace of the A's Fall Classics. Bender, a member of the Chippewa tribe, compiled 18 victories in his first year of professional baseball, and in 1910, his most productive year with the A's, he posted a 23–5 record and earned the victory in the deciding game of the 1910 World Series, a performance he managed to repeat in 1911.

With that kind of talent, Connie Mack was able to capture the American League pennant four times in five seasons and win the World Series three times in four seasons (1910, 1911, and again in 1913). Philadelphians seemed to live and die with those early A's teams. As long as Mack was cultivating young talent, the turnstiles kept clicking. But when they stopped, he became "Mack the Knife" and ruthlessly dismantled the team. The breakup began at the end of the 1914 campaign when the Tall Tactician found himself with a $60,000 deficit, despite winning a fourth pennant.[24] He believed that the fans had become too complacent with winning and that his players were no longer a team but rather a collection of talented individuals, more concerned about salary than performance.[25] In fact, six members of the team were called in by the Internal Revenue Service for failing to report their World Series bonuses. Another five were accused of breaching their contracts by engaging in salary negotiations with the Federal League while still on the A's payroll.[26]

Shortly after the A's lost the 1914 World Series, Mack asked waivers on Bender, Plank, and Coombs. Before the 1915 season, he sold Eddie Collins to the Chicago White Sox for $50,000. Home Run Baker, aware of his manager's plans and not wanting to play on a decimated team, sat out the 1915 season in a salary dispute with Mack and was sold the following season to the New York Yankees. McInnes and Barry, the only remaining members of value, were sold to the Red Sox during the 1915 season.[27] By 1916 all the high-priced stars were gone and Mack began the rebuilding process with a team that dropped 117 games and is still widely regarded as the worst team ever to have played the game.[28] The A's would finish in last place for seven consecutive seasons before emerging from the cellar in 1922.

Despite the poor performance of these teams, it was during this same period that Mack became a symbol of the enduring values of the national pastime. He emphasized team commitment rather than catering to individual stars and preserved the integrity of the game by extolling the virtues of clean living and total abstinence among his players. Rarely did he display anger and never did he engage in profanity; he let his feelings be known with a stare or question that would stifle the most unruly player. Mack even dressed the part of a gentleman. Believing that uniforms were meant for players, he preferred to dress in a three-piece business suit, keeping the jacket on during the early spring and removing it only in the most intense heat of the summer. Although his shirtsleeves were occasionally rolled to the elbow, Mack still wore a necktie, a detachable collar, and a derby or straw skimmer. Thus, the congenial Irishman cut quite a dashing figure as he waved his trademark scorecard from the edge of the dugout, positioning outfielders with the skill of the unmistakable baseball genius he was. Such genuine dedication and love for the game served to endear him and his hapless Athletics to the city's youngsters.

At the same time, Connie Mack was an enterprising business-man capable of offering top dollar for a prospect if the player, in his estimation, was worth it.[29] On the other hand, he ran a tight payroll, having nothing against selling off a team for top price to field a much cheaper one. When attendance dropped, he did perhaps the only log-ical thing a businessman could do: He sold his commodity while it still retained value and waited for the higher demand on the market before producing another winner. That demand came in the mid–1920s and not a moment too soon.

At the "seasoned" age of 66, Mack's managerial skills were being called into question by many a sportswriter.[30] After all, the A's had not won a pennant since 1914 and many Philadelphians suspected that the A's skipper had lost his ability to judge talent and to create a team of winners. Besides, his last World Series title had come dur-ing the dead ball era, when the strategy of the game emphasized pitching and manufacturing runs by executing the bunt, stolen base, and sacrifice fly. Could Mack succeed in the age of the "lively ball" where the home run captured the imaginations of the fans and power hitters reigned?

Mack was vindicated by a second championship dynasty that began in 1929. His two consecutive world championships, followed by another pennant in 1931, put his detractors to rest. Mack's star-studded squad featured quite a colorful cast of characters as well, including four future Hall of Famers.

There was Lefty Grove, the ace of the team, who posted a 20–6 record, 170 strikeouts and a 2.81 ERA in 1929. Widely considered the greatest left-hander of the era, he won 28 in 1930 and had his best season ever in 1931, posting a 31–4 record and a 2.06 ERA. The only thing hotter than Grove's exploding fastball was his temper. When he lost, the southpaw was known to tear through the clubhouse lay-ing waste to lockers, watercoolers and, on occasion, a teammate or two.[31]

Even more competitive was his catcher, Mickey Cochrane. Known as "Black Mike" to a legion of admirers, Cochrane was known to respond to a loss by weeping, pulling his hair, and butting his head against the dugout wall. Despite this behavior, Cochrane was an articulate, intelligent individual and the uncontested field general of the team. His exuberant spirit—as well as his .346 batting average—sparked the A's to three consecutive flags.[32]

None of those pennants would have been possible, however, without the slugging combination of first baseman Jimmie Foxx and leftfielder Al Simmons. Though much has been made of the Yankees' tandem of Ruth and Gehrig, Simmons and Foxx presented some formidable competition to the Bronx Bombers. Foxx, the legendary "Double X," was an intimidating power hitter known to launch home runs even farther than the Bambino himself. Simmons could be just as vicious, working himself into a homicidal rage against pitchers before going to bat. His unorthodox style earned him the name "Bucketfoot Al."[33] Idiosyncrasies aside, the duo's statistics were impressive, to say the least.

In 1929, Simmons beat out both Ruth and Gehrig for the RBI title, knocking in 157 runs. Foxx did the same in 1932 and 1933 with 169 and 163 respectively. Simmons won the American League's batting title in 1930 with a .381 average and again in 1931 with a .390 mark. Foxx succeeded him in '33 by winning both the batting title and the American League MVP Award. More impressive was his home run tally. Beginning in 1929, Foxx hit 30 or more round-trippers for 12 successive seasons, and in 1932 he just missed tying Ruth's record of 60 homers when a rainout erased two of the homers he had hit. All four of these A's were elected to Baseball's Hall of Fame between 1947 and 1953.

There were others who contributed as well. The '29 pitching staff was solid. Grove was complemented by George Earnshaw (24–8, 3.28 ERA), Rube Walberg (18–11, 3.59 ERA), and closer Ed Rommel (12–2, 2.84 ERA). A scrappy infield anchored the team's defense. Joe Boley, the A's slick fielding shortstop, made his mark as a clutch hitter. Second baseman Max Bishop, who was the club's leadoff man, hit only .232 in 1929, but he walked almost once a game for a total of 128 free passes that season. Jimmy Dykes, a Philly native, played the hot corner. Nothing seemed to get past him or his protruding tailgate in '29. He was just as deadly at the plate, compiling a .327 average, 79 RBIs and 13 homers. Outfielders Bing Miller (.335, 93 RBI, 8 HR) and Mule Haas (.313, 82 RBI, 16 HR) rounded out the lineup.

The success of the 1929 Philadelphia Athletics allowed Connie Mack to stand head and shoulders above all other managers, proving that his advanced age did not blunt his judgment or ability to win, in spite of a wholly new approach to the game. Surprisingly, considering how diligently and lovingly the sport has been chronicled, hardly anyone remembers the team that outdistanced the New York Yankees by 18 games to become champions of the baseball world.[34] It was *the* team that earned Connie Mack his unique place in baseball history.

Time has not been kind to the '29 A's. It has left them in the shadows of the 1927 Yankees, widely considered "the greatest team ever assembled." That the 1927 Yankees have enjoyed that singular honor is largely due to the fact that they played in New York, a media-rich haven where sportswriters have always blurred the distinction between myth and reality. They began shortly after the Yankees had crushed the Pittsburgh Pirates in the '27 World Series, when James Harrison of the *New York Times* dubbed the team "the greatest in the more than fifty years of baseball history." Not to be outdone, H.I. Phillips of the *New York Sun* called them "a team out of folklore and mythology."[35] The mythology has been fueled for over three-quarters of a century now by some of baseball's most celebrated writers, including Ring Lardner, Grantland Rice, Arthur Mann, Damon Runyon, and Paul Gallico. That many of these writers hailed from New York is not coincidental. Nor were their selective memories, which chose, over the years, to forget that their famed "Murderers' Row" was executed by a White Elephant.

Trying to single out one team as the "all-time best" is an entertaining pastime, but it is also inevitably a futile exercise. Nevertheless, sportswriters have engaged in it since 1944 when *The Sporting News* made the first attempt. Of the 140 members of the Baseball Writers' Association who were polled, 71 (or 50.7 percent) of the respondents voted for the 1927 Yankees. Only four other teams received at least five votes, including the 1929 Philadelphia Athletics, who garnered six. Twenty years later, the Academy of Sports Editors, a Boston-based organization whose 100 members represented newspapers with a circulation of at least 100,000, repeated the exercise. Again, the '27 Yankees were the winners by an overwhelming margin over the runner-up '29 A's. In 1969, the Baseball

Writers Association took yet another poll on the occasion of professional baseball's centennial year. Once again, the '27 Yankees came out on top. As recently as 1988, the editors of *The Sporting News* reassessed the question and again concluded that the '27 Yankees "have yet to be eclipsed in superiority."[36]

Because there is no more exalted team in the annals of sports history than the New York Yankees, the '29 Athletics have unfortunately fallen victim to their mystique. Lost to the world is the fact that although the 1927 Yankees might have had stronger hitting, the '29 A's had better pitching and defense, along with a better bench.

The purpose of this book is *not* to claim that the 1929 Philadelphia Athletics were a better team than the 1927 New York Yankees and therefore the greatest collection of ballplayers ever assembled. To do so would be just as irresponsible as it is to crown the Yankees the all-time diamond kings. Instead, *Connie Mack's '29 Triumph* chronicles the rise and fall of the 1929 Philadelphia Athletics and their six-year rivalry with the New York Yankees, spanning the period from 1927 to 1932. Based primarily on contemporary newspaper accounts, the book tells the story of Connie Mack, the "Grand Old Man of Baseball" and one of the most misunderstood figures in the game's history. It is also a story about a colorful era when many a young man chased after his dream to become a major leaguer, caught up with it, and lived it. Ultimately, it is a story that gives long overdue credit to a forgotten team that was *arguably* the greatest ever to have performed on a baseball diamond.

Chapter 1

PHILADELPHIA IN THE ROARING TWENTIES

The 1920s were an era of excitement, restlessness, and change for Philadelphia. World War I had just ended. Business was booming. Radio, movies, tabloid journalism, and the recording industry radically altered the rhythms of everyday life. Almost overnight, the automobile became an institution, freeing people to travel where they pleased. City and country were brought together by an expanding network of hard-surfaced roads and public transportation. New factories and pleasant suburbs flourished where a few years before there had been miles of farmland. Happiness, success, and enjoyment—the "good life"—were increasingly defined by what a person owned or the freedom they enjoyed. New manners and new morals made it a good time to be alive, especially for the young. Old rules were changing. Women were shortening their hair and their skirts. The tin lizzy was quickly becoming a four-wheeled sofa for youth determined to listen to their libido and only their libido. Bootleg booze, flappers, and pinstripes were the new rules. The dance was the Charleston, the music, jazz.

At the same time, the 1920s ushered in an era of deep and persistent tensions, with ethnic, racial, and geographic overtones. Over the course of a decade, Philadelphia, with it's small town atmosphere and mixed neighborhoods, was transformed into a large industrial metropolis. More than two million people of different social backgrounds, skills, wealth, and power shared the city.[1] Natives began to relocate from the shabby, rundown sections of the old city to suburban areas with new homes, new industry, and accessible transportation. Newcomers arrived from the small towns and farmlands of rural Pennsylvania, New Jersey, and Delaware. Others came from more distant places. The presence of large ethnic communities attracted immigrants with family ties and those who were simply looking for a familiar culture. The great migration of African-Americans begun during the World War I years also contributed to Philadelphia's growth, as blacks continued to leave the rural South in search of greater economic opportunities. This natural growth resulted in segregated neighborhoods largely dictated by income and ethnicity.[2]

Irish, German, and Polish enclaves surfaced in the northeast neighborhoods of Kensington, Richmond, and Frankford, areas that had traditionally been comprised of English and native American workers. Here, along the Delaware River, were located the wharves, shipyards, and warehouses of the city's port as well as the mills, foundries, and chemical plants that formed the backbone of its heavy industry. The district had an old-fashioned atmosphere, much like a 19th century mill town where immigrants from the same European background tended to live and work together. Life was characterized by community solidarity and discipline, which was reinforced by the unions, benefit associations, ethnic clubs, and fraternal orders these immigrants established and frequented. But as the financial opportunity presented itself, some residents relocated to the more affluent districts of the city.[3]

South Philadelphia was home to Jews, Italians, and blacks. Most were poor, some ambitious. Yet, each group had its own distinctive lifestyle. Jews were the most prosperous, running the street markets and small shops of the district. Their strong sense of kinship and family loyalty allowed them to weather the seemingly endless crises of poverty that hit this part of the city during the decade. The most successful left for the tree-shaded lawns of Oak Lane and Cheltenham, or the nicer homes of Wynnefield and Strawberry Mansion.

The Italians were more divided. A small, middle-class minority

established themselves as skilled craftsmen, emphasizing the importance of a good education as a means for advancement in society.
The fact that the public schools stressed vocational training for the
children of immigrants greatly irritated them, proving to be the root
of their anxiety over assimilation. Nor were they content with the
rowdyism of the blue collar majority who labored on the wharves
and in the terminals of the Port of Philadelphia, or were employed,
irregularly, in the construction, transport, and garment industries.
Most of the Italians remained in South Philadelphia, though some
did eventually resettle in the suburbs in hopes of greater educational
opportunities for their children and better jobs for themselves.

At the other end of South Philadelphia's social spectrum were
blacks who worked at whatever low skill, low paying jobs they could
find and congregated in the city's ghetto. Located in the cramped
streets and alleys between Spruce and South streets, this area was a
haven for gambling, prostitution and bootlegging. Despite the overwhelming temptation to engage in these activities, many blacks found
refuge in stable family lives, some managing to move to the north-
ern suburbs.[4]

Downtown Philadelphia was populated primarily by lawyers,
engineers, architects, brokers, and public relations men who served
the city's large firms. J.B. Lippincott book publishers, Baldwin-Lima-
Hamilton locomotive works, Smith, Klein & French chemicals, and
Hardwick and McGee rugs were just a few of the many businesses
that had downtown office buildings with branches across the nation.
Adding to the allure of center city were some of the largest, most
glamorous stores located on six blocks of Market Street from Litt
Brothers on the east at 7th Street to John Wanamaker's on the west
at 13th Street. All of these enterprises depended on the kind of rapid,
intercity communication that could only be provided by Philadelphia's central post office, telegraph and telephone exchanges, as well
as its two train terminals for passenger service to New York, Pittsburgh, Chicago, and Washington. What's more, the downtown had
an extensive system of public transportation, allowing the upper-
and middle-class professionals who worked there easy access to the
Main Line communities of Haverford, Bryn Mawr and Villanova
where they lived.[5] Downtown also had its poor section, located along
the corridor of Lombard Street in the neighborhood of Mother Bethel

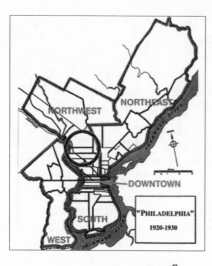

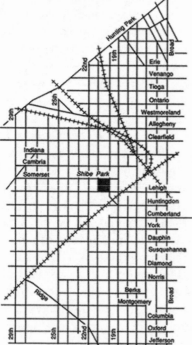

Philadelphia maps showing location of Shibe Park, 1920s. (Circled area at top represents detail below.)

A.M.E. Church, as well as in the neighborhoods of the fourth ward adjacent to South Philadelphia. These neighborhoods were home to poor blacks who held jobs as street and sewer cleaners, trash collectors, and domestic servants.[6]

West Philadelphia was the most modern of the commuter suburbs. Its residents were a mix of groups, including blacks who made a steady living, Jews and Italians who prospered enough to leave the ghetto, and, most populous, the Irish and native American who ran the stores and offices of the downtown. West Philadelphia did not have the same strong neighborhood loyalties that characterized other sections of the city, though. Friendships were often based on business contacts. Most residents sought entertainment or recreation outside of the district, taking advantage of the freedom the automobile afforded them. Nor was it a very attractive place to live. Miles of red-brick row houses and brand-new efficiency apartments dominated an area once known for its beautiful, old Victorian mansions.[7] If Philadelphia had a "stepping stone" to a life of "bigger and better," West Philadelphia fit the description.

The largest and most popu-

The North Philadelphia neighborhoods surrounding Shibe Park during the late 1920s. (Courtesy of Temple University Urban Archives.)

lated of all the city's districts, however, was Northwest Philadelphia. It was an area bounded to the northeast by Germantown Avenue, to the west by the Schuylkill River, and to the south by 6th and Vine streets. Within these boundaries, the racial, ethnic, and economic composition of the district reflected the same pattern of urban growth of many other American cities.[8] Alongside the downtown was the poor neighborhood, inhabited largely by blacks. Next came Strawberry Mansion, home to a large Jewish community. These were the merchants of the business district who lived above their shops. Further north were the mills, with the working class and aging middle-class row houses of North Philadelphia. While Italians lived in the eight square blocks that ran north from Cambria to Erie Avenue, known as North Penn district, second-generation German and English families inhabited their own small enclaves within these blocks. Just beyond were the factories—Midvale Steel, Exide Battery, Budd

Company, Heinz Food Co., Hornung Brewery, and Tastykake Bakeries—which dominated the blocks between Allegheny and Hunting Park avenues. Finally, on the other side of Hunting Park, were the spacious Victorian houses of Germantown and East Falls, where more affluent families resided.[9] At the heart of the district was a sizable working-class Irish enclave called "Swampoodle."[10] Located in the area that bordered 22nd Street and Lehigh Avenue, Swampoodle gave the entire 38th Ward a distinctively Irish reputation as a tough, but proud and family-oriented neighborhood.

Collectively, these five districts comprised 48 wards, all of which were controlled by Republican party boss Boies Penrose and Congressman William S. Vare. Penrose, a descendant of Philadelphia's early merchant Quaker aristocracy, had dominated Pennsylvania's Republican Party ever since 1897, when he was elected to the United States Senate. Disdainful of his social peers and independently wealthy, he sought no graft for himself. But his appetite for power spurred him to serve the industrial tycoons of his era faithfully.[11] Vare's power base, on the other hand, existed among the ethnically defined slum wards of the downtown and the crowded row house neighborhoods, shipyards, docks and factories of South Philadelphia. His politics were fundamental as well as pragmatic. Vare possessed a unique understanding of ward leadership and how to use it to his own advantage. He controlled each ward through patronage, false voter registration, stuffing the ballot box, and purchasing votes, as well as by the force of his charismatic personality. A hefty war chest that he enhanced through lucrative contracts won by his own construction company allowed Vare to strengthen his authority.[12]

So complete was the Republican hegemony of Philadelphia that even the chairman of the city's Democratic Party, as well as the rest of the city council, yielded to the wishes of the machine.[13] All attempts at reform were effectively negated by the city charter of 1919, which had given primary authority to the council at the expense of the mayor. Since the voters continued to elect the same politicians to council, mayoral campaigns were the substitution of one Republican nominee for another.[14]

Nevertheless, Philadelphia was able to weather the corrupt politics, as well as a brief postwar depression that hit the city. Then came Prohibition. Bootlegging became a popular pastime shortly after the temporary wartime restriction on alcohol was made permanent by the Eighteenth Amendment. The law proved difficult to enforce because of the city council's refusal to increase the police force and the refusal of ethnic groups to abide by it. Rumrunners obeyed the law of supply and demand, breaking all the rest. Their profits ran into the tens of thousands. There were a few staged raids on illicit breweries and speakeasies, but by 1923 the increased incidence of alcohol-related gangsterism, as well as Philadelphia's infamous tendency to obstruct the enforcement of liquor laws, had earned the city a national reputation.[15]

Forced to act against the rampant lawlessness, Mayor W. Freeland Kendrick, in 1924, hired a Marine Corps general, Smedley D. Butler, as head of the police department to clean up the city. Butler's strong arm tactics did not go over well with the magistrate courts, though. Apparently, he was cutting into their share of the take. After repeated raids on politically sensitive bootleg operations, he was relieved of his duties. Butler left Philadelphia in disgust. Upon his departure he quipped, "Until the people of Philadelphia stop playing the game of 'Enforce the laws against others, but not against me,' they will not win the fight against lawlessness!" Butler's remark proved to be a prophetic one. Law and order were not restored until 1928, when gangland warfare became so severe that Judge Edwin O. Lewis ordered a grand jury investigation into the connection between bootleggers, police, and gambling rings.[16]

If nothing else, Philadelphia's politicians did manage to change the landscape of the city. Streets of row houses were constructed out of what were once underdeveloped areas within the city's limit. Downtown and country were united by an expanding network of hard-surfaced roads and public transportation. Roosevelt Boulevard, constructed northeast of the old Hunting Park race track, and the Frankford Elevated, which wove its way along the Delaware River, gave access to more rural areas. Old York Road connected the affluent suburbs of Cheltenham, Jenkintown, and Abington with the urban center. Broad Street, one of downtown's two main thoroughfares, was gradually expanded to the north and south, while a subway was tunneled beneath it. And a Parkway, lined with such monumental buildings as the Free Library and the Art Museum, was created, bringing the green of Fairmount Park into the heart of the downtown.[17]

The Roaring Twenties also brought a new popularity to base-ball. Despite the ethnic differences that existed among Philadelphians—or perhaps because of them—the national pastime held a special appeal to the city's diverse population. The game was, after all, a symbolic representation of the American Dream, offering each individual the opportunity to step up to the plate and seize the chance for glory. The ability to compete on even terms with an opponent, as well as the "rags-to-riches" implications of the sport, were so cherished among the city's immigrants that they embraced the game and encouraged their children to play it. For them, baseball was an important step in the assimilation process, providing a common meeting ground for the various social, ethnic, and religious groups of the city. Youngsters, too, chose to play the game. They had grown up with it in school, on the streets, and in the newspapers. It was *their* pastime. Like their immigrant fathers, the second generation became, at best, incredibly single-minded about the importance of

Aerial view of Shibe Park, circa 1929. (Courtesy of Temple University Urban Archives.)

the game. At worst, they were mean and ornery. Their response depended on whether the hometown team was winning or losing. It was behavior characteristic of Philadelphia's urban culture in the 1920s when baseball had a remarkable grip on people's hearts and minds and reflected the excitement and restlessness of the era.

The ball was livelier than ever before. Prior to 1920, baseball was a low-scoring game. It emphasized the hit-and-run, stolen base, squeeze play, and bunt. The ball remained largely inside the park and teams focused on manufacturing runs, inning by inning. But in 1920, the "inside game" yielded to the lively ball. Home runs were flying out of ballparks at a record pace, especially in the American League. Led by a young Babe Ruth, the power hitting outfielder of the New York Yankees, baseball became a high scoring game. After Ruth smashed the previous home run record with his 29 circuit clouts in 1919, attendance soared throughout the American League. Such was the case at Shibe Park, home of the Athletics.

Located at 21st Street and Lehigh Avenue in the heart of North Philadelphia, Shibe Park was best known, in the 1920s, for its obstructed views and absence of Sunday games. The park, built in 1908 and opened on April 12, 1909, was the first steel and concrete stadium in the nation.[18] It was named for Benjamin F. Shibe, principal owner and president of Reach Sporting Goods. Shibe Park was a handsome facility, giving the appearance of a French Renaissance castle from the outside. Its two grandstand walls were joined at 21st and Lehigh where the domed tower of the main entrance stood. The first base foul line ran parallel to Lehigh Avenue; right field to center field, 20th Street; center field to left field, to Somerset; and the third base line, to 21st Street. Shibe had a seating capacity of 23,000, and an additional 10,000 fans could stand behind ropes on the banked terraces in the outfield. Another 10,000 seats were added in 1925 when upper decks were attached to the bleachers. After the renovation, the park's dimensions were shortened in right field from 340 to 331 feet and in left field, from 378 to 334 feet. Center field remained a very respectable 468 feet.

As the 1920's unfolded so did the fortunes of the A's. Their winning ways resulted in increased attendance. Mack accommodated those growing crowds—as well as his own pocketbook—by constructing a mezzanine with 750 box seats between the upper and lower decks in 1928. A year later, when the A's captured their first World Series in 16 years, he added another 3,500 seats to the grandstands, along with a small press box located under the roof of the second deck. The pillars supporting the upper deck obstructed the view of many lower deck fans, but they also increased the seating capacity to 33,500, where it remained until the stadium closed in 1970.[19] It still wasn't enough, though.

From 1929 through 1931 fans crowded onto the rooftops on the other side of 20th Street. From that vantage point, they had a clear view of the entire field over the 12 foot high right field wall. According to one neighborhood resident, "You could put up to 80 people on the roof of one house. Plus you could seat about 18 more in the bay window of the front bedroom. There were bleachers that extended from one end of the block to the other. Sometimes you'd get a couple thousand people up there. You'd charge 35¢ during the regular season. We got $5.50 per person during the World Series."[20]

Because most residents had a backyard staircase that led up to the second story of the house, there was easy access to the roof. Others put up ladders in the bathroom so fans could climb through the skylight. Some residents even sold hot dogs and sodas. Rooftop squatting became such a lucrative business by the mid–1930s that Mack, who felt cheated out of additional income, had a 22-foot addition of corrugated sheet iron affixed to the existing 12-foot wall in right field. The renovation raised the height of the wall to a total of 34 feet, completely blocking the view from the 20th Street rooftops. Known as the "spite fence," the wall stirred both amusement and resentment among the local fans of North Penn.[21]

Pennsylvania's blue laws also hurt the A's attendance. Dating back to 1794, the blue laws were a host of ordinances that prevented drinking, gambling, and sporting contests on Sunday. As early as 1911, Connie Mack attempted to have the laws rescinded, arguing that if the wealthy could play croquet, gulf, and tennis at their private clubs, then the common man should be able to enjoy a baseball game. When that line of argument proved unsuccessful, he complained that prohibiting Sunday baseball placed the A's in debt. In 1926, Mack went so far as to test the ban by playing a Sunday game at Shibe, a 3–2 victory over the Chicago White Sox. Afterward, Mack publicly stated his wish that "all those who oppose Sunday baseball could have been there to see that we are not causing a lessening in church attendance."[22] Still, he failed to convince the authorities, who stopped the A's from further play on the Sabbath. So determined was Mack, however, that he and club owner Benjamin Shibe tried to pressure the city's politicians by threatening to move Sunday games across the river to Camden, New Jersey. Bickering over the site continued until 1934 when the state finally passed a local option law that permitted the A's to play Sunday games between the hours of 2:00 and 6:00 p.m.[23]

Nevertheless, 21st and Lehigh was the focal point of adventure for many Philadelphians during the Roaring Twenties. On game day, the blocks surrounding the Shibe became the scene of controlled pandemonium. Most fans arrived by public transportation. Clanging bells of the street trolleys, ooo-gahs of car horns, and piercing shrills of the traffic cops' whistles cut the air. People scurried to buy tickets — 50¢ for bleachers, $1.25 for grandstand seats, and $2.00 for box seats — and poured through the turnstiles at the main entrance or, alternatively, crowded onto the rooftops of the houses lining 20th Street. Inside the park, batting practice commanded the attention of the early arrivals. Pitchers warmed up along the sidelines, adjacent to the stands. Vendors made their pitch: "Getchur scorecard lineup!" "Peanuts!" "Ice cream!" At 3:15 p.m., the national anthem was played. Shortly after, the ballpark announcer called out the starting lineups through his megaphone and the home plate umpire cried, "Play ball!" Outside the streets became quiet. All that could be heard was the clamor of the neighborhood kids who congregated along 20th Street in hopes of retrieving a ball that sailed over the right field wall.

Once the game began, all eyes focused on the pitcher and the hitter. Each inning became a series of individual contests that added up to six outs, each and every one having its own unique drama. After a side was retired, the players would toss their gloves onto the field and head into the dugout to boast about their most recent play or to trade insults with the opposing team. An impressive pitching performance or extra base hit by the hometown A's was greeted with enthusiastic applause. And a bad play was met just as easily with a flying seat cushion or a raucous jeer.[24]

There was a special intimacy to Shibe. Spectators felt the excitement of the game. Players responded to their approval and rejection.

It was as if the fans were part of the unfolding drama itself. Each visit seemed to provide another story to remember. Every home run became a history of its own, inevitably hitting one of the rooftops across the street, breaking a front window, or disturbing an afternoon nap. Babe Ruth, for example, was credited with hitting a homer over two rows of houses and breaking a window 500 feet from home plate. Not to be outdone, the A's own Jimmie Foxx and Al Simmons tried to replicate that performance during many a batting practice.[25] An enterprising youngster could collect one of those batting practice balls, take it home, clean it up, and return by game's end to sell it to some naive tourist as a home run ball.[26]

Neighborhood kids had a special way of inventing their own excitement during the game. They didn't even need a ticket. Some would lie down on the sidewalk on Somerset Street to catch the action by peering through a half-inch crack that formed between the pavement and one of the two iron doors. By closing one eye and focusing the other, one could see the pitcher and catcher as well as the first and third base bags. Many a kid would surface from that position after an inning or two half-paralyzed from lying on the sidewalk and half-blind from squinting with one eye. Not surprisingly, the turnover rate was fairly high. It was still possible to follow the game without that kind of effort though. The noise of the crowd often signaled the fortunes of the team at bat. A sharp roar meant a single. A longer roar that suddenly broke off meant either a double or a triple. And an especially solid contact, followed by the mixed crescendo of stomping feet, clapping hands, and, ultimately, a deafening roar, could only mean one thing—a home run.[27]

After the game, the neighborhood kids would hang around the park to cadge autographs from the players, sometimes following them home. It wasn't that far. Most of the A's great stars lived within a few blocks. Lefty Grove rented a place on Lehigh Avenue. Mickey Cochrane had a room at Rush's boarding house on 22nd Street. Al Simmons had a home at 2745 North 20th Street, behind the right field stands. Unmarried players doubled up, renting a room at Mom Keyborn's boarding house on 23rd Street. Max Bishop lived with a dentist and his family on Somerset. Still others lived at the Lorraine or Majestic hotels on Broad Street.[28] In fact, there really weren't many options for a ballplayer looking for room and board. Most were working

A street-level view of Shibe Park, ca. 1910. (Courtesy of Jerome Romanowski.)

class individuals who did not have a car for transportation or the financial income to live in the suburban neighborhoods where doctors, lawyers, and businessmen resided. They naturally gravitated to the area around the ballpark which was inhabited by people from the same socioeconomic class as themselves. Over the years, a natural affinity developed between the A's and the residents of North Penn.

"We'd treat them just as if they were neighbors," recalled Joe Barrett, who was raised in the neighborhood. "Many of them were our neighbors. Since the ball games were played in the afternoon, you'd see the A's sitting out on their front steps in the early evening, or at Schilling's ice cream parlor, or even at the movie theater. Sometimes the single ballplayers would stand out on the corner at 23rd and Lehigh and challenge the neighborhood kids to a game of stick ball."[29] Another neighborhood resident, Bill Brendley, recalls, "In 1929 I bought a new baseball and took it around to the main gate at Shibe. Just inside, I saw Mickey Cochrane. I yelled, 'Hey Mickey, how about getting the ball signed for me?' He said, 'Sure, kid,' and took the ball in the clubhouse with him. A few minutes later, he came back with it, and the whole team, including Connie Mack, had signed it."[30] These kinds of simple gestures earned the fellow who wore an A's uniform the hero-worship of the youngsters.

Divided loyalties didn't exist. Philadelphia was an American League town. The Phillies couldn't win to save their lives. Only the most loyal fan could endure their losing ways. Besides, Connie Mack's crop of colorful—as well as highly talented—personalities, inspired an almost religious devotion among fans of all ages. With names like "Bucketfoot Al" Simmons, Robert "Lefty" Grove, and Jimmie "The Beast" Foxx, the A's had little difficulty capturing the imagination of the Quaker City. They were sharp-witted and strong, reckless and carefree, brutally candid and shamelessly self-indulgent—much like the time period itself. It was the Jazz Age, the Roaring Twenties. The dead ball was gone, the lively ball had arrived, and so had the Philadelphia A's.

Chapter 2

REBUILDING THE A'S, 1920–26

By late September 1920, Connie Mack's A's were on their way to a sixth consecutive last-place finish. Nearly 50 games behind the first-place Cleveland Indians, the team was flirting with a .300 winning percentage. Chances seemed remote that the Tall Tactician would ever see the first division again. He had no money, no talent, and no hope of getting much of a return at the gate. In fact, things had become so bleak that Philadelphia sportswriter Bugs Baer quipped that for the A's "a base on balls constitutes a batting rally."[1] Mack was going nowhere, he knew it, and he was extremely dejected.

With only a few games remaining in the season, he arrived at the ballpark on that last Saturday afternoon hopeful that his club would at least be competitive and the attendance more than a few thousand. Outside the clubhouse, one of his players remarked, "A great crowd today, Mr. Mack!" Rather than acknowledge the sarcasm, Mack simply proceeded up the runway to the A's bench in utter silence. To his amazement, he was greeted by the applause of 15,000 fans. It was Philadelphia's way of saying, "We're behind you, even in the hard times!"[2]

Connie Mack and the A's weren't the only ones experiencing

hard times in 1920. Baseball itself was wracked by tragedy and scandal. On August 16, at New York's Polo Grounds, Yankee pitcher Carl Mays, notorious for brushing back hitters with his submarine delivery, beaned Cleveland shortstop Ray Chapman on the side of the head. Chapman staggered out of the batter's box and fell to the ground. He never regained consciousness, dying the next day—the first and only fatality in major league baseball. Mays insisted that the pitch that killed Chapman would have been called a strike had he managed to duck out of the way. But Chapman hugged the plate so closely that his head was actually in the strike zone and he was unable to see the worn, discolored ball as it sped towards his skull. The incident compelled baseball's rule makers to outlaw trick pitches and introduce the practice of keeping clean baseballs in play throughout the game. Both changes not only improved the safety of the game, but they also ushered in the lively ball era by giving a decided advantage to the hitter.[3]

If Chapman's death shook the baseball world, the Black Sox scandal brought the national pastime to the brink of disaster. Gambling scandals had been a part of baseball since the 19th century, but the ultimate corruption was revealed in September 1920, when a grand jury exposed eight members of the Chicago White Sox who had agreed to throw the 1919 World Series in return for $100,000 from New York gambling interests. Though the soiled Sox were acquitted, the scandal cast a long shadow over the game. Fans wondered whether baseball deserved any serious following at all if one of its greatest teams could betray a national trust by fixing games and be exonerated in a court of law.[4]

Fearing for baseball's survival, club owners replaced the old three-man National Baseball Commission with a single commissioner, Judge Kenesaw Mountain Landis. The 48-year-old Illinois judge, who had played a major role in securing an out-of-court settlement with renegade players from the Federal League, agreed to serve on the condition that he had complete control without any interference from the owners. The owners complied, and on November 12, 1920, Landis was unanimously elected to the new post of Commissioner of Major League Baseball. One of his first official acts was to ban for life the eight members of the Black Sox whose acquittal was rumored to have been arranged by the powerful White

Judge Kenesaw Mountain Landis' appointment as baseball commissioner in 1920 restored public confidence in the national pastime after the Black Sox episode of 1919. (Courtesy of the National Baseball Hall of Fame.)

Sox owner Charles Comiskey. "Regardless of the verdict of juries," Landis ruled, "no player that entertains proposals or promises to throw a game, no player that sits in a conference with a bunch of crooked players and gamblers where the ways and means of throwing games are discussed, and does not promptly tell his club about it, will ever again play professional baseball."[5] The lifelong ban branded the expelled players as villains who had betrayed the game, but it was needed to restore public confidence in organized baseball, as well as to reestablish the game's institutional integrity.

The Black Sox scandal greatly troubled Connie Mack. It reflected the egoism and selfish attitudes he had come to disdain and was, unfortunately, becoming characteristic of the men who played the game.[6] "Organized baseball has suffered an embarrassing moment," he bemoaned. "It has been caused by lapses of character on the part of some of its best-known figures. The game cannot afford to field a single player who cannot stand in the light of the sun as an example, in both private and public life, for youngsters to follow."[7] To be sure, while he would never disgrace the national pastime by betting on the game, Mack had not always been an innocent bystander. But he paid for his own indiscretion. His earlier raiding of the Phillies' roster caught up with him in 1914. After winning the World Series in 1910, 1911 and 1913, many of his own stars were attracted by the prospect of selling their services to the newly formed Federal League where they could earn more money. Instead of committing themselves to winning a fourth world championship, the A's bickered. "Some were merely playing out the string, waiting to jump to the new league," according to baseball writer Red Smith. "Others, who weren't going, were envious and discontented because they weren't going to get the same money. Mack just barely held them together to win the pennant in 1914 and I think was not too greatly astonished when they lost the World Series to the Boston Braves in four straight games."[8]

Poetic justice can be a bitter pill to swallow if you're on the losing end as Mack was in those years. He found himself $60,000 in debt and with players whose selfish attitudes he disdained. And so, in 1915, Mack began to break up his championship dynasty. "If the players were going to cash in and leave me to hold the bag, there was nothing for me to do but cash in too," he reasoned. "I might be broke financially, but I am also full of ambition. It will be like starting all over again for me. I love to build teams. I have done it once and I will do it again."[9]

In fact, Mack didn't make much of a profit at all. He ended up giving away star pitchers Chief Bender and Eddie Plank as well as

Jack Barry to Boston. The only real money he made was on the sale of Eddie Collins to the Chicago White Sox for $50,000. Desperate to balance his books, Mack, in 1916, proposed to his players a profit-sharing system whereby their salaries would be based on a percentage of the gate receipts. But because the A's were floundering in last place with no hope of getting out in the near future, the players wisely opted for salaries that were guaranteed by contracts.

After the disbandment, Mack's Athletics finished last for seven consecutive seasons, with their worst year coming in 1916, when the team dropped 117 games. But never did Mack stray from his basic philosophy that "there is room in the baseball profession for gentlemen and the owners have a responsibility to cultivate them."[10] To this end, Mack crafted his own code of conduct for the players, rules that he sometimes struggled to enforce over the next forty years.

- I will always play the game to the best of my ability.
- I will always play to win, but if I lose, I will not look for an excuse to detract from my opponent's victory.
- I will never take an unfair advantage in order to win.
- I will always abide by the rules of the game—on the diamond as well as in my daily life.
- I will always conduct myself as a true sportsman—on and off the playing field.
- I will always strive for the good of the entire team rather than for my own glory.
- I will never gloat in victory or pity myself in defeat.
- I will do my utmost to keep myself clean—physically, mentally, and morally.
- I will always judge a teammate or an opponent as an individual and never on the basis of race or religion.[11]

During those lean years when the A's were perennial losers, the fans might have cursed the team, or worse, deserted them. But they didn't. Rooting actually became more a labor of love than genuine entertainment. "Wait till next year!" became the eternal hope. "Next year" finally arrived in 1922 when the A's emerged from the cellar. Though they finished only seventh, there was a bright future on the horizon.

With the death of Benjamin Shibe in January, the presidency

of the A's was assumed by Thomas Shibe, Benjamin's son. The younger Shibe deferred to Mack on most of the club's administrative affairs, especially in player transactions and development.[12] What's more, a decade earlier Mack had purchased another quarter interest of the A's from newspapermen Frank Hough and Sam Jones, the original share holders, making him, in effect, an equal partner with the Shibe family. His strategy was simple: "You've got to spend money to make money."[13] Almost immediately, he put into practice what he preached. Mack renovated Shibe Park before the season began, covering the left field bleachers and adding new seats in front of the left field fence. The shortened fence not only accommodated more fans, which meant more gate receipts, but it also generated more home runs. So prodigious was the A's production in 1922 that they even outdistanced Babe Ruth and the Yankees in homers with a total of 111 to New York's 95.

Mack also began building a contender. He tailored his team from a combination of young, unproven talent and seasoned veterans, realizing that it would take about five to seven years to experience success. "A chap who starts, let us say, at twenty-two after graduating from college doesn't attain his full baseball maturity for five or six years," he reasoned. "That makes him about twenty-seven. He stays at the peak of his games for another five or six years, which take him to thirty-three. From then on he may have a few years of active play left in his legs and arms. After they've been used up, he still has remaining the greatest asset in baseball: the 'know how' of the game."[14]

The first cog in his experiment was a barrel-chested, scrappy infielder by the name of Jimmy Dykes. A Philadelphia native who was purchased by Mack in 1918 to play second base, Dykes was a temperamental fireplug who was playing for Seaford, Delaware, in the Eastern League when the Tall Tactician discovered him. Just 22 years old when he played in his first major league game, Dykes had an inauspicious beginning, striking out four times in as many plate appearances. After taking him out of the game, Mack, who always managed to find the humorous side of a dismal situation, told his young infielder, "I suppose you know why I took you out. You see, the American League record for striking out is five times in one game, and I didn't want you to tie it in your very first big league game."[15] Dykes would prove to be Mack's most reliable player, averaging 125 games through 13 full seasons with the A's. In 1920, Dykes was joined by Eddie Rommel, a successful spitballer with Newark of the International League. As a rookie, the 23-year-old went 7–7. Two years later, in 1922, he pitched 294 innings for the A's, posting 27 wins, or nearly half of the team's 65 victories that year.

Throughout the early 1920s, Mack also took a number of chances on promising young players who, unfortunately, never realized their potential. He seemed to have a soft spot for pitchers, especially from the South. Among these "here-today-gone-tomorrow tailenders," as they became known, were Bryan "Slim" Harris and Rollie Naylor, pitchers who both hailed from Texas; Chick Galloway, a shortstop from Clinton, South Carolina; Frank "Boog" Welch, an outfielder from Birmingham, Alabama; and Bob Hasty, a pitcher from Clayton, Georgia. There were so many of these revolving door acquisitions that Dykes and Rommel soon considered themselves to be the "old guard of the team." "As we saw the players come and go," recalled Dykes, "we would look at one another and say: 'I guess we're next.' But somehow we weathered the storms."[16] To their great relief, other more successful players were added over the next few years as well.

Mack acquired Bing Miller from Washington in 1921. Miller was a dependable, graceful outfielder who immediately contributed a powerful bat to the A's lineup, hitting 21 homers during the 1922 campaign. That same year Mack purchased twenty-two-year-old first baseman Joe Hauser from Milwaukee. Doc Johnson, the A's regular first baseman was, at age 35, beginning to show some vulnerability at the position. "One day he dropped a couple fly balls and was hit on the ankle by a sharp grounder," recalled Hauser. "The next day some of the players put all the catching equipment in his locker. They figured he needed it so he wouldn't get hurt. I played first base that day and never looked back." Though Hauser was a little rough around the edges, he possessed the skill and power to become a dangerous hitter in the big leagues. During his first season with Philadelphia, Hauser demonstrated his potential, knocking out 9 home runs and 21 doubles in 111 games for a .323 average.[17] Infielder Sammy Hale and Pitcher George "Rube" Walberg were acquired from Portland of the Pacific Coast League for $75,000 in 1923. Hale proved to be a smart fielder and valuable utility man who platooned at third base with Jimmy Dykes during these early years, while Walberg became one of Mack's most consistent and durable pitchers despite a bad case of nervousness that often cost him sleep the night before a starting assignment.[18]

With his new additions, Mack was able to finish in sixth place in 1923 with a record of 69–83 for a .454 winning percentage. More impressive, the A's had a taste of what it was like to contend, if only for a brief period. For the first two and half months of the season, they were the only team to chase the powerful Yankees, who were on their way to a third straight pennant. Their offensive attack was led by Hauser (.307, 16 HR, 94 RBI) and Miller (.299, 12 HR, 64 RBI), while Rommel headed the pitching staff with an 18–19 record and a 3.27 ERA. Unfortunately for the A's, the high tide of that season came in late June with a 16–7 whitewashing of Walter Johnson and the Washington Senators. During the next series, against the Yankees, the A's were humbled: 4–3, 10–9, 6–1, and 4–0. They went into a sharp skid after the sweep and never recovered, finishing in sixth place just ahead of Chicago and Boston.

They resumed their losing ways in 1924. From May 5 to August 8 the team languished in last place. Again, the Yankees managed to humble the A's. Ruth was on his way to his only career batting title that season, Wally Pipp led the league in triples, Bob Meusel was hitting well over .300, and former Athletic Jumpin' Joe Dugan proved to be an offensive sparkplug for New York, scoring 105 runs that season. The Yanks weren't the only team to bring the A's to their knees, though. Washington, which would go on to capture the pennant, was also tearing up the league. Walter Johnson enjoyed an MVP season in which he led the league in strikeouts with 158, wins with 23, shutouts with 6, and posted an ERA of 2.72. After 19 years in the majors, Johnson finally pitched for a team that could provide him with some offensive punch. Among the Senators' heavy hitters that year were Hall of Fame outfielder Goose Goslin, who hit .344 with a league-leading 129 RBI; Sam Rice, who hit .334 and scored 106 runs; and Joe Judge, who batted .324. Together, the Yankees and Senators combined to make most of the '24 campaign a nightmare for Mack and his White Elephants. Mack's own miscalculation seemed to do the rest.

Signed by Connie Mack in 1918, infielder Jimmy Dykes proved to be the A's most reliable player, averaging 125 games through 13 full seasons in Philadelphia. (Courtesy of the National Baseball Hall of Fame.)

Paul Strand, the A's prized rookie that season, proved to be a costly flop. Strand, who had briefly pitched in the majors, converted to the outfield and was scouted by Mack himself during the 1923 season. Playing with Salt Lake City in the Coast League, he compiled a .394 average in 194 games, hitting 66 doubles, 13 triples, 43 home runs, and 187 RBIs. So impressed was Mack that he purchased the young player's contract for $70,000. Then, in 1924, Strand hit a lowly .228 in 47 games. At midseason Mack traded him along with pitcher Rollie Naylor to Toledo and acquired outfielder Bill Lamar to fill out the roster.[19] The sportswriters were predicting another tailender for the A's, and worse, some began to question Mack's ability to scout as well as manage. "The only salvation for the A's is to get rid of Connie Mack," wrote one Philadelphia scribe. "So long as this old fogy directs the team it will never get anywhere."[20] The 62-year-old Mack might have begun to entertain doubts himself. Perhaps that is why he asked his son Earle to return to the A's as a coach, after eleven years of managerial experience in the minor leagues.[21] He needed someone he could trust, possibly someone to replace him if, indeed, the critics were correct. Fortunately, they weren't.

The A's emerged from their slump in mid–August and played the best ball in the league for the remainder of the season, finishing in fifth place with a record of 71–81. The turnaround was largely due to the hitting of newly-acquired outfielder Bill Lamar, who batted .330 in 87 games; Bing Miller, who finished the season at a .342 clip; and Joe Hauser, whose 27 home runs were second only to Ruth's 46 round trippers that year. But the big surprise for the A's that season was the emergence of 22-year-old rookie Al Simmons.

The son of polish immigrants in Milwaukee, Aloysius Szymanski modeled his American name after a hardware store ad, making it easier for the sportswriters to remember.[22] He began playing ball for semipro teams in Milwaukee in the early 1920s. Signed by the minor league Brewers in 1922, Mack purchased Simmons for $50,000 the following season when he hit .398 in 24 games. It was a risk. Other major league clubs were unimpressed with Simmons. A right-handed hitter, he pulled his left foot away from the pitcher and toward the dugout with every swing. Scouts predicted that his odd batting stance would prevent him from ever hitting major league pitching with any success.[23] The media only seemed to add insult to injury.

On opening day in 1924, a photographer asked the young rookie to pose with his foot in a red water bucket. Angered by the request, Simmons refused and came cursing into the clubhouse.

"What's wrong kid?" asked Jimmy Dykes.

"Oh, some cheese picture-taker out there wants me to pose with my foot in a water bucket!"

Overhearing the discussion, Mack asked, "Have you always hit like that?"

"It's the only way I know," replied Simmons.

"Then keep doing it, son."[24]

The idiosyncrasy earned him the nickname "Bucketfoot Al" while his success at the plate earned him the respect of pitchers throughout the league. Despite his unorthodox style, Simmons still managed to generate remarkable power from his hips and upper body, especially on the low, outside curve that he would hammer against right-field fences.[25] He "bucketfooted" his way to a .308 average that season, becoming a regular in the A's outfield.

Later, when asked why he didn't try to change Simmons' hitting style, Mack recalled: "I noticed Al's unusual batting stance the first time I saw him play. Ordinarily, I would have suggested that he try to correct it. But he did so well at batting even in spite of his unorthodox procedure that I never suggested he try to remedy it. If he can hit with 'one foot in the bucket,' or even with both feet there, I am inclined to let him alone. A player will always do a thing better if he does it naturally than if some other technique is forced upon him. Besides, it's hits we want, not beauty."[26]

Simmons became the A's cleanup hitter and one of the most feared sluggers in the American League. Over the next decade, he would drop below .340 only once. Mack's $50,000 gamble had paid off in spades. What's more, he was willing to spend even greater sums to build a second championship dynasty.

In the spirit of the progressive twenties, Mack spared no expense when he found a prospect he really wanted. Many came from Jack Dunn's Baltimore Orioles of the International League. A talented scout with a fierce determination to win, Dunn discovered great players from the Baltimore sandlots, reform schools, and colleges and molded them into a winning team. Because the International League was exempted from the major league draft, Dunn was able to hold

Al Simmons would work himself into a homicidal rage before stepping up to the plate, considering the pitcher his mortal enemy. (Courtesy of the National Baseball Hall of Fame.)

on to his talent until he was offered market price.[27] While he antagonized major league owners by doing so, he angered other International League franchises by monopolizing the championship title for seven straight seasons between 1919 and 1925.

Dunn was no wealthy sportsman pursuing a hobby. He was a

serious businessman who made his living from the game. Though several major league clubs tried to lure him out of Baltimore, he always refused, enjoying his unique place as a maverick in organized baseball. Mack understood him and liked him. While other major league owners believed that the minor leagues existed for the sole purpose of supplying the majors with a pool of talent at a low cost, Mack sympathized with Dunn's financial predicament. Aside from the fact that he was experiencing his own financial difficulties, Mack realized that operating a minor league team was a money-losing proposition. Thus, theirs was an understanding based on trust. They both knew what Dunn's players were worth. They both had confidence in each other's baseball judgment. And there was no expectation of charity from either side.[28] Perhaps Dunn's insistence that his ballplayers conduct themselves as gentlemen made him even more partial to Mack who had an impeccable reputation for clean living.

Whatever the case might have been, Dunn had offered Mack one of his finest pitching prospects as early as 1914—George Herman Ruth. Dunn had signed the young southpaw out of St. Mary's Industrial School in Baltimore that year and in one of his first appearances for the Orioles, Ruth pitched a complete game victory in an exhibition contest against the A's. His continued success endeared Ruth to the feisty little manager who assumed legal guardianship for him and by season's end he was being called "Dunnie's Babe."[29] Facing financial ruin though, Dunn offered Ruth to Mack for a song. The A's manager rejected the offer. He was in the process of selling off his own championship team. And though the decision not to acquire the strapping young hurler no doubt proved regrettable, Mack believed the poor financial circumstances of both clubs at that time didn't warrant such a deal. "I didn't turn Jack Dunn down because I didn't think Ruth was good," Mack admitted years later. "He was already a star in Baltimore. But Jack didn't have any money in those days and we didn't either. I remember I told him, 'No, you keep that fellow, Jack. Sell him where you can get some money. You can use it as well as I.'"[30] Dunn took Mack's advice and sold Ruth to the Boston Red Sox for $2,900.[31] Nevertheless, the trust that developed between the two owners resulted in several major transactions during the 1920s.

The most famous deal came in 1925 when Mack purchased

Robert "Lefty" Grove, a 6'3" southpaw who had already become a legend in Baltimore. Raised in the coal mining region of Lonaconing, Maryland, Grove dropped out of school after the eighth grade and went to work in the mines. At age 19, he tried out for Martinsburg of the Blue Ridge League and made the team as a first baseman. Shortly after, Grove switched to pitching with extraordinary success. After watching him strike out 60 hitters in 59 innings of play, Dunn purchased his contract for $3,100.[32] In his first year with Baltimore, Grove posted as 12–2 record. The next year he went 27–10 and set International League records in innings pitched with 303 and strikeouts with 330. Keenly aware that the market for his young pitcher's talent would rise, Dunn waited to sell Grove. Dunn's patience paid off: Mack purchased the star pitcher in 1925 for the unprecedented sum of $100,600, exceeding the $100,500 the Yankees paid for Babe Ruth five years earlier. (Arguably, Ruth's price totaled as much as $135,000 with all the incentives, but the base figure was $100,500.)[33] Mack also purchased Oriole second baseman Max Bishop for $25,000. A great two-strike hitter who was also adept at drawing a walk, Bishop soon became the A's leadoff hitter.

Two other acquisitions would also figure prominently in the A's fortunes as the 1920s unfolded. Mickey Cochrane, a Massachusetts farm boy who starred at halfback for Boston University, was purchased from Portland of the Pacific Coast League. Cochrane compiled a .338 average and demonstrated exceptional speed on the base paths in his single season with Portland. While he preferred the outfield, he was often asked to go behind the plate. Mack was so taken by the young man's competitive spark, work ethic, and aggressive play that he purchased the entire Portland franchise to secure his services. "I spent a little money for Cochrane," mused Mack, "$50,000 to be precise. Actually, to get him we bought the entire Portland club. It isn't often that you buy a whole club to get one player. He wasn't a very good catcher either. But there was something in the way he played that made me think we could do something with him. He was a real dynamo on the field, full of energy, trying all the time, never letting up. Every manager wants a player like that."[34] Perhaps a more likely candidate to become the A's catcher was another farm boy by the name of Jimmie Foxx.

Foxx grew up doing chores on his father's dairy farm in Sudlers-

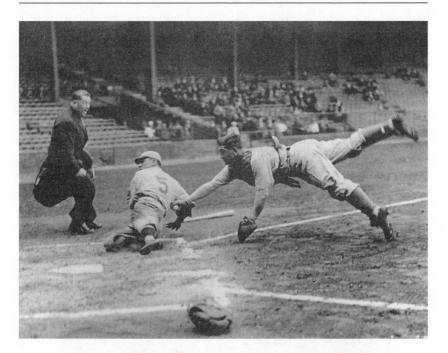

Mickey Cochrane tagging out a base runner in a 1928 game.

ville, Maryland. The labor made him unusually well developed for his age. He was so physically mature, in fact, that he tried to join the army at age 10 and almost fooled the recruiters into taking him![35] Instead, Foxx turned his attention to sports, most notably baseball, where he proved to be a successful power hitter. At age 16, he caught the eye of Frank "Home Run" Baker, the third baseman of Mack's first championship dynasty, who was then managing Easton in the Eastern Shore Class D league. Baker recruited the muscular adolescent in 1924. Foxx played in 76 games that season, mostly at catcher. He quickly proved to be a clutch hitter and home run threat. So impressed was Baker that he contacted Yankee manager Miller Huggins and offered to sell the adolescent to him for $2,500. Huggins declined. He was coming off a second place finish in 1924 after having captured a world championship in 1923, along with three straight American League titles. He intended to keep his team intact and saw little chance of a youngster like Foxx cracking the lineup anytime in the near future. Baker then approached his former manager. Mack

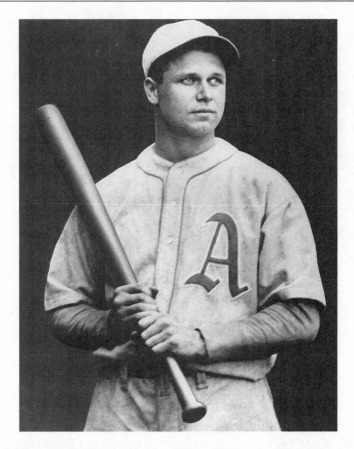

Jimmie Foxx signed with the A's at age 16, in 1924, and quickly became one of the most feared power hitters in the major leagues. (Courtesy of the National Baseball Hall of Fame.)

was hesitant at first because he had already signed Cochrane. But he realized that if the youngster could hit, he could put him anywhere in the lineup. Baker insisted he could: "Mr. Mack, this kid is a hell of a ballplayer. He can run, field, throw and hit and he can also help your ball club." Mack took Baker's advice and signed him for the same asking price of $2,500. Shortly after the signing with the A's, on December 1, 1924, Foxx dropped out of high school, despite his mother's objections. Two months later he boarded a train bound for Fort Myers, Florida, where the A's held their spring training. It would be the first of his 21 seasons in professional baseball.[36]

Players like Dykes, Hauser, Cochrane, Foxx, and Simmons typified the kind of players Mack preferred. They were big, strapping young men who could run, hit, and throw with equal skill. In fact Mack identified what he considered to be the "ideal physique" for a major league player as "5'10" to 6' in height, 175 to 185 pounds in weight, with a body built in proportion." He claimed to favor this kind of build because, as he put it, "baseball can be a somewhat rugged sport where endurance counts and, under those circumstances, size and muscle pay off."[37] At the same time Mack was willing to sign a player who didn't fit that mold. He was known to favor tall pitchers because he believed they had a distinct advantage over the hitter. Lefty Grove and Rube Walberg both stood at 6'2", for example, and could hurl a ball with such ferocity that it would break across the plate at an angle difficult for any batter to hit squarely. On the other hand, a player of smaller stature like Max Bishop or Bing Miller would also be signed "if he had the ability to compensate for his lack of brawn." Specifically, the smaller-built players had to demonstrate "a strong throwing arm; power enough in his bat to hit the ball squarely and hard; fleetness of foot for fielding and running the bases; a good, sure pair of hands; and good eyesight."[38]

Above all, every prospect—regardless of size—had to possess a certain degree of intelligence. Earlier in his managerial career, Mack had a soft spot for dim-witted roustabouts. He signed a fair share of them to build his first championship dynasty. But as the years unfolded, he came to realize that "the fellow with the ability to think and to think fast, will forge ahead of the player who makes decisions slowly because baseball is a game of quick decisions boldly followed out."[39] Thus, Mack, increasingly placed a high priority on signing more experienced veterans as well as college players. Jack Quinn was a fine example of the kind of veteran Mack preferred.

Quinn, a spitballer who helped pitch the Yankees to their first pennant in 1921, came to Philadelphia in 1925 at the age of 41. "Jack Quinn is a wonder," said Mack. "He's never out of shape, works like a Trojan, and seems to improve with old age."[40] Quinn himself attributed his success to "clean living, proper rest, and daily exercise that includes a lot of running to improve the wind."[41] Mack knew that Quinn would be a good role model for the young pitching staff he was developing, and the veteran hurler didn't disappoint him. Quinn was known to stress the following points in counseling young pitchers:

1. Develop the pitching arm slowly until it is strong.
2. First practice control with the fastball alone.
3. Next practice control with the curve.
4. Then practice control with the change of pace.
5. Spend hours fielding your position and covering first.
6. In pinches always use your most effective form of delivery.
7. Try to be a ball player as well as a pitcher. Get your share of batting practice and get the full extent of running speed you possess.
8. Don't let bad breaks or errors dishearten you and never criticize teammates. Always be confident.[42]

Finally, Quinn advised, "Don't feed the hitters what they like. Pitch to their weakness. Study the batter, get control and remember there's eight other fellows to help you out when the ball is hit. That's all there is to pitching. I don't believe in straining the arm when there's no need to. If a youngster wants to pitch for a good many years, let him learn control first, how to pitch in the pinch, and to have something in reserve at all times."[43] But there was more to Quinn's longevity in the majors than his pitching knowledge and physical regimen. He also threw the spitter, one of only a handful of hurlers permitted to throw the pitch after it was outlawed in 1920. "The secret to Jack's effectiveness," claimed Joe Boley, who later played shortstop for the A's, "was his use of the 'straight pitch' or a 'dry ball' to confuse batters who were expecting one of his versions of the spitter—a 'straight drop,' an 'in-drop,' or an 'out-drop' on the corner of the plate."[44]

Collegians were also favored by Mack. "A chap who plays on his college baseball team is really getting the same experience that he would get in the minor leagues," he reasoned. "In addition to his experience, he is getting an education, which is just as important as anything in his life."[45] While not all of his more recent prospects could boast of a college education like Cochrane, all of them seemed to possess a natural instinct for the game. Mack was so excited about their potential that he predicted a "contender" in 1925.[46]

At the A's spring training camp in Fort Myers, Florida, Jimmie Foxx caught the attention of teammates and sportswriters alike when, in an intrasquad game, he hit a mammoth home run that was called "the longest ever seen in Fort Myers and one that would have easily cleared the center field wall at Shibe," which was 468 feet from home plate.[47] The 17-year-old's catching skills were just as impressive. The scribes wrote that he "showed real class behind the plate" and was "surprisingly smooth in handling pitchers."[48] Cochrane, on the other hand, was a disappointment. Hitting wasn't a problem. Cochrane could tear the proverbial cover off the ball. But his catching left much to be desired. Mack complained that his rookie backstop was "crude at receiving the ball. His stance and his crouch were both wrong. And on foul balls, he was simply pathetic!"[49] So disappointed was Mack that he actually considered shifting Cochrane to third base or the outfield. Instead, he assigned the rookie to Cy Perkins, who had been the A's regular catcher for the last six years. Perkins was an excellent defensive catcher, but a light hitter. Together with A's coach Kid Gleason, Perkins mentored Cochrane. Gleason endlessly drilled the rookie, hitting him pop-ups until he learned how to discard his mask quickly, scan the sky for the ball, and catch it. Perkins proved to be an exemplary role model on the field and an able tutor off of it. He quizzed Cochrane on a host of subjects ranging from how to handle the pitching staff to defensing the bunt, ultimately transforming the youngster into a defensive model of himself.

First impressions can be deceiving though. While Cochrane learned well and ended up catching 134 games for the A's in '25, Foxx found his place on the bench. Through the first part of the season, he was used almost strictly as a pinch hitter and a batting practice catcher. In late June, Mack optioned him to Providence of the International League where he could be mentored by Frank Shaughnessy, one of the most highly respected managers in organized baseball.[50] There, Foxx played a number of positions, including catcher, right field and first base. Wherever he played, Foxx consistently hit .300 or better. In 41 games at Providence, he compiled 33 hits for a .327 average. Predictably, Foxx returned to Philadelphia in September where he would stay for good. Years later, Foxx recalled how the demotion helped to build his confidence: "The A's bought me as a kid of 17 with nothing but a bunch of muscles and a big desperate lunge at the ball. I think one of the greatest things Mr. Mack did for me was to give me confidence by allowing me to prove myself in the minors. When I returned to Philadelphia, he seldom raised his voice if I made a mistake on the field. If he ever did lecture me, all he would do was five words. Another manager would relish the opportunity for a half-hour."[51] To be sure, Mack had no intention of rushing the youngster. He believed that a 17-year-old could learn more by playing in Providence than riding the bench in Philadelphia. When Foxx was promoted in September, Mack knew that his rookie had gained the confidence necessary to play at the big league level and, more importantly, that he could contribute.

If there was a disappointment that spring, it came in a preseason exhibition game against the Phillies when first baseman Joe Hauser suffered a freak injury. Hauser, who had become one of the A's most dependable hitters, fractured his left kneecap while moving to cover first base. The injury was so severe that it tore the bone apart, sidelining him for nearly the entire season. Mack had no choice but to fill the hole with Jim Poole, a promising infielder he brought up from the A's newly purchased Portland club. Nevertheless, the A's would field a much improved team in 1925 and, consistent with Mack's preseason prediction, challenge for the pennant.

The Yankees, who had just missed out on a fourth straight flag in 1924, expected to return to their pennant-winning ways. But what they didn't expect was the "Bellyache of the Bambino." Their star outfielder's prodigious appetite for greasy food, alcohol, women, and the good life itself, caught up with him on April 8th as the Yanks were in the final stages of spring training. Ruth keeled over on the playing field, suffering from an intestinal abscess. Abdominal surgery kept him out of the lineup until June. Even after he returned, Ruth's performance was hardly acceptable on or off the field. By September, when Manager Miller Huggins slapped him with a record $5,000 fine for insubordination and constant breaking of club training rules, the aging Yankees were languishing in seventh place, where they finally finished the season, 28 games out.

With the Yankees out of competition, the A's and Senators battled it out for the pennant. From May 9th to June 29th, the A's were in first place. The most dramatic contest came on June 15th against the Cleveland Indians at Shibe Park. The A's overcame a 15–4 eighth inning deficit to score 13 runs, giving them a 17–15 victory. It was one of the greatest comebacks in baseball history. Al Simmons hit a titanic three-run homer onto the left field roof that capped an inning featuring nine hits and four walks, including a two-run triple by Jimmy Dykes. Though the A's fell to second in early July, they recaptured first-place by the middle of the month and held a five-game lead over the Senators in mid–August when they embarked on their last western road trip. The team's beat writers dubbed the road trip the "Pennant Special" and traveled along to chronicle the events leading to Mack's seventh pennant. But things did not go as expected. The A's dropped three straight against the Browns on their first stop in St. Louis. Two more losses followed in Chicago before Slim Harriss and Sammy Gray gave the A's a reprieve, turning back the White Sox with 6–1 and 3–0 victories. Then the Mackmen went into a 12-game tailspin. It began in Cleveland, where they came away empty-handed in three games. Another three-game sweep followed in Detroit. Their fortunes didn't improve when they headed back east either. The A's blew two games in Washington and another pair to the 7th place Yankees in New York.

Despite their miserable road trip, the A's were greeted by 70,000 when they returned to Philadelphia for a Labor Day weekend doubleheader against Washington. Unfortunately, they fared no better, dropping both games 2–1 and 7–6 for their 11th and 12th straight defeats. Although Gray and Harriss put an end to the misery the next day, combining on a 6–4 victory over the Senators, the damage had already been done. The A's were nine games out, in second place, and their hopes for a pennant were dashed.

Washington repeated in 1925, going 96–55. Their fortunes came on the arms of an aging pitching staff that posted a 3.67 ERA and was widely regarded as the best in baseball. Walter Johnson, now age 37, slipped a bit to 20–7 with a 3.07 ERA. But the staff was bolstered by 35-year-old Stan Coveleski, who came over from Cleveland to notch 20 more victories, and 33-year-old Dutch Reuther, who posted 18 more wins after being picked up on waivers from the National League. If the starters faltered, they could rely on Firpo Marberry, one of baseball's first great relief pitchers, who led the American League in games with 55 and saves with 15.

Still, Connie Mack's youngsters showed great promise. Rommel was quickly becoming an ace, chalking up another fine season with a 21–10 record, 67 strikeouts, and a 3.67 ERA. Slim Harriss went 19–12 with 95 strikeouts and a 3.50 ERA. Sammy Gray even managed to post a 16–8 record, 80 strikeouts, and a 3.39 ERA, in spite of being out a month with a broken finger. And though rookie Lefty Grove only registered 10 victories against 12 defeats, he surpassed the great Walter Johnson in strikeouts 116 to 108, showing some of the awesome potential that would characterize his pitching in the near future. The A's hitting was even more remarkable, leading the American League with a team average of .307. Seven hitters compiled averages of .318 or better: Al Simmons (.384); Walter French (.370); Bill Lamar (.356); Sammy Hale (.345); Mickey Cochrane (.331); Jimmy Dykes (.323); and Bing Miller (.319). On the horizon was Jimmie Foxx, who in the closing weeks of the season collected six hits in nine at bats for a .667 average.

Such colorful players as Simmons, Cochrane, and Foxx demanded a new kind of press coverage. Predictably, sportswriting reached a pinnacle in the Roaring Twenties with a style and jargon that hasn't been equaled since. There seemed to be at least one great baseball writer in every major league city: Shirley Povich, *Washington Post*; Burt Whitman, *Boston Herald* ; Ed Burns, *Chicago Tribune* ; Harold Heffernan, *Detroit News* ; Stuart Bell, *Cleveland Press*; and Herman Wecke, *St. Louis Post-Dispatch*. New York was, of course, loaded with talent, including Ford Frick of the *Evening Journal,* Paul Gallico of the *Daily News,* John Kieran of the *Times,* Frederick Lieb of the *Telegram*, Grantland Rice of the *Herald-Tribune*, Damon Runyan of the *American*, and Joe Vila of the *Sun*. Philadelphia had its share of talent as well. Among the best known writers were Jimmy Isaminger of the *Inquirer,* Bill Brandt of the *Public Ledger,* and Stoney McLinn of the *Evening Bulletin*. Tucked away in the press box, which was sandwiched between the roof and the upper deck grandstand at Shibe, some writers delighted in the use of sarcasm, others praised athletic prowess with inspirational prose, and still others were moved to poetry. Whatever the writer's approach, the A's were a team that made for good copy.[52]

While the morning newspapers captivated baseball fans with box scores and yesterday's news, radio provided instant gratification. KDKA Radio in Pittsburgh broadcast the first baseball game in

August of 1921. Two years later, the 1923 World Series between the Yankees and Giants was broadcast live to listeners in the New York metropolitan area. By 1926, radio had become so popular that it was estimated that every third home across the nation had a radio and many stations dedicated their afternoon airtime to baseball. Baseball and radio seemed to be made for each other during an era when the national pastime was the most popular form of entertainment. Even when the hometown team played on the road, local announcers would recreate the game by receiving pitch-by-pitch details from a Western Union telegraph and then using a variety of sound effects and their imagination to broadcast the contest. At the same time, broadcasting was controlled because of the owners' fear that gate receipts would decline if the fans could listen to games at home for free. Thus, certain restrictions were established, such as banning radio on Sundays and holidays except when the biggest crowds were expected at the park.[53] Nevertheless, radio enhanced the colorful personalities of Connie Mack's young A's, bringing them right into living rooms across the city.

The Athletics made another run at the pennant in 1926. While the sportswriters predicted that Chicago and Cleveland would be the Yankees' closest competitors, the A's ran second to New York throughout the spring. It was a distant second, though. There was no race during the first half of the season. The Yanks held a commanding eight to ten game lead through most of it. Shortstop Mark Koenig and second baseman Tony Lazzeri, both rookies, solidified the Yankee defense, and the big three of Murderer's Row—Babe Ruth, Lou Gehrig, and Earl Combs—were all having big years at the plate. Together with the solid pitching of Waite Hoyt, Urban Shocker, and Herb Pennock, it looked as if New York was on its way to another A.L. flag.

By late June, the A's still had 12 games to play against the Yankees, who, at that point, had already beaten the Mackmen six out of ten meetings. The A's would have to add more stability to their pitching staff as well as more punch to their batting order if they were to challenge for the flag. Though Lefty Grove had posted 83 strikeouts by that time and was being acknowledged as "the fastest pitcher in baseball," he only had seven victories in 16 starts. Nearly all five of his losses came by one-run margins because the A's couldn't support him at the plate. Walberg, Gray, and Rommel were pitching into the same hard luck. Because it was such a young pitching staff, their frustrations began to mount, especially when they were losing by one-run margins.

Joe Hauser, who had been one of the league's most feared sluggers in the past, was struggling to come back from his knee injury in 1926. When he fell below the .200 mark in June, Mack benched him indefinitely, replacing him with young Jim Poole at first base.[54] Other dependable bats also fell silent. Simmons, Dykes, and Lamar all struggled at the plate. They were youngsters who were doing their best, but did not have the experience to battle through a slump.

Desperate to overcome the A's ten-game deficit, Mack engineered a three-team deal he hoped would put his club over the top. Bing Miller was traded to the St. Louis Browns for another outfielder, "Baby Doll" Jacobson, who, in turn, was dealt to Boston along with pitchers Slim Harriss and Freddy Heimach for veteran righthander Howard Ehmke. Ehmke, a submarine baller, broke in with the Federal League in 1915. He came to Boston by way of Detroit in 1923 and immediately made his mark, posting 20 wins for the Red Sox that season. Another 19 victories followed in 1924. His fortunes changed after that. Laboring for the cellar-dwelling Bosox in 1925, Ehmke went 9–20 and, until he was traded to Philadelphia, had posted only three wins against ten defeats in 1926. But Mack liked him and believed that the veteran would not only rediscover his winning ways pitching for a contender, but also become a valuable mentor to his young pitching staff.[55]

The A's fortunes began to change on July 5, when the Yankees came to Philadelphia for a doubleheader. Grove won the first game, 2–1, demonstrating extraordinary control. He didn't issue a single walk, nor did he throw more than two called balls on any batter. Instead, Mack's young southpaw fanned 12 batters, including Babe Ruth to end the game. The Yankees could manage only one run on four hits, and even that score came on an error when Bill Lamar misplayed a fly ball. Grove returned to the mound as a reliever in the second game, combining with Rube Walberg to defeat the Yanks, 6–3.[56] Later that week, the A's took three out of four from the White Sox. Poole single-handedly defeated Chicago in the first game of that series with a grand-slam home run for an 8–7 comeback victory. Just as dramatic was his performance in the second game when, in the tenth inning with two outs, he clouted a solo homer over the right field wall for a 2–1 win. Poole went on a tear through mid–July, collecting 23 hits in 64 at bats for a .344 average. So inspired were his teammates that they also found their batting strokes. The most noticeable improvements were Simmons, Lamar, and Dykes. No less inspired were the A's faithful. Rarely did daily attendance drop below the 10,000 mark. Saturday games attracted over 25,000 fans. Baseball was booming at Shibe Park. Then, the A's slumped.

A seven-game losing streak that began on July 17 in Detroit and continued in Cleveland forced the A's out of the pennant chase by early August. Only once in those seven games did the A's score more than two runs. Things became so bad that Al Simmons was benched for the first time since he joined the team in 1924. He had played 394 straight games for the A's before Mack sat him against Cleveland. To make matters worse, Grove split Mickey Cochrane's throwing hand with a fastball in one of the earlier games against Detroit. Cochrane would be out for three weeks. An inexperienced Jimmie Foxx, who had been used almost exclusively as a pinch hitter and utility man up to that point, would have to assume the catching duties.

The Yankees, on the other hand, managed to weather their own storms. July proved to be a problem-filled month. Outfielder Bob Meusel and catchers Benny Bengough and Pat Collins were lost to injuries. Babe Ruth and Joe Dugan played on gimpy legs. Hoyt suffered through his own pitching woes. And rookie Mark Koenig allowed the derisiveness of the New York fans to send him into a nervous collapse, both at the plate and in the field. But by August 5, the Yankees were sitting atop the American League with a commanding nine game lead over second-place Cleveland. Naturally, Yankee skipper Miller Huggins took nothing for granted. "It is very unwise to claim the pennant at this stage of the race," he stated. "There isn't a soft club in the American League. Even the [last-place] Red Sox have become dangerous as of late. So it is well to take nothing for granted and play as hard as we can the rest of the way."[57] The Yankees, of course, went on to capture the flag, going 91–63. Despite Ruth's four-home-run performance, the World Series went the full seven games that year. The Yankees dropped a nail biter in Game 7, falling 3–2 to Rogers Hornsby's St. Louis Cardinals.

The A's finished in third place, six games behind New York and three behind the second-place Cleveland Indians. Though they enjoyed the best pitching staff in the league and a tight, scrappy defense, Mack was frustrated with his team's performance. Again, the sportswriters began to question whether the aging manager could still win it all. One of the most scathing analyses came from Jim Nasium of *The Sporting News*, who suggested that Mack was still wedded to the "scratch-hit, rough-and-tumble baseball of the dead ball days when he built championship teams" and that the "lively ball has effectively put the kibosh on that style of play." Nasium added, "Unless Mr. Mack can make the adjustment, the A's will never see another world championship."[58]

In fact, Mack had made the adjustment. His acquisition and careful nurturing of power hitters Al Simmons and Jimmie Foxx underscored his determination to win in the lively ball era. What's more, he realized that the home run was worthless if a club didn't have the pitching to keep the opposing hitters in check. To that end, Mack had put together the best staff in the American League. Nor did he have to apologize for his team's speed or defense. Mack had crafted a well-balanced team. If he had a problem winning the pennant, it was due to his young players' lack of experience. His main tasks over the next few seasons would be to give them the playing time they needed to gain that experience and to sign a few more veteran ballplayers who could mentor them, contributing their baseball knowledge and experience.

Chapter 3

COBB COMES TO TOWN, 1927

O n the evening of February 8, 1927, the Philadelphia sports-writers held their annual banquet at the Hotel Adelphia. Nearly 800 people gathered in the elegant Crystal ballroom to pay tribute to baseball's greatest star, Ty Cobb, who had retired as player-manager of the Detroit Tigers at the end of the previous season. The large turnout underscored the remarkable support Cobb enjoyed in the baseball world during an especially difficult winter.

During the off-season, rumors spread that Cobb was, in fact, forced out of baseball by American League President Ban Johnson for conspiring to fix a game in 1919. Cobb maintained his innocence, but Johnson declared that "whether guilty or not, he was through playing in the American League." To Johnson's dismay, the public rallied behind Cobb, putting pressure on Commissioner Landis to end the investigation. On January 27, lacking any hard evidence against the former Detroit outfielder, Landis proclaimed the star's innocence.[1]

Cobb wanted more than Landis' pardon though. He wanted vindication and, like the way he played the game itself, he wanted it on his own terms. Refusing to leave the game under a cloud of suspicion, the 40-year-old outfielder was determined to play another season to vindicate himself.[2] Detroit was not an option. He was at an impasse with club president Frank Navin. While Navin criticized him for causing dissension on the team and making bad trades, Cobb believed that Detroit couldn't win with the players they had. He wanted to go to a contender.

For nearly two weeks after his name was cleared, American League clubs bid for Cobb's services. The Athletics were among his top choices.[3] Philadelphia's sportswriters knew it too. That is why they gathered in such great numbers at their annual banquet. Cobb didn't disappoint them.

At the appointed hour, he stepped to the podium and, in words choked with emotion, said, "If I had the ability, perhaps I could tell you this in better words. I only want to say that I am happy beyond words to tell you that I will play next season for the Athletics."

There was instant bedlam. The crowd rose to their feet and applauded wildly for nearly ten minutes, some even standing on chairs. Cobb, clearly overcome with emotion, tried to mask his feelings with a slight smile. When the cheering subsided, he continued, "I only wish that I had come to Philadelphia while I still had a little more spring left in my legs, when I could go out on the field knowing just what I could do. But I'll be out there, you can depend upon it, giving my best. I am happy to be with the Athletics."[4]

It was a strange twist of fate. Cobb had feuded with the Athletics and their fans for most of his career, beginning in 1909 when, in the heat of a pennant race, he ruthlessly spiked third-baseman Frank "Home Run" Baker. Mack was so angered by the incident that he campaigned to have him thrown out of the league. Calling Cobb a "back-alley artist," Mack declared that he "wouldn't let him play for me if he did it for nothing." The A's fans were more subtle. They sent him anonymous death threats and, on one occasion, posted a placard on the outfield wall showing Cobb with a knife protruding from his chest. Predictably, the Detroit star required his own entourage of policemen whenever he appeared at Shibe Park.[5] But time has a way of healing even the most serious rifts. In this case, the needs of Mack and Cobb transcended their bitter rivalry, making good friends of old enemies.

Shortly after signing an A's contract worth $70,000, Cobb admitted that he and Mack had been "bitter enemies on the field." "I gave

A smiling Ty Cobb prepares himself for the 1927 season at the Athletics' spring training site in Ft. Myers, Florida. (Courtesy of Shawn M. Murray, The Bruce Murray Collection.)

everything I had to beat his ball club every time we met," he confessed, "but I believe that Mr. Mack is also the symbol of everything decent in the game. He deserves to be on top again if any man ever did. And I'll break a leg or an arm, I'll do anything to win for him this summer."[6] Mack was just as flattering in his praise of Cobb. Referring to his new outfielder as "the greatest ball player who ever lived," Mack claimed that Cobb was "very much misunderstood by the fans. But he still has a lot of good ball in him and there is no player in the history of the game who can surpass him in all-round ability and baseball knowledge."[7] To be sure, Mack's young Athletics would capitalize on both Cobb's ability and knowledge of the game.

But Cobb wanted to do more than simply finish his playing career on a pennant winner. He wanted to secure his place in baseball history as the greatest ever to have played the game. Many sportswriters didn't hesitate to remind him that he had already seen his heyday, having been eclipsed by Babe Ruth. And it infuriated him. To be sure, Cobb typified the earlier, dead ball era, when the objective was to keep the ball inside the park. Teams would manufacture runs base by base, bunting to first, stealing second, sacrifice to third, and base hit to drive in a run. It was a thinking man's game where teams played for the lead and relied on their pitching and defense to keep it. But once Ruth entered the game, the approach changed. Baseball had become a power hitter's game; the home run, with all its excitement and drama, was the attraction. But not for Cobb. "Given the proper physical equipment, which consists solely in the strength to knock a ball 40 feet further than the average man can do it," he insisted, "anybody can play big league ball today. Science is out the window." Cobb, then, was seeking to prove that he could be successful at a wholly new game, as much as he despised the power hitting that now dominated it.[8]

Ty Cobb wasn't the only big name signed by the A's in 1927. Mack brought his former second baseman, Eddie Collins, back to Philadelphia. The cornerstone of Mack's "$100,000 Infield," Collins was sent to the Chicago White Sox when the Tall Tactician disbanded his first championship dynasty. As one of the honest players on the 1919 Black Sox, Collins shined during his 12-year tenure in the Windy City and returned to Philadelphia with a .333 average and well over 700 stolen bases. Mack had a great deal of respect and affection for Collins, considering him "one of the greatest team players in the history of the game." Mack also knew that his "superb playing set a high standard for the others players on the team."[9] The manager planned to use him as a player-coach and mentor to young second baseman Max Bishop. Not surprisingly, Collins was also Mack's choice to replace him as manager of the A's at some undetermined future date.[10] Also joining Cobb and Collins was thirty-eight-year-old Zach Wheat, who starred in the Brooklyn Dodger outfield for eighteen years. A graceful, line-drive hitter, Wheat was a quiet team leader who routinely batted over .300. Though his legs were failing him, Mack believed that the veteran outfielder still had value as a pinch hitter and spot starter.[11]

The A's began their spring training camp in Fort Myers, Florida, with great enthusiasm. Almost immediately, the veterans took to their mentoring roles, helping to instruct the younger A's. Cobb took Al Simmons under his wing. Collins did the same with Bishop. Along with Wheat, both veterans also gave special attention to Jimmie Foxx, who was quickly becoming the most promising power hitter in the majors.

When the exhibition schedule began, many of the baseball aficionados were curious to see whether Cobb would second-guess Mack, especially in the positioning of players. But Cobb soon learned that his new manager knew the hitters, the park's air currents, and the sunshine factor so well that he never hesitated to follow orders when the Tall Tactician shifted his outfielders with his scorecard from the dugout.[12] By the time the A's broke camp, the graybeards and youngsters had performed with such an exceptional blend of power, speed, and intelligence that the sportswriters were predicting a pennant winner. Billy Evans of the *Sporting News* wrote, "Of all the ball clubs I have looked at in the South, the Athletics are by far the most impressive. The club doesn't appear to have a single weakness. They have a strong defense, a highly efficient pitching staff, plenty of reserve power, and oodles of gray matter." Evans believed that the addition of Cobb, Collins, and Wheat to an "already very good ball club," had made the A's a "great one."[13] Even some of the New York writers begrudgingly gave their nod to the A's, over their own beloved Yankees, on the strength of the three veteran acquisitions. "After all, the Yankees have a much younger club than the

Ty Cobb, Zack Wheat, and Eddie Collins were signed by Mack in 1927 to provide the kind of baseball knowledge and experience that would benefit his young A's. (Courtesy of the National Baseball Hall of Fame.)

Athletics," pointed out Joe Vila of the *New York Sun.* "Manager Miller Huggins is preparing for the future and isn't wasting time with old players."[14] Though the A's were much improved, they hardly provided competition for the Yankees in 1927, something that was abundantly clear on opening day in New York.

Connie Mack and Yankee manager Miller Huggins before the opening game of the 1927 season at Yankee Stadium in New York. (Courtesy of the National Baseball Hall of Fame.)

Nearly 70,000 fans jammed Yankee Stadium on April 12, 1927, to see the first of four games between New York and Philadelphia. It was the largest crowd in the history of the game to that date. Lefty Grove faced Waite Hoyt, New York's strong-armed fastballer better known as "Schoolboy" because his father signed him to a major league contract at the age of sixteen. Grove held Murderer's Row at bay through four innings. In the first, with Combs on third base, he struck out Babe Ruth on four pitches and followed by punching out Gehrig to retire the side. The Yankees threatened again in the fourth, this time with Koenig on third. But Grove got Ruth on a pop-up in foul territory to end the inning. In the fifth, with Hoyt on third base and Combs on second, Gehrig doubled in the two runners. Grove was relieved in the sixth. But by that time the score stood at 6–0 in favor of New York. Hoyt, on the other hand, had an effective change of pace and used it to shut down the A's for an 8–3 victory. It wouldn't get any better for the Mackmen either.

The next day, the Bronx Bombers pounded Sammy Gray and Howard Ehmke for ten runs, while Dutch Reuther held the A's bats to four. In the third game, the two teams played to a 9–9 deadlock before the contest was called because of darkness and a quickly descending freezing spell.[15] When it was replayed on April 15, the Yankees won 6–3, completing a three-game sweep of the A's. Ruth broke out of his slump by stroking the first of 60 home runs that season. Collins went to bat 15 times in the series and didn't collect a single hit. Cobb didn't fare much better. Their poor performances were received by the New York scribes with smug reassurance that their best days were behind them. "Once again the baseball boys have forgotten that a good label may hide a damaged can," wrote Ed Frayne of the *New York American.* "The Pennant-Picking Society took a frightful pasting at Yankee Stadium. It appears that the horsehide sophisticates were sadly mistaken in their appraisal of Messrs. Ty Cobb and Eddie Collins. They were good goods in their day, but they have been on the shelf too long. In a word, they're shot."[16] James Harrison of the *New York Times* was less dismissive: "The season is young yet, but so far the apathetic Athletics have displayed nothing that should cause a Yankee fan to walk the floor restlessly at night. Connie Mack, at first blush, appears to have an interesting but not highly valuable collection of antiques."[17] Their words were a bit premature. When the Yankees traveled to Shibe Park for another three-game series later that month, the outcome would be different.

On April 20, a record crowd of 40,000 watched Lefty Grove and 42-year-old reliever Jack Quinn hold Ruth hitless while the A's bats exploded against spitballer Urban Shocker. Collins and Cobb sparked two late-inning rallies and Cochrane led the attack with a triple and a home run. When it was over, the A's had capped an 8–5 victory. Not to be outdone by the New York scribes, John Nolan of the *Philadelphia Evening Bulletin* sarcastically boasted, "Connie Mack's so-called 'Antiques' reared up on their hind legs, flourished in two dashing late inning rallies, pummeled two pitchers and gained their first triumph over the Yankees this season."[18] The Yankees won 13–6 the next day on home runs by Lou Gehrig and Tony Lazzeri. But the A's rebounded behind the pitching of Rube Walberg in the final game of the series to win 4–3. Despite the loss, the series proved to be uplifting for the A's after their disastrous showing in New York earlier in

Cobb stealing home at Boston, April 26, 1927, on pitcher Tony Welzer of the Red Sox. Umpire Billy Evans and batter Dudley Branom look on as Cobb eludes Grover Hartley's tag. (Courtesy of the National Baseball Hall of Fame.)

the month. What's more, Cobb began to play like his old, unrelenting self. By the beginning of May, he was hitting at a .400 clip and fielding his position flawlessly.

Trailing the Red Sox, 7–3, in the seventh inning of a game at Shibe, Cobb stretched a single into a double. On the next pitch he stole third. Bill Carrigan, the Bosox manager, brought in right-handed reliever, Tony Welzer. More concerned with closing down the A's rally than he was with Cobb, Welzer ignored the star base stealer as he edged off third. Despite the fact that the left-handed hitting Walt French was at the plate, Cobb was determined to steal home in order to ignite a rally. As Welzer swung into his delivery, Cobb took off for the plate. The startled reliever attempted to redirect his throw to nail him, but Cobb's hook slide didn't give the catcher much more than a toe to tag. Cobb slid into home safely, making the score 7–4. The A's picked up three more runs in the eighth. In the ninth, with the score tied at 8–8, Dykes doubled and Cobb knocked him in with another double for a 9–8 victory. The next day, Cobb's ruthlessness caught up with him.

With Boston leading 3–2 in the eighth inning, Cobb came to bat and drove the first pitch over the right field fence just inside the foul line. As he began his trot around the bases in what he believed was a game-tying home run, plate umpire Emmett Ormsby ruled the ball foul and called him back. Al Simmons, who was on deck, suggested in rather colloquial language that Ormsby was blind. Cobb didn't appear to contest the decision, but once he stepped back into the batter's box he took a liberal practice swing that caught the umpire on the shoulder. Since there had been a history of bad blood between the two, Ormsby believed the act to be intentional and ejected Cobb. When the A's star insisted that it was an accident, Ormsby refused to change his decision. Cobb then shoved his nemesis, setting off a bottle-throwing riot in Shibe Park. It took two dozen policemen to contain the mayhem. Ormsby subsequently filed a complaint with the American League office, accusing the A's of "umpire baiting." Never a big fan of Cobb's, Ban Johnson suspended him, along with Simmons, for their roles in the incident.[19] When he returned to the lineup the following week, Cobb, perhaps more out of obstinacy than anything else, went on a 21-game hitting streak. Unfortunately, the team didn't fare as well.

May was a tough month for the A's. Scheduling inequities had them on the road through most of it. Hard luck put them on the losing end as well. After dropping a series in Cleveland and another in St. Louis, the A's managed to win a few games in Detroit and earned an even split in Chicago. Their luck wasn't much better when they returned to Philadelphia for a four-game Memorial Day weekend series against the Yankees. The A's took the first game of the series, 8–9. Babe Ruth won the second game with an 11th inning, tie-breaking home run that gave the New Yorkers a 6–5 victory. But the highlight of that game came in the fourth inning with one of the most unusual plays in major league history. With one out, Cobb at first and Collins at second, Al Simmons hit a foul pop fly near the A's dugout. Johnny Grabowski, the Yankee catcher, went after the ball and caught it, falling over the railing into the Philadelphia dugout. Before he emerged, both Collins and Cobb crossed the plate, tying the score at 2–2. When Huggins protested, chief umpire Roy Van Graftan declared the catch similar to a sacrifice fly and the runners entitled to score. Huggins appealed to the other two umpires and, after a lengthy conference, the crew reached a compromise decision: Collins' run would score, but Cobb was sent back to third. Despite Mack's fierce protestations, the ruling stood.[20]

The following day, the Yankees swept a doubleheader from the A's, 10–3 and 18–5. Grove, who started the first game, was getting hit pretty badly early on. Returning to the dugout after an especially bad inning, Mack greeted his young pitcher with a word of encouragement and a simple suggestion on how to pitch to Ruth and Gehrig. After he finished, he picked up his scorecard and began walking way. Grove, who was not known for his tactfulness, stood there angrily glaring at his manager and muttered, "Oh, go take a shit!" To his great surprise, Mack was still within earshot and heard the remark. Visibly angered, the Tall Tactician put down his scorecard and walked the length of the dugout to where Grove sat. Placing himself squarely in front of his short-tempered pitcher, Mack stood motionless for a moment, then said, "*You* go take a shit, Robert!" Then, in a dignified manner, he returned to his seat as the team struggled to control their laughter.[21]

Unfortunately, Mack's advice didn't do much good. Both Ruth and Gehrig homered in that first game, and the Bambino followed it up in the second game with his sixteenth home run of the season. In the two games, the Yankees pounded out 37 hits, six home runs, four triples, four doubles, and a smattering of singles. Despite the lopsided scores, the games proved entertaining, if for no other reason than the comic relief the players provided. The Babe, for example, batted right-handed in his final plate appearance, and Al Simmons, who had grown weary of chasing batted balls to the fence, finally climbed the ladder at the centerfield scoreboard to sit and watch the line drives as they soared overhead.[22]

The final game of the series, on June 1, was a hard-fought duel between Rube Walberg and Myles Thomas through eight innings. In the top of the ninth, with the scored tied at 1–1, two Yankees on base, and two outs, Jumpin' Joe Dugan came in to pinch hit. The Philly fans immediately began to razz the A's former third baseman with a chorus of "I wanna go home!" But Dugan quickly silenced them by hitting an 0–2 fastball into center field to give the Yankees the go-ahead run, which would prove to be the game winner.[23]

By the end of that series, the Yankees had captured nine of the 13 games they had played against the Athletics. Four of the last five games were victories at Shibe Park. Mack blamed the poor performance of the A's on the pitching staff, particularly Howard Ehmke.

He couldn't understand how the veteran pitcher who always baffled teams when he was with the last-place Red Sox could pitch so poorly for a contender. With a 6–9 record, Ehmke had been of virtually no use to the A's. Worse, the team lost Cobb, Collins, and Wheat to injuries.[23] By July 4, the Mackmen could not escape the fact that there was not going to be any pennant race in the American League that season. The Yankees, who had been in first-place from the very first day, were playing .700 baseball and held a commanding 9½ game lead over second-place Washington. Instead of setting the pace as the sportswriters had predicted, the A's found themselves floundering in 5th place, 13½ games back.[24] It created wonderful press in New York.

Ed Sullivan, sports editor for the *New York Graphic*, couldn't resist the temptation to take a jab at his former boss, Bill Brandt, at the *Philadelphia Public Ledger*. Writing at the conclusion of another series in which the Yanks took three of four games from the A's, Sullivan quipped,

> Bill Brandt, called "Doc" out of consideration for his early try at horse doctoring, is one of the veteran writers traveling with the Philadelphia Athletics. Bill, like most veterinarians, has horse sense, and has developed plenty of baseball savvy. I was interested in what he had to say yesterday. "It is against all the legends of baseball," he said hoarsely, "for a team to hit over a stretch the way the Yankees have been slugging. If their hitting falls off, the Yankees are licked. That infield will cost them the pennant if Ruth, Gehrig, and Lazzeri go into any considerable slump. Gehrig is not a high-class defensive player, Dugan is old enough to play on the Athletics, and Gazella is below championship team caliber. Morehart, Lazzeri, and Koenig are good defensive men, but first base and third base are in and out. If the Yanks lose their punch and have to depend on tight defensive play, that infield will crack." Inasmuch as the Doc is traveling with the Athletics, it might be suspected that the wish is father to the thought.[25]

The A's fortunes began to change after the Yankee series. They won 13 of their next 23 games, taking two of three from Cleveland, four straight from St. Louis, three of five from Washington, and splitting series with Detroit and Chicago. Cobb made history in Detroit when on July 18 he collected his 4,000th hit—a first-inning double off Sam Gibson.[26] Al Simmons was also setting records of his own. The temperamental leftfielder, who was hitting around .360 at the end of June, boosted his average to .433 during the A's win streak, which gave him the lead over Gehrig in the A.L. batting race. Although the team lost Simmons to injury for six weeks in late July, the A's continued their winning ways through August and September. While they won 36 of the 40 games they played during that stretch, Washington and Detroit, who were in second and third place respectively, were in the grip of losing stretches. By mid–September, the A's held sole possession of second place. That's where they finished the season, 19 games behind New York, who set a new American League record with 110 wins.

The 1927 New York Yankees were unquestionably among the greatest teams ever assembled. Having captured their fifth pennant in seven years, New York had established itself as the perennial powerhouse in the American League. The World Series took only four days, as the Yankees quickly dispatched the Pittsburgh Pirates, outscoring them 23–10 in the four-game sweep.

Yankee owner Colonel Jacob Ruppert, who liked to win pennants early and often, provided the money for a baseball dynasty. As president and owner of one of New York's great breweries, Ruppert purchased the franchise in 1914 for $450,000 from original owner Bill Devery, who had fallen on hard times. Success was not immediate, though. The Yankees finished in the second division until, in 1920, the Colonel hired Edward Barrow, the manager of the Boston Red Sox, as business manager, and Miller Huggins, the peppery player-manager of the St. Louis Cardinals, to manage his team. While Ruppert provided the financial support and Huggins the field expertise, Barrow had the vision and network to build a Yankee dynasty.[27]

In a series of transactions that have gone down in baseball history as the "Rape of the Red Sox," Barrow took advantage of his Boston connections to secure the services of his former superstars, including pitchers Bullet Joe Bush, Sam Jones, Waite Hoyt, and Herb Pennock; starting infielders Everett Scott and Joe Dugan; and catcher Wally Schang. But his greatest purchase was that of Boston's great slugger Babe Ruth for $100,000. Ruth's sale by Red Sox owner Harry

The 1927 New York Yankees. Front row (left to right)—Julie Wera, Mike Gazella, Pat Collins, Eddie Bennett (mascot), Benny Bengough, Ray Morehart, Myles Thomas, Cedric Durst. Middle row—Urban Shocker, Joe Dugan, Earle Combs, Charlie O'Leary (coach), Miller Huggins (manager), Art Fletcher (coach), Mark Koenig, Dutch Ruether, Johnny Grabowski, George Pipgras. Back row—Lou Gehrig, Herb Pennock, Tony Lazzeri, Wiley Moore, Babe Ruth, Don Miller, Bob Meusel, Bob Shawkey, Waite Hoyt, Joe Giard, Ben Paschal, (unknown), Doc Wood (trainer).

Frazee was considered such a heinous act in New England that one Boston newspaper ran a cartoon showing Faneuil Hall draped with a For Sale sign.[28] Ruth had, indeed, become a baseball institution in Boston and would have an immediate impact in New York. In 1920 he led the Yankees to a third-place finish, compiling 54 home runs, 137 RBIs, and a .376 average. Attendance more than doubled, and the Yankees enjoyed the first of many banner years at the gate. The following year Ruth's 59 homers paced a power-hitting lineup that included Bob Meusel, Frank Baker, Wally Pipp, and Roger Peckinpaugh. Each player had at least hit eight home runs and 70 RBIs that season, earning them the nickname "Murderer's Row." Though the players would come and go, the moniker would remain. By 1927, Murderer's Row consisted of Ruth, Meusel, Earl Combs, Tony Lazzeri, and Lou Gehrig. Their late afternoon hitting rallies were referred to as "five o'clock lightning."[29]

The cornerstone of the Yankee lineup, however, was the duo of Ruth and Gehrig. The pair of sluggers formed one of the most devastating one-two punches in professional baseball. Gehrig introduced himself to the Yankee batting order in 1925 with 20 homers, 68 RBIs and a .295 average. The next year he improved his average to .313 and contributed 16 home runs and 107 RBIs to the Yankee attack. Huggins was so impressed with his young first baseman's performance that, in 1927, he moved him into the cleanup spot, ahead of Bob Meusel and behind Ruth. Gehrig responded by challenging the Bambino's home run mark. The two men ran neck and neck throughout most of the 1927 campaign. Ruth pulled ahead in September and, on the last day of the season, stroked his 60th round-tripper. Never one for much humility, Ruth circled the bases and, returning to the bench, cried out, "Sixty! Count 'em, sixty! Let's see some other son-of-a-bitch match that!"[30] Gehrig ended the season with 47 home runs and 175 RBIs, which gave him the league title in that category ahead of Ruth's 164. While their slugging feats and hitting statistics were similar, their dispositions could not have been more opposite.

Babe Ruth was both a product as well as a catalyst of the Roaring Twenties. Outgoing and boisterous, Ruth loved being the center of attention. Not only did he revolutionize the game with his home-run hitting, but his personal excesses were legendary. He indulged himself with the finest clothing, a twelve-cylinder Packard, and an eleven-room suite at the exclusive Ansonia Hotel on New York's Upper West Side. He had a gargantuan appetite and a remarkable capacity for alcohol and tobacco. "I've seen him at midnight, propped up in bed, order six club sandwiches, a platter of pigs' knuckles and a pitcher of beer," Ty Cobb once confirmed. "He'd down all that while smoking a big black cigar. The next day, if he hit a homer, he'd trot around the bases complaining about gas pains and a bellyache. Then he'd let out a magnificent belch or fart at will."

A big spender known for his womanizing, Ruth also hungered for female affection, most likely because of a neglected youth. Women were eager to please him, and rarely did he ever turn them down. Once, when the Yankees were playing in St. Louis, he announced that he was going to go to bed with every girl in the local whorehouse that night—and did. On another occasion, after the Yankees had clinched the pennant in Detroit, Ruth rented four hotel rooms with connecting doors and threw an all night party. Midway through the evening, he stood on a chair with a beer in one hand and a sandwich in the other and announced: "Any girl who doesn't want to fuck can leave now!" Few of them did, allowing Ruth to set yet another record—the most legendary orgy in baseball history. On still another occasion, Gehrig discovered him, naked and half-drunk, in a hotel bedroom with two girls. Sitting at the side of the bed, Ruth was sobbing because, after a night of sexual gymnastics, he was now unable to service both of them.[31]

According to teammate Waite Hoyt, Ruth did whatever he pleased, on and off the field. "Babe seemed to believe that his mere presence in the lineup was all he owed to the club," recalled the Yankee pitcher. "He paid no attention to curfew, never took the room assigned to him, and often trotted into the clubhouse just barely in time to make the game."[32] Tired of the all-night carousing and constant breaking of team rules, Miller Huggins was determined to discipline his star player during the 1927 season. Backed by Ruppert and Barrow, the Yankee skipper fined Ruth $5,000 and suspended him for nine days. When he returned to the lineup, the slugger understood who was boss and improved his behavior.

Gehrig, by contrast, was modest and reserved to the point of shyness. A devoted family man who worshipped his mother, the young first baseman would eventually settle into a quiet married life. He was never a big drinker, watched carefully what he ate, and was extremely frugal with his money. His salary peaked at $39,000 in 1938, but it didn't come close to the $80,000 Ruth commanded one year during his prime. Despite being the highest paid player of his day, Ruth often threatened to hold out for more money, whereas Gehrig's devotion to the game and his loyalty to the Yankees prevented him from asking for a cent more than management offered to pay him. While Ruth overshadowed Gehrig both on and off the field, the quiet first baseman apparently accepted his subordinate position without envy or resentment. "I'm not a headline guy," he once said. "I'm just the guy on the Yankees who's in there every day. I'm the fellow who follows the Babe in the batting order. If I stood on my head, nobody would pay any attention."[33]

That Gehrig didn't capture many headlines was a mixed blessing, even though some New York writers predicted that that would change. As Gehrig was closing in on Ruth's home run title in 1927, Paul Gallico of the *New York Daily News* wrote, "The most astonishing thing that ever happened in organized baseball is the home run race between Babe Ruth and Lou Gehrig. If anything looked to be permanent, it was the Babe's record of 59 home runs in one season. Now Gehrig is a sure thing to break the mark within a few years." Gallico admitted that Gehrig could "not approach Ruth as a showman, but there is time for that." In an insightful comparison to Ruth, Gallico predicted that Gehrig's true nature would reveal itself when "he runs up against the temptations that beset a popular hero." He pointed out that Ruth,

> without temptations, might be a pretty ordinary fellow. Part of his charm lies in the manner with which he succumbs to every temptation that comes his way. That does not mean that Henry Louis must take up sin to become a box office attraction. Rather one awaits to see his reactions to life, which same reactions make a man interesting or not. Right now, he seems more devoted to fishing and hitting home runs. For this reason, it is a little more difficult to write about Henry Louis than George Herman. Ruth is either planning to cut loose, is cutting loose, or is repenting the last time he cut loose. He is a news story on legs going about looking for a place to happen. He has not lived a model life, while Henry Louis has, and if Ruth wins the home run race it will come as a great blow to the pure.[34]

Both men, however, were very concerned about their public image. That is why they hired Christy Walsh, a quick-thinking, ambitious agent to become a financial advisor and public relations man. While Walsh spent fifteen years persuading Ruth to invest some of his money and healing his reputation, he persuaded Gehrig to pose for several beefcake photographs as Tarzan and to exploit his quiet masculinity in a Hollywood Western titled *Rawhide*. But as Shirley Povich, who covered baseball for the *Washington Post* in the 1920s, pointed out years later, neither player really needed Walsh from an image-making standpoint. "They were special," he insisted. "*Everyone* knew what Babe Ruth and Lou Gehrig meant to the game. After all, who can 'boo' a home run? Even Ruth's excessive behavior, which would be exposed in this day of baseball writing, was simply ignored at that time."[35]

Beyond the power-hitting duo of Ruth and Gehrig, the Yankees had remarkably effective starting pitchers. Waite Hoyt, Herb Pennock,

Urban Shocker, and rookie Wilcy Moore were the workhorses of the staff. All four pitchers topped .700 in winning percentage, and together they led the American League in ERA (3.20), shutouts (11), and fewest walks (409). After these four hurlers, Yankee pitching was questionable. Had it not been for the effectiveness of Moore, who collected 13 saves—many of them in relief of Shocker, who was terminally ill and had difficulty finishing—New York would not have held the commanding lead they enjoyed throughout the season.[36]

Despite their solid pitching and the home run prowess of Ruth and Gehrig, the 1927 Yankees did have their weaknesses. Aside from Gehrig and Lazzeri (.309, 18 HR, 102 RBI), their infield left much to be desired. Shortstop Mark Koenig's average hovered around the .280 mark through most of the season, but he did not possess the range, hands or glove of a quality middle infielder. His 52 errors the previous season led the American League, and four more in the 1926 World Series led to the Cardinals' winning rally in the seventh and deciding game. He would commit another league-leading 47 errors in 1927. Joe Dugan, at third, had already seen his heyday. That season he hit only two home runs, with 43 RBIs and a .269 average. His defensive skills were also lacking, and he was platooned with a mediocre Mike Gazella (.278, 0 HR, 9 RBI) during the season.[37] The catching duties were shared by Pat Collins, Johnny Grabowski, and Benny Bengough. While all of them were fairly dependable behind the plate, none of them could hit. Collectively, the three backstops produced only seven home runs and 71 RBIs. The Yankees realized that their fortunes at that position rested with a young Bill Dickey, who was purposely left in the minors to gain more experience. Thus the Yankees pitching staff enjoyed the luxury of a deadly batting order that could boast of a league-leading .307 average and all the runs they needed to win.

Though disappointed in their second-place finish, the Athletics had demonstrated marked improvement over previous years. Lefty Grove had become the indisputable ace of a solid pitching staff. Posting a 20–13 record with nine saves and an ERA of 3.19, Grove also led the American League with 174 strikeouts. His most effective performance came on September 3, when he handed the Yankees their first and only shutout of the season, 1–0. Grove recorded a total of nine strikeouts, three of which came in the second inning, when he retired the side—Meusel, Lazzeri, and Dugan—on just 10 pitched balls. Though not as impressive as Grove, the other pitchers were more than reliable. Rube Walberg (16–12, 3.97 ERA), Jack Quinn (15–10, 3.17 ERA), Howard Ehmke (12–10, 4.22 ERA), and Eddie Rommel (11–3, 4.36 ERA) were the other starters, and Sammy Gray (9–6, 4.60 ERA) was used primarily in relief.

The infield was also strong. Jimmy Dykes was quickly becoming one of the league's best defensive first baseman and was hitting as well. Max Bishop had replaced Collins as the A's regular second baseman, having developed into a smooth, sure-handed infielder. Though he wasn't a dangerous leadoff hitter, his keen judgment of the strike zone allowed him to work his way on base and then manufacture runs with his speed. His keystone partner was a 29-year-old rookie, Joe Boley, who hit .311 that season. Mack, who purchased Boley from Baltimore earlier in the year, considered him "the best shortstop in America" because of his uncanny ability "to make the tough plays look so confoundedly soft and a bat to go with it."[38] Sammy Hale proved to be a more than dependable third baseman, while compiling a .313 batting average. Collectively, the infielders posted a .967 fielding average, while committing only 71 errors. Additionally, Mack had the pleasant problem of trying to find a regular position for Jimmie Foxx, who was coming on strong at the plate. Originally a catcher, Foxx was inserted at first base in May and platooned at that position with Poole and Dykes. In 37 at bats that season, Foxx collected 42 hits and 20 RBIs for a .323 average. He also demonstrated some impressive power with six doubles, five triples and three home runs. His first four bagger came in the second game of a Memorial Day doubleheader against Yankee spitballer Urban Shocker. A week later, in St. Louis, he hit his second. Though his third and final home run of the season didn't come until late September against the White Sox, it proved to be the margin of victory in a 5–4 contest. So impressive was the 468-foot shot that it was described by one sportswriter as a "lick of Ruthian might."[39] Predictably, A's fans began to demand more playing time for the youngster, and at times their demanding nature could be simply insufferable.

Philadelphia was known, among other things, for its scrutinizing fans. While they made plenty of strange noises in the stands, their favorite expression was "boo." And the jeers were not always directed at the opposing players. During an early season slump, the heckling became so severe that after the seventh inning of one whitewashing, Dykes asked Mack if he could go into the bleachers to settle the score against two brothers who were riding him. One sat along the first base line, the other along third, and they'd take turns insulting the first baseman. Both had deep, powerful lungs and particularly enjoyed razzing Dykes because they knew it got to him. Mack, in his great wisdom, advised, "Jimmy, there's only two out there now; by the time you get up in the stands, there will be five more; and shortly after that there might be twenty-five. So, as I think you're a pretty valuable man on this team, I feel you might just as well spend the afternoon at first base. Have a good sleep on it, and by tomorrow, you'll forget it ever happened."[40] But even Mack became fed up by the end of the season. He was so perturbed by the abuse laid on by one fan, Harry Donnelly, whose voice carried throughout Shibe Park with the "resonance of a three mile loud speaker," that he sought legally to restrain him. At a September 15th game against the Chicago White Sox, Mack had the young man arrested. The following day, at a hearing before a local magistrate, the Tall Tactician testified against him. "There are several people who come out to the park just to ride the players and umpires," he said. "Yesterday, Mr. Donnelly rode third baseman Sammy Hale until he had him so nervous he would have missed the ball had one been hit to him. In this game an error might have meant defeat." Mack added that the heckler's raspberries not only broke up the morale of his team, but also forced him to trade a valuable player, Bill Lamar. "Lamar," said Mack, "was one of the best outfielders I ever had. But a group of fans, of which this man was the ringleader, kept riding him until he wasn't any good to me and I had to trade him away." Mack concluded his testimony by saying, "It seems that this young man pays his $1.10 to come and ride the players. Why doesn't he save it and meet them outside after the game? We want him to stay away from the park." The magistrate, a big A's fan himself, held Donnelly on $500 bail to keep the peace and threatened to fine him if he were arrested again for "handing out raspberries."[41]

When they weren't razzing the players, A's fans were complaining about ticket prices. At one point, the grievances became so petty that James Isaminger of the *Philadelphia Inquirer* wrote: "Men

Premier power hitters of the 1920s: Jimmie Foxx, Babe Ruth, Lou Gehrig, and Al Simmons. (Courtesy of the National Baseball Hall of Fame.)

who darn their own socks have been complaining that Shibe Park tickets have been advanced in price. 'Isn't it terrible!' 'Let's write to the papers,' etc. As a matter of fact, the ticket schedule is the same as last year: 50¢ for the bleachers, $1.10 for grandstand, and $2.20 for box seats."[42] If the fans had a legitimate gripe, though, it was the ban on Sunday baseball.

After several appeals by Connie Mack failed to rescind the ban, the A's manager went ahead and challenged the ruling by playing a Sunday game against the Chicago White Sox in August of the previous season. His action resulted in legal proceedings by the Pennsylvania Supreme Court, which, on June 25, 1926, upheld the ban, declaring, "We cannot imagine anything more worldly or unreligious than professional baseball being played on the Sabbath." The ruling produced a storm of criticism from fans and Philadelphia sportswriters alike. As one writer pointed out, "There are 2,000 games played every Sunday in Pennsylvania and admission is charged too.

This does not only apply to semipro and independent games, but the International League and the New York and Pennsylvania Leagues, members of organized baseball, which play regularly on Sunday. So, the sum total of the whole business is that Sunday baseball can be played anywhere in Philadelphia or the state of Pennsylvania except at the three major league parks."[43] Another writer was even more antagonistic: "It's a laugh to pick up a Philadelphia newspaper on Monday morning and read sermons whose ministers genuflect the supreme court 'for saving Sunday from baseball' and then turn to the sports section and see a page of box scores of minor league and independent games that were played all over the state on the Sabbath."[44]

The absence of Sunday baseball—as well as a pennant race—hurt the Athletics at the gate. The team drew well until after the Labor Day series against Washington. By defeating the Senators in those three games, the A's assured themselves a second-place finish. There was no chance that they could catch the powerful Yankees. Fans lost interest and stopped attending the games. Mack was forced to cut his payroll.[45] The most obvious choice was to release Cobb, the highest paid player on the team.

Two weeks before the season ended, Cobb had asked and received permission to quit the team. Rumors had been circulating that some teammates were unhappy with his selfish attitude, believing that he played to pad his own statistics rather than for the good of the team. Mack squelched the rumors by crediting Cobb for the A's second-place finish. Declaring that he "never handled a finer baseball man," Mack insisted that he would keep the Georgia Peach if he could come up with the money to pay his salary.[46] Despite the fact that the A's didn't capture the pennant, Mack still paid Cobb the additional $15,000 he promised for the A.L. flag. After all, the Georgia Peach had given Philadelphia fans a tremendous season. He drove in or scored 197 runs, stole 22 bases, and hit .357, fifth best in the American League. After 1927, even Babe Ruth admitted, "Sure, Cobb's a prick, but God Almighty, how that old man can still hit and run."[47]

Chapter 4

CHALLENGING THE YANKEES, 1928

C onnie Mack's baseball fortunes were clearly changing by 1928. No longer were his A's finishing in the second division, and, despite the need to tighten his payroll, Mack had still managed to put together a serious contender. His personal life was also flourishing.

A widower for several years, Mack remarried and began a second family. His new wife, Katherine Hallahan, was a very stylish woman and a dedicated mother who provided a stable home life for the Tall Tactician. He maintained a healthy relationship with the children from his first marriage—Roy, Earle, Marguerite—and seemed to enjoy raising the children from his second—Mary, Connie Jr., Ruth, Rita, and Betty. By 1928, his elder sons were working for the Athletics and Connie Jr. was developing into an impressive prep school athlete at Germantown Academy. While he adored all of his children, Mack took special pride in his namesake, a strikingly handsome boy who inherited his father's 6'4" frame as well as his gentlemanly disposition.[1]

Connie Jr.'s athletic achievements made his father extremely proud. At Germantown Academy, he excelled in both amateur boxing and baseball. While he won the school's championship in the former, he was one of the most talented prep school pitchers in the latter, thanks to Eddie Rommel. Connie Jr. and his best friend, Rudy Baizley, would spend their summer days at Shibe Park with the A's. "During the morning practice sessions, which went from 9:30 a.m. to 11:30 a.m.," recalled Baizley, "we'd play some pepper and shag fly balls in the outfield while the players did their infield and hitting. Near the end of practice, Eddie Rommel would come over and work with Connie Jr. on the mechanics of pitching and Cy Perkins would catch. Afterwards, Mr. Mack would take us up to his tower office where we'd have lunch. The afternoons, of course, were spent watching the game."[2]

Mack's personal financial circumstances had also improved. He was able to relocate his family from the working class neighborhoods of North Philadelphia to the more affluent suburb of Germantown. He purchased a spacious, three-story home at 604 Cliveden Street, bordering Fairmount Park. Ruth Clark, Mack's daughter, recalled the sizable proportions of the house:

> You entered through a vestibule into a center hall. Off to the left was a large parlor, which had a grand piano in one corner. Next to the parlor was a living room where the family would often sit in the evenings after dinner. To the right, there was a large dining room and behind it, a pantry, a breakfast room, and the kitchen. In the pantry there was a back stairway leading to the second floor where there were three large bedrooms, two baths, a huge walk-in closet, a sitting room, an enclosed sun porch, and a sewing room. On the third floor, there were four bedrooms, a storage room, and a bath. There was also a basement with a large laundry area and a coal bin, which, during the early thirties, was converted to gas heating. It was a very comfortable, as well as beautiful house in which to raise a family.[3]

On a summer Sunday afternoon after church, Mack could be found sitting out on the front porch with his family, entertaining the neighborhood children, or watching his son play baseball on the vacant lot adjacent to the house. Though he was in his mid–60s at the time, Mack retained a youthful outlook by surrounding himself with children. He delighted in their company and took every opportunity to interest them in baseball.[4]

Just as important to him was his Catholic faith. A devout member of St. Madeline Sophia's on Green and Upsal streets, Mack sent all the children of his second marriage to Catholic elementary school. The girls then matriculated to Mount St. Joseph Academy, where Mary, Mack's oldest daughter, seriously considered taking vows to become a nun.[5] "When the A's played at home," recalled his daughter, Ruth, "he always attended Sunday mass at St. Madeline Sophia's with our family. On the road, he always accompanied his Catholic players to mass after Sunday breakfast."[6] Unlike the Protestant establishment that controlled Philadelphia politics, Mack

Pitcher Eddie Rommel became the mainstay of Mack's bullpen. (Courtesy of Jerome Romanowski.)

saw no contradiction between baseball and religion. For him, professional baseball on the Sabbath was nothing more than good, healthy recreation, just like the independent contests that were allowed to take place within Sunday church leagues.[7]

Mack's Catholicism was best demonstrated in the service he performed for others. Several of his younger players enjoyed a college education because of his generosity.[8] He never forgot his former ballplayers, either. Eddie Collins once said that he "didn't know of any needy old ballplayer who was ever turned down by Mr. Mack for a loan." Instead Mack helped those in need without any fanfare or publicity. "A few years ago, a frail-legged hunchback, Louis Van Zelst, drifted into our ballpark one morning and never saying a word to anybody minded our bats," Collins recalled. "He needed a job but was too proud to ask. Mr. Mack, being the kind man he is, understood the situation and put Little Van on the payroll as our team's mascot. Mr. Mack's generosity can be seen in other ways as well. At his orders, our old uniforms are sent to an Indian Reservation in Oklahoma and used baseballs are boxed up and sent to the Eastern Penitentiary for the convicts to use."[9]

At the same time, it is difficult to know just how much of Connie Mack's genteel, almost saintly disposition was calculated and how much of it was natural. He was, after all, very reserved about his personal life and just as quiet, though authoritative, on the baseball diamond. "My father was very human," admitted Ruth Clark, "and, like us all, not perfect all the time. Yet, as close as I was to him, I could never understand how he accepted all the responsibility of managing a professional ball club as long as he did. It was constant work and worry, but never did I hear him complain."[10] By his mid–60s, the adoption of a calm, tranquil exterior may have been necessary for Mack to continue in a profession that was wrought with pressure and rowdyism. His daily regimen reflected an extraordinary self-discipline. *The Philadelphia Record* once ran the following account of his summer daily routine.

> Mack awakens at 7:00 a.m. and dresses in a dark business suit with a fresh, tall white collar. Breakfast is at 8:00 a.m. sharp. He has grapefruit or sometimes baked apple or prunes followed by oatmeal or cream of wheat and coffee. He reads the *Philadelphia Record* as he eats of course.
>
> Then it's off to Shibe Park and his tower office where he spends 30 minutes reading about the other American League teams in out-of-state papers, opens mail, receives visitors, and dictates for about an hour. He keeps his office door locked.
>
> Lunch is taken at 1:00 p.m. promptly. He spreads a towel across a chair to serve as a table cloth. His house servant James packs him sandwiches and vegetable soup and Mack brings it to the ball park in a wicker basket and thermos bottle.
>
> After lunch he takes a one hour nap, reclining on his office sofa. At 2:45 p.m., Mack leaves for the clubhouse where he makes out the batting order and talks with the players. At 3:10 p.m. he leaves the clubhouse, picks up his

scorecard and takes his place on the steps of the dugout. For the next two hours, he manages the game. Mack admits that those two hours are the toughest and that he is physically and mentally drained after a game.

After the game, he returns home and has dinner at 6:00 p.m. He then retires to the living room where he turns on the radio and listens to boxing. Later in the evening he joins Mrs. Mack to play bridge or to go to the theater. He is always in bed by 11:00 p.m.[11]

To be sure, Mack enjoyed an impeccable reputation as a clean-living gentleman and paternalistic manager to a tremendously talented but volatile collection of personalities. Never one to upstage his players, the Tall Tactician downplayed his own importance to the team. Except for a pregame meeting, he rarely entered the clubhouse, and since he preferred not to wear a uniform, he was prohibited from stepping onto the field. By dressing in street clothes, Mack created the distance between himself and his players he believed necessary to achieve their respect. "In my early years, when I managed in Milwaukee, I was in uniform," he recalled.

During those years, I dressed with the players and there were the usual arguments after we lost a tough game. And trying to fix the blame, hot words were often spoken on both sides. Then one day something came up that made me real sore: I was so mad I knew I couldn't talk calmly. So I waited around until all the players had dressed and gone home. I was still hot when I went home, but when I awoke the next morning I realized that it was just another ball game we had lost. It was a bonehead play, yes, but ballplayers are human, and it was all part of baseball. From that time on, I never again dressed with my players, either in Milwaukee or afterward in Philadelphia. My coaches are in the clubhouse, but I do not go near the players unless I have something I especially want to take up with them. I save my own feelings as well as theirs that way. If we are on the road, I see the player who may have made a mistake in the hotel lobby or call him to my room. If we are home, I let it go until the next day. By then we both are calm and can discuss the matter with no bitterness. Often I am able to point out to the player his mistakes, show him how the play should have been made; and, if the player has the natural ability, he may learn from his mistake.[12]

Connie Mack, the Tall Tactician of the Philadelphia Athletics. (Courtesy of the National Baseball Hall of Fame.)

Nor did Mack fine his players, though he did express his displeasure when a player broke training rules or the midnight curfew. Instead he tried to serve as a role model for them. He never argued with an umpire during the game, but was known to give them a piece of his mind as they made their way to the clubhouse afterwards. Above all, he demanded that his players be accountable. "Don't give alibis!" he admonished them. "If you've made a mistake, or a misplay, take the blame for it good-naturedly. You will only gain stature in the eyes of your teammates if you do so."[13] Mack was a strict disciplinarian who didn't hesitate to lay into an unruly player with subtle sarcasm if it was warranted. Only when was he extremely angry did he use profanity. Though he once admitted that "goodness gracious" was the closest he ever came to swearing, there was at least one sportswriter who disagreed. According to Red Smith, Mack was "always painted as a plaster saint in the newspapers. He was quoted as saying 'my goodness' or 'goodness gracious' as the strongest expletive he ever used. It was not. He had grown up on baseball benches where you hardly could use that language. I never saw him blush either listening to or occasionally borrowing some of the language." Nevertheless, Smith accorded Mack the utmost respect. Though he, like other sportswriters, often referred to the A's manager in the press as the "Spindly Strategist," the "Tall Tactician," or simply as "Connie," he always addressed him as "Mr. Mack" in person—a practice that was also followed by his players.[14]

By achieving a necessary distance between himself and the players, as well as by his strict but paternalistic approach to managing them, Mack cultivated a special chemistry that placed team success above individual achievement. "Baseball is played by teams, not by individuals," he reminded his players.

> It is inevitable that in the course of a game or a season or even over a period of years, certain players will be outstanding on offense or defense or both. The names that get into the headlines are those of the heavy hitters or champion base stealers, or those who stand out in a spectacular play. But no man ever won a game by himself. Behind him were not only the eight men on the playing field but the substitutes, the pinchhitters, the coaches, and, if I may modestly say so, the manager. The greatest ball teams in history have always been those where the friendliest relationships prevailed between the individual players and where there was present that most essential element called "team spirit." You cannot have a winning ball club where there is dissension and divided loyalty. Nor can you have a winning team when there is jealousy of one or two men that happen to be outstanding.[15]

It was this philosophy that convinced Mack to retain Ty Cobb for another season, despite the differences some of his younger players might have had with the former Tiger.

At almost 42 years of age, Cobb's batting eye was still sharp, but his legs were gone. It was questionable whether he would be able to beat out a bunt or take the extra base or steal with the same ease he once did. Nor did he have anything more to prove. The 1927 campaign gave him the vindication he sought. He certainly did not need the money. His success in the stock market, as well as a series of lucrative contracts, assured that he would live comfortably for the rest of his life. But he did have an emotional need to stay in the game. That is why he agreed to a pay cut and signed for two-thirds of the salary he earned the previous year.[16] Perhaps in an effort to make Cobb feel more comfortable, Mack signed his good friend Tris Speaker, who had also been accused of game fixing. Together with Collins and Gleason, Mack now had four ex-managers on his team.[17]

The A's, sporting new uniforms, opened their spring training camp in Ft. Myers, Florida, in late February. No longer would they wear the white elephant emblem over the left breast of their jersey.

It was replaced with a script letter "A." To go along with their new look, Mack's regulars returned physically fit and ready to play. Right handers Ehmke, Rommel, and Quinn, who had had their problems the previous year, looked to be capable of pitching good ball from the start, while left handers Grove and Walberg, who were expected to bear the burden of the starting rotation, appeared to be in excellent shape.[18] Accompanying the regular infielders—Dykes, Boley, and Bishop—was first baseman Joe Hauser, who was making a comeback after an injured knee. The outfield looked to be particularly strong. In addition to the projected regulars—Cobb, Speaker, and Simmons—the A's sported a platoon of talented reserves, all of whom batted above the .300 mark during the previous season. Bing Miller, returning to Philadelphia from St. Louis in exchange for pitcher Sammy Gray, hit .328 for the Browns, while Walt French hit .304. DeWitt Lebourveau brought a .346 average with him from Toledo, while George Haas of Atlanta batted .323 in the Southern Association, and Oswald Orwell, a former Athletic making a comeback as a pitcher-outfielder, hit .370 in the American Association. But once the exhibition games began, there was cause for concern.

Only occasionally did the A's perform well. They beat the New York Giants and Boston Braves twice, and earned solitary victories over the St. Louis Cardinals and hometown Phillies, while losing the same number of games to the same opponents. They fared even less well when they played minor league clubs. Baltimore beat the A's in both of their games and Buffalo split a two-game series with the Mackmen. That gave the A's a total of seven wins and nine losses in the South.[19] If anything, the final record was deceiving. The A's inconsistency had more to do with their inability to field a regular lineup than anything else.

Mack alternated between Hauser, Dykes, and Foxx at first base, and at third he platooned Dykes and Foxx. The outfield was worse. Cobb, after being in camp less than a week, had to return to Georgia to be with his wife as she was undergoing an operation. In his absence, Mack played musical chairs with Simmons, Speaker and the other reserves. What's more, Simmons, who had a reputation for improving his performance as the season unfolded, complained of a bad back throughout the spring.[20] Predictably, his playing was erratic at best.

Still there were positive signs. The pitchers seemed to be ahead of the hitters in the last few contests. Grove fanned seven batters in his first three innings of work against the Braves and turned in a similarly effective performance against the Phillies. Rommel also pitched effectively, going a total of nine innings in two games against the Giants and holding them to only one run. Even Ehmke and Quinn, who were questionable going into the camp, pitched more effectively than they had the previous spring. Perhaps the most pleasant surprise, however, was the hitting of Hauser, Miller, and Haas, who broke camp with .400 averages.[24] Mack was so impressed with Haas' power that he often boasted it "packed the kick of a mule," thereby coining a phrase.[22]

The A's opened against the Yankees at Shibe Park. Unfortunately for them, the game was a repeat of the 1927 opener. Bitter cold temperatures and a high wind added to the A's misery, as Herb Pennock pitched New York to an 8–3 victory over Lefty Grove. Heavy rain that turned to snow caused the following day's game to be canceled. The series resumed the following day when a warming sunshine attracted 23,000 to Shibe. The game proved to be a home run contest. Gehrig opened the slugfest in the second, drilling a shot over the right field fence and into the open window of a house on Twentieth Street. Combs and Meusel followed with solo homers of their own, and by the bottom of the third inning, the Yankees held a commanding 7–0 lead. Before the game ended, however, the A's added a few blows of their own. Joe Hauser contributed two homers and a triple to the A's attack, while Cochrane added a solo shot in the losing cause.

The A's misfortunes continued when the Senators came to town, as the team dropped a two-game series to Washington. Lefty Grove turned things around with a 2–1 victory against the Bronx Bombers in New York. Tris Speaker batted in the first run with a single in the sixth inning. Then, in the ninth, Cobb tripled over Comb's head and Speaker brought him in with a sacrifice fly. Walberg made it two straight by blanking the Yanks, 10–0, the following day. It was the worst defeat the Yankees had suffered at home in recent memory, and the first time they were swept at home since 1926. Returning to Shibe, the Mackmen took two more games from Boston, 11–6 and 3–2. In the first game, Speaker collected two doubles and two triples and, in the second, doubled in the first Athletic run in the fourth. Cobb figured in the winning run in the sixth by smacking a double, stealing third, and scoring on a sacrifice fly. The A's won seven of the next eight games on the road. When they returned to Philadelphia, the fans came out en masse to greet them. Nearly 30,000 turned out to see the opening game of a series against Detroit. The Macks didn't disappoint them.

Dramatic home runs by Sammy Hale, Joe Hauser, and Jimmie Foxx thrilled the crowd and accounted for seven of the ten runs scored by the A's in the Friday opener. Cobb provided more excitement with his baserunning. After hitting a single, he loafed down the first base line and with a burst of speed dashed for second and made it. Later in the game, he was leading off first when Speaker scorched a grounder just inside the line. Detroit first baseman Sweeney stopped the ball, but Cobb forced an overthrow when he took off for second and came around to score on the error. On Saturday, another 35,000 turned out to see Tris Speaker blast a game-winning, two-run home run over the right field wall. In the Sunday finale, Grove held the Tigers to five hits while fanning nine in a 10–0 victory.

The A's combination of effective pitching and powerful hitting presented a serious challenge to New York. The entire batting order from Bishop down to Boley was scorching the ball. Miller, who replaced the injured Al Simmons in the outfield, was hitting above .400, while Hauser became the A's big RBI man in Simmons' absence. Not to be outdone, Cobb and Speaker were delivering in the pinch. Even Foxx, who was being platooned at three different positions, was murdering the ball.

By May 24, the A's had whittled the Yankees' lead to only three and a half games when New York came to town and took four of five games from the Mackmen. Although Cobb and Speaker continued to hit the ball as well as ever, they were becoming a defensive liability. Between the two veterans, many a fly ball was dropped or misplayed. They performed so poorly against the Yankees that the *New York American* printed an amusing little cartoon of their miscues titled "Philly Phollies."[23] Simmons, who had recently returned to the lineup, was forced to retrieve many a misplayed ball during the series. After the final game, he complained, "If this keeps up, by the end of the season I'll be an old man myself."[24]

Beset by failing legs and an assortment of injuries, both Cobb and Speaker were replaced in the lineup by a younger, more mobile outfield of Simmons in left, Bing Miller in center, and Mule Haas in right. In mid–June, Mack strengthened his pitching staff by purchasing an impressive righthander, George Earnshaw, from the Baltimore Orioles and also made some changes in the infield. Foxx became the A's regular third baseman and Hauser, whose average began to slip, was being platooned with Jimmy Dykes at first base.[25] Mack could no longer afford to keep Foxx out of the lineup. He was emerging as one of the most productive power hitters in the game and one whose slugging feats were being compared to Babe Ruth's. In a July 21 game against the St. Louis Browns, the young power hitter tagged curveballer John Ogden for a titanic, 450-foot home run, the first ever to clear the roof above the left field double deck at Shibe. Similar blasts earned Foxx and his 42 ounce bat a regular spot in the lineup, hitting fifth behind Cochrane and Simmons.[26]

Cobb, never accustomed to sitting on a bench, became irascible. Instead of mentoring the younger players as was expected of him, he began to harass them. Joe Hauser insists that Cobb was personally jealous of his success. "He came up to me in spring training and offered to help me with my hitting," recalled the A's former first sacker. "But I was already hitting around .400. I didn't need his help. Still he kept heckling me. By June my average had slipped to the .320 mark, so I began listening to him. Nothing I did was right for him. He told me to change my grip, my stance, my swing—everything! A month later my average dropped to .260 and I was riding the bench. I never spoke to that S.O.B. again!"[27]

Although Hauser finished the season with a .280 average, Jimmie Foxx was quickly emerging as a power-hitting first baseman with much more speed on the basepaths. Hauser became expendable. Mack sold him back to the Brewers at the end of the season. He returned to the majors briefly in 1929 as a reserve infielder with the Cleveland Indians. Afterward, Hauser, hampered with injuries, spent the rest of his career as a minor leaguer. His best year came in 1933 with the Minneapolis Millers of the American Association where he set a professional baseball record for home runs, knocking out 69 round trippers and collecting 178 RBI. After retiring in 1937, Hauser returned to Sheboygan where he became a minor league manager.[28]

Although his mind and his batting eye were as sharp as ever, Cobb's legs had betrayed him by 1928. At age 43, he always seemed to be a step behind, unable to take the extra base, steal third, or catch a rapidly sinking line drive. (Courtesy of the National Baseball Hall of Fame.)

Cobb, on the other hand, continued to add to his already impressive career totals during his final season in the game. He remained a fierce competitor whenever he got the chance to play, doing anything to win—he had to win. When the opposing pitcher was warming up before the game, Cobb would belittle him just to get an edge.[29] He intimidated opposing infielders with threats and epithets, though increasingly he wasn't able to back them up because of his age. In one game against New York, Cobb hit a long drive to right center. He rounded first base, roared past second, and headed for third. On the way, the Yankees' rookie shortstop, Leo Durochur—quite a fierce competitor in his own right—gave him the hip, knocking Cobb to the ground. He was easily thrown out at third by twenty feet. Getting to his feet, the Georgia Peach wheeled on Durocher, cursing him. According to Babe Ruth, both Cobb and Durocher refused to back off.

"If you ever do that to me again, I'll cut your legs off!" Cobb threatened.

Durocher laughed at him, "Go home, Grandpa, you might get hurt playing with us young guys."

No one ever dared to speak to Cobb that way, certainly not a rookie. Cobb started to say something, but Durocher cut him off.

"And listen, Grandpa," he added, "you're not going to cut off anybody's legs. You've gotten away with murder for a lot of years, but you're through, see? I'll give you the hip every time you come around my way, and if you try to cut me, I'll ram the ball right down your throat."

Cobb was so angry he became almost dizzy with rage and started after the loudmouthed rookie. But before he could get to him, both benches emptied; eventually peace was restored.[30] Durocher had a different recollection of the incident.

> No fight ever took place. After knocking down a Cobb line drive in short center field, I was scrambling after it and happened to get in his way, accidentally, of course—forcing him to pull up just enough so that I was able to throw him out at third to end the inning. As I'm passing Cobb on the way into the dugout, he says to me, "You get in my way again, you fresh busher, and I'll step on your face!"
>
> I hadn't said a word to Cobb and still didn't. But Ruth, who was coming in from left field, wanted to know what Cobb said to me. After I told him, he said, "Well kid, the next time he comes to bat, call him a penny pincher."
>
> What I didn't know was that Cobb had a reputation for being very tight with a dollar and had been ready to fight at the drop of "penny pincher" for years. I called him the name during his next at-bat. He turns and points his finger at me and the umpire has to restrain him.
>
> When the game was over, Cobb races over to me

> ready to kill. I'm looking for a place to run when Ruth
> comes to my aid. Putting an arm around Cobb, Ruth says
> to him, "Now what are you going to do? You don't want
> to hit the kid do you?" And while the Babe has his atten-
> tion, I'm up the stairs like a halfback into the locker
> room.[31]

Whatever the case might have been, it is clear that Cobb continued to play with the same fire that elevated to the pinnacle of the
game. Off the field, however, Cobb was a loner. He alienated himself from the team on the road, choosing to dine by himself and
spend most of his time in his hotel room. Once, when he offered to
buy a few players a drink in a New York bar, he was told, "No thanks
Cobb, it's too late. You've been a bastard for too long."[32]

While the A's were struggling, the Yankees were flourishing. They
got off to a quick start in 1928, going 51–18. By July 4th, they held a
commanding 13½ game lead over the second-place A's. Of the 18 contests they had already played against the Mackmen to that point in
the season, the Yankees had won 13 of them. But when the New York
sportswriters began predicting that the Bronx Bombers could con-
ceivably win the league by 25 games, the A's quickly regrouped. They
went 25–8 for the month of July, closing the gap to only four and a
half games. By the end of August, only two games separated the Yankees and A's. And on September 7, in Boston, the Mackmen tied New
York for first place, sweeping both ends of a doubleheader while the
Yanks lost to Washington. The following day, the A's defeated the
Red Sox in another twinbill, 7–6 and 7–4. Despite a Yankee win, the
Athletics enjoyed a half-game lead over injury-riddled New York.

A climatic four-game series at Yankee Stadium followed. An
estimated crowd of 85,256 were on hand to see the opening doubleheader played on Sunday, September 9. It was the largest crowd
in baseball history to that date. Lines began forming the night before.
Thousands had assembled by the time the gates opened at 9:00 a.m.
Train loads of A's fans traveled to New York to bellow their best
wisecracks, some only to be turned away at the gate. By noon, the
unreserved seats had been sold out and battalions of mounted police
were brought in to keep the peace. Inside Yankee Stadium, the stands
were packed, four, five, and six deep, as a record-breaking crowd of
85,265 packed the ballpark. The crowd was so dense that even the

scorecard vendors, who could usually get anyplace to sell their goods, were shoved out to the periphery. It was, as *Philadelphia Inquirer* sportswriter Jimmy Isaminger called it, "a pickpocketer's paradise."[33]

Eddie Collins, Jr., who attended the doubleheader with his father, still insists that "nothing has ever reached the peak of that four-game series for me. It was such a phenomenal comeback for the A's just to be there, half a game in front of New York. And the overwhelming number of A's fans that came out to see the games attests to that fact."[34] Babe Ruth was less impressed. As the A's came out of the dugout to take batting practice, Ruth was waiting for them. "Well, how does it feel to be in first place, fellas?" he asked. "Take a good look at it, you bums, because you'll be in second when the day is over!"[35]

In the first game, Yankee ace George Pipgras held the A's to nine scattered hits while the A's Jack Quinn was only able to hold New York scoreless for five innings. The Yankee bats erupted for three runs in the sixth. Rommel came in relief and surrendered two more runs. The A's had their best scoring opportunity in the eighth inning when they loaded the bases. But with two outs, Foxx fanned to end the inning and the A's went on to lose the opener, 5–0. Game two was a more closely fought contest. New York took a one-run lead on Comb's triple in the first, but were held scoreless by Walberg through the next five innings. In the sixth, Simmons hit a two-run blast that put the A's ahead, 2–1. The Mackmen added another run in the seventh, when Simmons batted home Bishop with a single. But Walberg couldn't hold the lead. In the bottom of that inning he became wild, surrendering two more runs. In the eighth, with the score tied 3–3, Bob Meusel hit a grand slam into the left field bleachers giving the Bronx Bombers a 7–3 victory.

Monday's game was rained out. The series resumed on Tuesday with Lefty Grove going for his 15th straight win and his 23rd of the season. The A's took a 3–0 lead into the bottom of the seventh. Then Grove walked Combs. Koenig followed and got on base on a throwing error by third baseman Jimmy Dykes. With Gehrig at the plate, Grove threw a wild pitch allowing Combs to score and Koenig to advance to second. Then Gehrig looped a 1–2 fastball into left to score Koenig and tie the game. He advanced to second on Simmons' throw to the plate. Ruth followed with a home run which sealed the 5–3 victory for New York. Afterwards, catcher Mickey Cochrane gave the Yankees just credit for their performance. "Grove had everything," he insisted. "His speed was tremendous. His heart and soul were in the game, but the Yankees crossed us up on two occasions— that hit of Gehrig's and Ruth's homer."[36]

The A's salvaged the final game of the series, 4–3. Ty Cobb made his final appearance, coming off the bench in the ninth inning to pinch hit for Jimmy Dykes. He lined out to shortstop Mark Koenig, and then trotted toward the dugout and into the history books. It was a sad, strange ending for a remarkably talented but bitter individual. His mind and his batting eye were as sharp as ever, but his legs had betrayed him. At age 43, he always seemed to be a step behind, unable to take the extra base, steal third, or catch a rapidly sinking line drive. Admittedly, he played that final season of 1928 out of "a sense of duty for Mr. Mack," but it was "hellishly hard."[37]

Cobb left New York with a lifetime batting average of .367— still the highest ever compiled in major league baseball—and the A's departed in second place, trailing the Yankees by one and a half games. "We broke their hearts," said Babe Ruth in a mock display of sympathy, though aside from his solitary home run he did little in the series to contribute.[38] In fact, Ruth managed to make the headlines in other, less admirable ways.

Having publicly endorsed Democratic presidential candidate Al Smith a few days before the series, Ruth caused a storm of controversy when he refused to pose for a photograph with Republican candidate Herbert Hoover, who attended the series. "No sir," replied the Bambino when asked. "Nothing doing on politics. But tell Hoover I'll be glad to talk with him if he wants to meet me under the stands." [39] When the newspaper headlines disclosed Ruth's rebuff on Hoover, Christy Walsh, Ruth's agent prepared a statement for the Babe, apologizing for the misunderstanding and later had the Bambino oblige the picture-taking request.

Since both the A's and Yankees had to make their last western road trips of the season, the Mackmen still had a chance to capture the pennant. They would have to play winning ball against Cleveland, Detroit, St. Louis, and Chicago and hope that the Yankees would stagger. But it was not to be. On the days the Yankees lost, so did the A's. Finally, on September 28, the Mackmen were mathematically eliminated when New York defeated Detroit to clinch the pennant by two and a half games. In the World Series, the Yankees defeated the St. Louis Cardinals in four straight games, becoming the first team to sweep two consecutive Fall Classics.

"I had a fixation about the Yankees," admitted Jimmy Dykes at the end of the season. "To put it exactly—I hated them. They not only beat us regularly in the days when we'd been the footstool of the American League, they rubbed our noses in the dirt. A long lead in early innings never satisfied Murderer's Row. They kept pouring it on in late innings when five o'clock lightening would complete the job. They were remorseless. They kept right on hitting until they were weary and we were flat. We gave them some resistance in '26 when we finished third. We were second to their devastating '27 team, but we really began to feel our strength this year. Next season will be different, it will finally be *our* year."[40] It was.

Chapter 5

REVENGE OF THE WHITE ELEPHANT, 1929

T he 1929 Philadelphia Athletics were not a long shot to capture the pennant, but they were hardly anybody's favorite. *The
Sporting News'* preseason poll of baseball writers picked the
Yankees to capture their fourth straight flag. "We come to the problem of finding someone to beat the Yankees," wrote Martin Corum,
summing up the feelings of his fellow prognosticators. "The Athletics? I hardly think so. Though the Athletics are a great ball club
with a screw loose somewhere, we must remember that the Ruppert
Rifles have always had the Indian sign on Mr. Mack's mournful
men."[1]

Yankee skipper Miller Huggins was more circumspect about his
team's chances. "Now don't quote me as saying the Yanks will cop
another pennant," he cautioned. "What I will say is that we seem to
have pennant power. I have confidence in the team, like their spirit,
and see no signs of ominous cracks in their morale, which is most
important to be kept intact in a team that has repeatedly tasted the
pleasures of victory."[2]

Huggins had reason to be optimistic. His star slugger, Babe
Ruth, not only reported early to the Yankees' St. Petersburg, Florida,
training camp, but broke from a personal tradition by arriving in

unusually good shape. Tony Lazzeri appeared to be fully recovered from the sore arm that had crippled him during the previous season. And the pitching staff proved to be more effective than ever before in preseason competition. But it was still unwise to discount the A's.

Mack made some important adjustments to his team during the off-season, changes that would give him a better chance to capture the flag in 1929. After Walter French and Ty Cobb announced their retirements and Tris Speaker became a free agent, the Tall Tactician bolstered his outfield by purchasing Homer Summa from the Cleveland Indians and limiting Ossie Orwoll to the outfield and, when needed, first base. The addition of Summa gave the A's a reliable fly chaser with substantial punch in his bat, while making Orwoll a reserve outfielder enabled Mack to give an occasional rest to the projected regulars, Simmons, Miller, and Haas. Changes were also made in the infield. While the keystone of Bishop at second and Boley at short would provide some regularity, the corners would be platooned. After releasing first baseman Joe Hauser, Mack intended to rotate Foxx, Orwoll, and Dykes at that position. If Foxx played first, Dykes would go to third and Orwoll would become the first outfield reserve. If Foxx started at third, then Orwoll would cover first. Sammy Hale and Joe Hassler were also retained for utility purposes.

Aside from these changes, Mack kept the status quo. Mickey Cochrane was the catcher and Cy Perkins would be his backup. They would handle an experienced pitching staff, including righthanders Quinn, Rommel, Earnshaw and Ehmke, and lefthanders Grove, Walberg and Yerkes. Eddie Collins, Kid Gleason, Ira Thomas and Earle Mack returned as coaches. Collectively, then, the A's had all the ingredients necessary to capture the pennant: a scrappy defense, powerful hitting, effective pitching, and the wisdom of three former big league managers to direct them. Perhaps more importantly, they had chemistry. "We enjoyed every minute of the game," said Jimmy Dykes. "We were all pals, a harmonious bunch of team players who ribbed each other, but also helped each other on the field and off. We had no cliques, no factions, no holdouts, no nonsense."[3] Shirley Povich, who covered the national pastime for the *Washington Post*, agreed: "The A's had a collection of players whose chief interest was

The 1929 Philadelphia Athletics. Front row (left to right)—Samuel Hale, G. Cochrane, Walter French, James Dykes, John Boley, Ralph Perkins, and Earle Mack (coach). Center row—Homer Summa, George Walberg, C. Yerkes, Connie Mack (manager), George Burns, George Earnshaw, and James Cronin. Back row—Bing Miller, Wm. Breckenridge, George Hass, Eddie Collins, "Kid" Gleason, James Foxx, Robert Grove, Howard Ehmke, and Al Simmons.

baseball. That's all they concentrated on. There were no other involvements. No divided attention. Above all, they played to win."[4]

The 1929 Philadelphia Athletics were one of the most cantankerous teams in the history of the game. They absolutely hated to lose, scratching and clawing their way to the top of the American League. Some of the players were so fiercely competitive that they allowed an obsession with winning to completely dominate their lives. Lefty Grove, for example, was so intense that on the day he was scheduled to start, he reported to the clubhouse with a scowl. He ignored his own teammates and snarled at the sportswriters. It was suicide for a photographer to try to take his picture because the pitcher would pick up a ball and throw it through the lens. His behavior only became worse if he lost. On those rare occasions, Grove was known to storm through the clubhouse, tearing off his uniform and destroying anything in sight, whether it be a water cooler or a teammate.[5] The lanky pitcher preached only three rules of conduct—rules he believed would guarantee success on the ball diamond: "attend to business," "get at least eight hours of sleep," and, ironically, "observe moderate habits."[6] Clearly, he had difficulty abiding by the last one.

Mickey Cochrane, the uncontested team leader, was just as ornery, sharing Grove's passionate disdain for losing. "Lose a one-to-nothing game and you didn't want to get into the clubhouse with him," said rookie Roger Cramer. "You'd be ducking stools and gloves and bats and whatever else would fly."[7] He also took it personally. "When we'd lose," recalled Bing Miller, "he'd weep and stomp and butt his head against the clubhouse wall. Mickey was the fiercest, scrappiest, and cryingest guy I ever saw."[8] At the same time, though, it was that kind of intensity that made Cochrane the finest catcher in the game. "Black Mike," as he was known to a legion of admirers, was "tough as a piece of flint" and most formidable when a base runner tried to challenge him at the plate. "Home plate was his," said Cramer. "You had to take it away from him ... if you could."[9] Connie Mack called his catcher "Ty Cobb wearing a mask" and insisted that Cochrane's level of play had improved so much by 1929 that he was the "greatest catcher in baseball."[10] Umpire George Moriarity, who witnessed many of Cochrane's impressive performances from behind home plate, agreed with the Tall Tactician. "There is no catcher quite like him in the game," he admitted. "When he fields a bunted ball in front of the plate, it is like a steam shovel operating because he also comes up with half the infield soil. Base runners idle in great fear of his throwing arm and wisely save steals for another day and another catcher. Nor does he shy away from contact. While many star catchers are weaklings in blocking off runners at the plate in fear of injury, Cochrane welcomes the challenge. Many an on-rushing base runner bounces off his shin guards like a school boy off a banana peeling."[11]

Al Simmons was cut from the same mold as Cochrane and Grove. He would work himself into a homicidal rage before stepping up to the plate, considering the pitcher his mortal enemy. Tommy Heinrich of the Yankees once called him "the most vicious man I ever saw at the plate." "When Al would grab hold of that 38 inch bat and dig in," he added, "he'd squeeze the handle tight and throw the barrel towards the pitcher, looking so blooming mad—and that was only in his warm-up swings!"[12] Simmons success certainly wasn't the result of a polished hitting technique. It was almost as if he succeeded through sheer determination and an unyielding desire to spite the pitcher. Arthur Daley of the *New York Times* was at a loss to

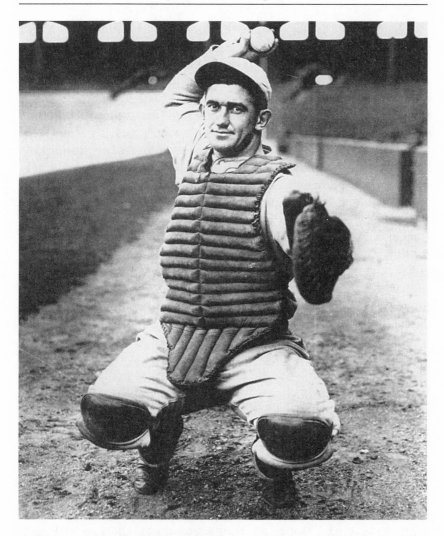

Mickey Cochrane, one of baseball's greatest catchers, was also the "fiercest, scrappiest, and cryingest player on the A's" according to teammate Bing Miller. (Courtesy of the National Baseball Hall of Fame).

explain Bucketfoot Al's hitting prowess. "Simmons was unquestionably the worst looking of all top hitters," he once wrote. "His style was atrocious. He should have been a sucker for an outside pitch. He wasn't. Curves should have troubled him. They didn't. In fact, he was the deadliest clutch hitter on the Athletics."[13]

Though not as fiery as Grove, Cochrane, or Simmons, the rest of the A's could be just as hot-tempered when things didn't go their way on the diamond. Jimmy Dykes, for example, became so enraged after being lifted for a pinch hitter in one game that he threw his bat at Mack, who had to jump out of its way.[14] Bing Miller and Mule Haas were quick to argue with the umpires. Nor was any member of the team ever known to shy away from a bench clearing brawl.

Philadelphia's fans loved the A's for their fiercely combative approach to the game. The team reminded them of an earlier, semi-mythical and perhaps more colorful era, when the city's baseball was dominated by such personalities as George "Rube" Waddell, Jack "Stuffy" McGinnis, Frank "Home Run" Baker, Albert "Chief" Bender, and "Shoeless Joe" Jackson. These players set a precedent for Philadelphia baseball as a "rough-and-tumble" game where you either "toughed-it-out" or "got out" of town. At the same time, the 1929 A's were even more admired because of their ethnic backgrounds. Diversity meant a lot in a city like Philadelphia, which was defined by its immigrant neighborhoods.

Prior to the 1920s, major leaguers came from predominantly white, Anglo-Saxon backgrounds. But with America's need for a cheap labor force to work the factories, mills, and coal mines of its industrial revolution, there was a great influx of new, unskilled immigrants to the United States. Many came from Poland, Ireland, and Germany, settling in the big cities along the East Coast where there were ample opportunities for work. These immigrants and their children embraced the national pastime as part of the assimilation process. Predictably, players of their own ethnicity were beloved. The A's didn't disappoint them. Fans of Polish ancestry embraced Simmons and Joe Boley, who had shortened his name from the original "Bolinski." Both were among the first of Polish ancestry to make it into the big leagues. Cochrane, Foxx, Quinn, and Mack were worshipped by the Irish. Those of German ancestry could boast about the pitching exploits of Rommel and Walberg. Even the Quaker blue bloods had a hero when George Earnshaw took the mound.

Philadelphia was an A's town in 1929. There were no divided loyalties. Not even the Yankees, whose winning ways had once allowed them to command a fairly sizable following in the City of

Brotherly Love, could compete for the affection of the fans. In fact, the Yankees had such a national following during the 1920s that they began, in 1929, to wear numbers on the back of their uniforms so the fans could identify their heroes more easily, a practice the A's adopted in 1931. Each uniform number corresponded to the player's position in the batting order. Babe Ruth, for example, wore number 3 because he hit third in the line up. He was followed by Lou Gehrig, who wore number 4 and hit cleanup. Still, the Yankees couldn't compete with the A's for the affection of the Philadelphia fans as the fortunes of the two teams reversed early in the 1929 campaign.

After losing their first three exhibition games in the Grapefruit League, the A's caught their stride and won four straight, beating Cincinnati and the Phillies in back-to-back two-game series. Dykes played remarkably well, both in the field and at the plate. Foxx went on a hitting rampage, his most memorable performance coming against the St. Louis Browns at Richmond, Virginia. The game was played at a ball park on Mayo Island, one of the larger isles on the James River. Double X hit two homers, the latter clearing the left field fence, sailing beyond the boundary of the island and landing in the river.[15] Before breaking their Fort Myers camp, the A's were invited to dinner at the Florida home of one of their biggest fans, Thomas Alva Edison. The great American inventor wintered in Fort Myers and attended many of their exhibition games. When the season began and the A's moved North, he would follow them and, on occasion, invite the entire team to his Menlo Park, New Jersey, estate for Sunday dinner.[16]

The A's opened the regular season at Washington on April 17. Despite losing Boley to a sore throwing arm and Simmons to a flare-up of rheumatism, the Mackmen won the game 13–4. Foxx continued his heavy hitting, going three for four, with a double and a home run. Heavy rains washed out the rest of the series and the A's resumed play at New York in a Sunday afternoon game. The Mackmen knocked out Yankee starter Henry Johnson in less than an inning, and scuffed up his reliever, Tom Zachary, before Dykes sealed the victory with a two-run homer to right field in the fifth. Grove was the winning pitcher.

The Monday game was called off because of rain, and the A's returned to Philadelphia, where a crowd of 26,000 came out to greet them for the home opener against Washington. Walberg started the game and surrendered two runs in the first. He regained his composure, however, and blanked the Senators for the next nine innings. The A's scored one run in the second and another in the sixth on a Mule Haas solo homer. With the score deadlocked at 2–2 in the eleventh, Washington tagged Walberg for two more runs. Though the A's rallied for another marker in the bottom of the inning, the game ended in a 4–3 defeat when Summa fanned with the bases loaded. The A's evened the series the next day when Al Simmons returned to the lineup. Though the A's had been winning without him, they lacked the batting punch and intensity that they would need to compete with the Yankees. "Simmons return," according to James Isaminger of the *Philadelphia Inquirer*, "had the biggest kind of effect on the team. It transformed all the players into fighters, showing the same irresistible spirit that marked them in midseason last year when they succeeded in passing the Yankees."[17]

Indeed it seemed as though the A's were firing on all cylinders with Simmons in the lineup. When the first-place Yankees made their first appearance at Shibe on April 25, they were given a rude awakening. Jack Quinn pitched brilliantly, going the distance in a 5–2 victory before a Friday afternoon crowd of 30,000. Quinn, the senior pitcher of the league, retired the side in order in seven of his nine innings of work, and he held Ruth to one single in four at bats while Gehrig came up empty-handed in the same number of tries. Walberg improved his record to 2–1 the following day, as the A's crushed the Yankees 10–1. Afterward, the Mackmen boarded a train for Boston where they took three out of four from the Red Sox. Jimmie Foxx continued to impress with his slugging power, hitting one of the longest home runs ever seen in Fenway Park in a 24–6 victory on May 1. The ball sailed high over the center field fence, cleared a nearby factory building, and landed on the tracks of the Boston and Albany Railroad. It was only the fourth of 33 home runs he would hit during a season that would earn him the nickname "Maryland Mauler."[18] The A's juggernaut moved on to Washington where they swept the Senators in four straight.

Returning to Philadelphia, the Mackmen won the only two games with Boston the weather permitted them to play. The A's were flying high when Washington, which had just swept a doubleheader with the Yankees, came to town on Thursday, May 23, for another twinbill. In the first game, Bump Hadley, the Senators' chunky curveballer, enjoyed an eight-run lead at the end of the third inning. In the fourth, the A's jumped on him for eight runs, tying the game. The next inning, Bing Miller hit his fourth homer of the season, ending the scoring in what proved to be a 9–8 victory for the Mackmen. The A's won the second game by the same score. Rube Walberg went the distance, winning his fifth contest of the season. Then on Friday, the A's handed the Griffs another loss, 10–3, and followed it up on Saturday with a fourth victory, 5–4, in 12 innings. Fortunately for the Senators, Sunday baseball was prohibited in Philadelphia, and they headed back to Washington before suffering a fifth loss. By week's

Pitcher George "Rube" Walberg, who joined the A's in 1924, became one of the team's most durable pitchers, despite chronic nervousness that often cost him sleep the night before a starting assignment. (Courtesy of Jerome Romanowski.)

end, the A's had completed an 11-game winning streak, going 22–5 for the month of May, and were comfortably ensconced in first place, four games ahead of the St. Louis Browns who had edged out the skidding Yankees for second.

Inadequate pitching, inexperienced catching, comparatively light hitting on the part of some regulars who used to murder the ball, and a glaring weakness at shortstop were the major reasons for the Yankees' slump. New York's pitchers had been a bitter disappointment. Pennock was still looking for his second win in half a dozen starts. Pipgras, Helmach, and Zachary were inconsistent. Wilcy Moore had blown more games than he had saved. Amidst this disaster, Waite Hoyt had been the one consistent hurler, pitching out of turn in order to keep the Yanks in the running. But the overworked righthander could not be expected to carry the burden on his own. Because of injuries to Benny Bengough and Johnny Grabowski, Bill Dickey had been doing most of the catching, in spite of his limited experience. Although it was no fault of his own, his inexperience probably added to the difficulties of an already vulnerable pitching staff.

Nor were the Yankee hitters faring much better. The bats of Ruth and Gehrig had fallen silent. Huggins, hoping that they would soon come out of their slumps, couldn't afford to replace them. Bob Muesel, on the other hand, was hitting so poorly that he was benched in Washington. Koenig was having a nightmarish season at shortstop and was replaced by Durocher, who wasn't fielding much better.[19] The A's only added to their troubles.

The Mackmen just couldn't seem to lose. Not only were they winning their games, but they were completely overpowering their opponents, getting an early lead and increasing it throughout the game. Though they had their 11-game winning streak snapped on May 27 in Boston, they started a new one the following day, defeating the Red Sox 7–1. On Memorial Day, the A's made a clean sweep of a double bill. Grove won the first game by a score of 9–2, and Quinn won the second by a margin of 9–3. The sweep marked the end of a string of 15 straight games played with Washington and Boston, both at home and away. Of those games, the A's captured nine straight from the Senators, and five out of six from Boston. What's more, the A's went 21–5 in May, ending the month in sole possession of first, six games ahead of second place St. Louis and seven in front of the third-place Yankees.

The A's opened the month of June by taking three out of four from the Detroit Tigers. Ehmke, who had posted victories in his last two appearances, won the first game, 9–6. Earnshaw and Grove followed with magnificent performances of their own, winning 11–2 and 3–2 in the second and third games of the series. Though the A's dropped the final game, 8–4, they quickly regrouped and took two out of three from St. Louis, three out of five from Cleveland, and swept Chicago in a three-game series. The most outstanding thing about those games was the way in which they dispatched their opponents with a sustained offensive attack. Few of the victories were close. The A's were defeating their opponents by six or seven runs and were very capable of erupting at any time for a ten-run inning. Only once had they lost as many as two games in a row, and of all their opponents, only Detroit had taken a series from them, garnering two out of three.

Leading the attack were Jimmie Foxx and Al Simmons. Foxx, who was leading the league in hitting with a .400 batting average, was having a spectacular spring. At every park the A's visited, he seemed to be establishing new hitting records, and his power was inviting comparisons to Babe Ruth, who was having much less success. Simmons, who was hitting cleanup, was just as devastating. A great clutch hitter, he was leading the league in RBIs and proving to be the lineup's most difficult out. Though they didn't pack the same power as Foxx or Simmons, Cochrane and Dykes were also effective batsmen. Cochrane ranked second to Foxx in the A.L. hitting race. Batting third in the lineup, he seemed to be the spark that ignited the offensive attack. Dykes, who occupied the eighth slot in the order, often completed what Cochrane had started, hitting well above the .300 mark.

The A's defense was equally superb. The three-man platoon of Foxx, Dykes, and Orwell at the corners was working better than Mack had expected. Cochrane, the uncontested field general, was in firm command of the infield as well as the pitching staff, and he rarely made a miscue. What's more, shortstop Joe Boley, who had been sidelined with a sore throwing arm, returned to the lineup on June 10. Just in case there were any further problems, Mack closed a quick deal with Portland, acquiring infielder Jimmy Cronin.

In spite of their overwhelming success, Mack barred the team from any talk of a pennant. When asked about the A's chances, he simply replied, "It's much too early to talk about a pennant." Even the Philadelphia newspapers downplayed the possibility of postseason play as if to avoid a jinx. When fans attempted to leave applications for World Series tickets at the Shibe Park windows, the box office politely turned them away.[20] Nevertheless, the fans and the players were locked in a mutual love affair, and nothing could discourage the city's affection for their Athletics.

Among the most adored players was Jimmie Foxx, whose good-natured personality underscored a genuine concern about youngsters. He never seemed to turn down a request to speak before them, often, encouraging them to make the best of their education. Before an assembly of 2,500 students at Philadelphia's Northeast High

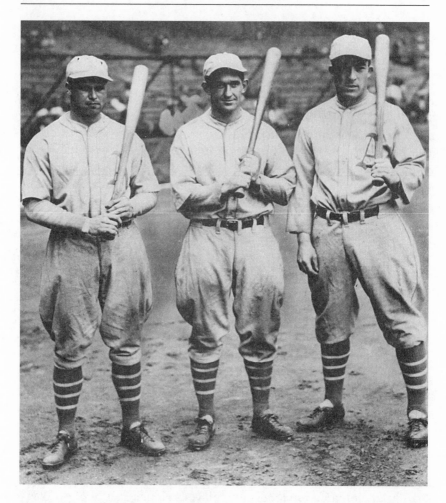

Jimmie Foxx, Mickey Cochrane, and Al Simmons (left to right) led the offensive attack of the 1929 Philadelphia Athletics, one of the most contankerous teams in the history of baseball. (Courtesy of the National Baseball Hall of Fame.)

School that spring, Foxx stressed the importance of education and spoke candidly about his own regret that he did not complete high school. "When I was in school, I took more interest in athletics than the books," he admitted. "It was a mistake. I wish I had studied more and gone to college. These days, a fellow needs all the knowledge he can obtain, since knowledge is what life's all about."[21] Lefty Grove was also known for a soft spot when it came to children. Spotting a

group of ragtag youngsters playing ball against another, better uni-
formed team one afternoon, he felt so badly that he not only outfitted
the entire group of kids but even provided brand new gloves and
balls.[22]

On June 21 the A's traveled to New York for a five-game series
with the Yankees. The A's took three of those games, 11–1, 7–3, and
7–4. Perhaps the most exciting performance came from Jimmie Foxx
in the first game. Facing Lefty Gomez, Double X got hold of a high
fastball and knocked it into the upper deck of Yankee Stadium, splin-
tering the back of a seat. It was a truly Ruthian clout, so impressive
that Gomez himself just turned to watch the ball sail high into the
seats. Forty years later, while watching the broadcast of Neil Arm-
strong picking up rocks during his moon walk, an elderly Gomez
reportedly said to his wife, "So there's the ball Foxx hit off me in '29."

A week later the Yanks came to Philadelphia for a three-game
series. Thirty-five thousand fans poured into Shibe for the first game.
They saw the A's dispatch the Bronx Bombers, 6–3, behind the masterful pitching of Rube Walberg who picked up his third win in as
many starts against the Yanks. Bing Miller also hit safely in his 28th
consecutive game, the longest hitting streak of the 1929 season. Rain
postponed the following day's contest and the series concluded on
Saturday when the Yankees, behind George Pipgras, pulled out a 7–5
victory. Ruth hit two homers to help his team's cause. The game also
marked the end of Miller's hitting streak. Nevertheless, the split
earned the A's some respect from the Yankees. The Mackmen had
won seven of the twelve contests they had with New York up to that
point in the season. That was quite a contrast to the total of six wins
they copped the previous season, losing exactly 16 times to the Yankees. It also disproved the earlier predictions of the so-called
"experts" who claimed that the A's would buckle at the sight of Yankee pinstripes.

The Yankees, on the other hand, seemed to be basing their pennant hopes on the assumption that the A's were going to have a severe
slump similar to the one they had experienced the previous season.
They had their work cut out for them though, since the A's continued to win throughout July, going 24–9. The A's were leading the
league in fielding and enjoyed a batting mark of .308, producing far
more runs than any other club in the circuit. Not surprisingly, the

A's won 13 of their last 16 games in July, sweeping Washington, Boston, and Detroit, winning another series against Cleveland, and breaking even with Chicago. The victories were not without incident, though. In one game against Cleveland, for example, Bishop and Dykes made back-to-back errors. Grove, who was pitching, was so angry that he berated his teammates and then proceeded to serve up home runs to the next two Indians. When the inning ended, Dykes and Bishop came into the dugout cursing the tall lefthander. Trying to retain some semblance of team spirit, Mack ordered them to "stop muttering," adding, "Do you want him out of there?" Before he could complete the question, the A's bench answered with a loud, resounding "Yes!" Mack complied. Grove didn't speak to anyone for nearly a week.[24]

On another occasion, Rommel, who hated relief pitching and was being used almost exclusively in that role, threw a temper tantrum in the clubhouse before a game against Chicago. "I don't give a damn what happens out there this afternoon," he screamed. "I don't care two hoops in Hades if ten pitchers get their domes knocked off and we drop a twenty-run lead. I'm not doing any relief pitching today. Not for Mussolini, Rasputin, or Al Smith. It's a lousy job. I ain't a relief pitcher and that's final!" When Mack called on the irascible hurler to come in for Walberg during the game, he dutifully obliged and sealed the victory.[25] Clubhouse blowups, hard play, and bench jockeying were commonplace that season. It was part of the A's hard-nosed, yet colorful and endearing, nature. It also made them the most unbeatable team in the American League.

As of July 30, the A's held a comfortable 9½ game lead over second-place New York, and no sign of a slump was in sight. Mack even confided to one Philadelphia sportswriter that "nothing but an earthquake can keep the Athletics from winning the pennant in 1929!"[26] Unfortunately, for the Tall Tactician, Bill Dooley of the *Philadelphia Record* didn't keep his confidence. "We have faith in Mack's prediction," he wrote in his July 25th column. "That is, faith in his personal belief that nothing but an earthquake can keep the A's from winning the pennant. Perhaps rival clubs are atrophying. A year ago the Yankees were wont to crow because they could knock the Athletics pizzle and upward for a whole series. They boast now because they can win one game from them. Either that is hardening of the arteries or the Yankees are experiencing a sensation of respect for Mr. Mack's literary notations on earthquakes."[27] Nevertheless, Mack's official position on the pennant issue remained, "Let's wait and see."[28]

The A's fortunes improved even more during the first week of August. On the first day of the month, the Mackmen increased their lead over the Yankees by another full game by defeating Detroit 7–4 while the Yanks lost a doubleheader to Chicago. On August 2, the A's gained another game by defeating the Tigers again, 11–10, while the Yanks dropped another twinbill to Cleveland. The Mackmen enjoyed an 11½ game lead—their biggest of the season—over second-place New York and their pitching seemed to be invincible. The A's top three pitchers had won a total of 49 games. Grove, with a record of 17–2, topped all major league hurlers. Earnshaw boasted a 17–5 record, and Walberg had posted 15 victories against 4 defeats.

Then the team began to lose. Weakened by the loss of Dykes and Boley to injuries and tired near the close of a successful homestand which saw them play three straight doubleheaders in 90 degree heat, the A's began to feel the pressure. They played five games with the Browns, won two, lost two, and tied one. Then they dropped two out of three to the Yankees. The road didn't prove to be any kinder. After a brief reprieve in Detroit where the A's won three of four and took two of three games in Cleveland, they returned to their losing ways. The Browns humbled them, taking all but one contest of their four-game series, and the White Sox did the same the following week. At one point, the A's had lost four straight, their worst performance of the entire season. Their misfortune gave the Yankees renewed hopes for a pennant race. But the Yankees self-destructed on their last western road trip of the season, losing their series with Cleveland, Detroit, and St. Louis. At one point the Yankees were playing so poorly that they went 30 innings without scoring a single run.

Despite their own misfortunes, the A's actually gained more ground on the Yankees, and on September 14 when George Earnshaw defeated the Chicago White Sox, 5–0, at Shibe, the A's had clinched their first pennant in 15 years. Six days later, Yankee manager Miller Huggins entered St. Vincent's Hospital in New York. He had been in poor health for weeks, but he continued to overexert himself in a desperate attempt to keep the Yankees from losing the championship.

On Wednesday, September 25, as his Yankees were playing the Red Sox at Fenway Park, the fiery little manager died of blood poisoning. He was only 49 years old. When the fifth inning ended, both teams met at home plate and observed a moment of silence as the flag was lowered to half mast.[29] A few days later, the Yankees gathered at his funeral to say good-bye. "We were a hard-boiled bunch, at least on the ballfield," recalled Babe Ruth, who had fought with Huggins during his early years in New York. "Tony Lazzeri, Waite Hoyt, Earle Combs, and myself—all of us—cursed Hug when he tried to harness our energies. We had scrapped with the little guy, but we had also played up to the hilt for him. As we knelt there at his coffin, there wasn't a dry eye when the minister spoke his last words. I cried like a baby."[30]

For the A's, on the other hand, there was much to celebrate. They finished their season with a record of 104 victories and 46 defeats, 18 games ahead of second-place New York. They finished with a winning record against all the A.L. teams but St. Louis, and they might have finished over .500 against them too if the final game between the two clubs had not been rained out. The Mackmen played winning baseball in every month of the season: they went 2–0 in October for a 1.000 winning percentage; 22–5 in May for .815; 24–9 in July for .727; 15–6 in September for .714; 19–8 in June for .704; 7–4 in April for .636; and 15–14–1 in August for .517.

Their pitching was nothing less than brilliant. The A's staff led the league in strikeouts with 573, saves with 24, and earned run average at 3.44. Individual hurlers led the league in almost every category as well. Lefty Grove, who posted a 20–6 record, led the A.L. in winning percentage (.769), ERA (2.91), strikeouts (170), and strikeouts per game (5.56). Earnshaw led the A.L. in victories (24–8), fewest hits per game (8.23), and was second to Grove in winning percentage (.750), strikeouts (149), and most strikeouts per game (5.27), while also finishing in the top five for ERA (3.29) and games pitched (44). Walberg, who compiled an 18–11 record, was among the top four hurlers in winning percentage (.621), fewest hits per game (8.61), and innings pitched (268). Rommel was one of the most effective closers in the league, posting a 12–2 record and a 2.84 ERA. Bill Shores was a fairly effective reliever himself, going 11-6, with a 3.59 ERA and seven saves. Even the old timers of the staff, 35–year-

Connie Mack waving his trademark scorecard from the steps of the dugout. (Courtesy of the National Baseball Hall of Fame.)

old Howard Ehmke and 45-year-old Jack Quinn had respectable numbers. Ehmke went 7–2 with a 3.27 ERA, and Quinn was 11–9 with a 3.88 ERA.

The batting order was just as productive. As a team, the A's hit .296, second only to Detroit, which compiled a team batting average that was three points higher. Opposing hurlers had great difficulty pitching around them since there really wasn't a weak spot in the order. Bishop, the leadoff batter, might have hit only .232, but he walked almost once a game for a league-leading total of 128. Haas, who hit second in the order, compiled a .313 average, with 16 homers and 82 RBIs in his first season as a regular. Cochrane, the third batter, hit .331 with seven homers and 95 RBIs. Miller, the number six hitter, was among the league leaders in triples (16) and stolen bases (24), while knocking out eight homers and compiling 93 RBIs and a .335 average. Dykes, with his .327 average, 13 homers, and 79 RBIs, followed Miller in the order. Though light hitting shortstop Joe Boley was the eighth hitter, he still managed to hit .251—well over his weight—and rap out two home runs and 47 RBIs. Simmons and Foxx, however, composed the meat of the order and gave the Yankee duo of Ruth and Gehrig some stiff competition.

Simmons, the cleanup hitter, led the American League in RBIs (157) and total bases (373). He finished second to Lou Fonseca of Cleveland in batting average (.365), second to Ruth in slugging average (.642), and third in home runs (34) and hits (212). Although Simmons wracked up bigger numbers, Foxx was quickly becoming the marquee player of the Athletics. He could also be found among the league leaders in seven categories: batting average (.354); slugging average (.625); home runs (33); total bases (323); bases on balls (103); home run percentage (6.4); and runs scored (123). He also drove in 117 runs and hit safely in 24 consecutive games. Double X had such extraordinary upper body strength that his tape-measure home runs quickly became the stuff of legends. One of his blasts at Shibe went off the flagpole in dead center field, a distance that was estimated to be 500 feet. Another one went over the roof in left center and sailed across two city blocks. It might have gone even further if it hadn't bounced off a building.[31] His hitting was so spectacular, his ability so exceptional that, at the tender age of 21, *Time* magazine put his picture on the cover of its July 29 issue. It was only the beginning of the good life for Jimmie Foxx. Within a year, he would be wearing striped flannel suits, brown-and-white shoes, silk ties, and soft felt hats. He would be driving an expensive touring car, living in a fashionable town house, and enjoying headlines on sports pages across the nation. Within the next month, he would also lead the Philadelphia Athletics to their sixth world championship and become the cornerstone of a baseball dynasty that would bid for the title "greatest to have ever played the game."

Chapter 6

THE 1929
WORLD SERIES

T he Chicago Cubs were the A's opponents in the 1929 World Series. After threatening for several years in the National League, the Cubs finally overcame a series of close races to win their first pennant since 1918. Their manager, Philadelphia-born Joe McCarthy, had grown up rooting for the Mackmen. But the loyalties to his boyhood team ceased once he crossed the foul lines for the opening game of the Fall Classic.

The Cubs awesome lineup came in to the series batting .303 as a team, seven points higher than the A's. McCarthy had an explosive outfield of Kiki Cuyler who hit .360 in right, Riggs Stephenson who hit .362 in left, and Hack Wilson who hit .345 and played in center. Though small in stature, being only 5'6" and 190 pounds, Wilson was a deceptively strong power hitter with 39 homers to his credit. He was especially dangerous in the clutch. The trio was considered the most fearsome righthanded-hitting attack in baseball history, combining for 71 homers, 337 runs, and 271 RBIs. Nor was the infield lacking for production, with National League MVP Rogers Hornsby, at second. Hornsby hit .380, slugged 39 homers, and drove in 149 runs. Additionally, the infield was bolstered by shortstop Woody English, who scored 131 runs.

Chicago's pitching staff, like its batting order, was dominated by righthanders. The only southpaw was 36-year-old Art Nehf who was already past his prime. Pat Malone was the ace of the staff, leading the National League with 22 wins. Charlie Root contributed another 19, and Guy Bush 19 more.

Many baseball writers were either unable or unwilling to declare a Series favorite. But none doubted that both teams would demonstrate a high quality of play. "If this year's World Series draws weather fit for baseball, it should produce the best competition seen in the Fall Classic for many a year," predicted Tom Swope of the *Cincinnati Post.* "Both are good teams which won their pennants far enough in advance of closing day to get thoroughly rested and prepared for a mighty effort in the big games. So it seems folly to attempt to pick one to defeat the other." Sam Carrick of the *Boston Evening American* believed the team that won the first game would win the series. "Past results have shown that the initial contest winner has come out on top in somewhat more than two-thirds of the Series," he insisted. "One game is 25 percent of the victories to be accomplished and that is a considerable margin."

Others favored the Cubs. Archie Ward of the *Chicago Tribune* gave four good reasons for his choice: "(1) The Cubs have been favored by the schedule, which will enable them to play a possible four out of seven games on their home field; (2) They have been exceptionally successful against left-handed pitching; (3) They have more men experienced in World Series competition and consequently will stand up better under the strain; and (4) The Cubs have a more devastating attack." Not all Cub partisans were from Chicago either. Arthur Mann of the *New York Evening World* gave the Cubs a slight edge in "six or possibly seven games." He based his prediction on the "A's mad quest for victories in the last weeks of the season" which has "shorn the team of its best pitchers and has leveled the sluggers to a point approximating mediocrity." Mann went on to write, "This disintegration is bound to tell in the Series. The Cubs, on the other hand, have swung along with no pretense at invincibility, winning three or four and losing one or two, since midseason they have accelerated and they are finishing in a blaze of hitting." Paul Gallico of the *New York Daily News*, evidently still smarting from the Yankees' recent fall from first place, seemed to give his vote to the Cubs based on little more than a personal animosity for the Athletics. "The whole thing apparently is a put up job to advertise Wrigley's chewing gum and Connie Mack's elephants—I believe it is elephants Mr. Mack sells—and I will have nothing to do with such out-and-out publicity schemes," he wrote in mock derision. "Our Yankees at least were playing for good Ruppert beer. The Cubs will win the Series in four straight games, so that a lot of sportswriters can perpetuate tear jerkers about poor old Connie Mack."

The A's had their devotees as well. Stuart Bell of the *Cleveland Press* made his prediction on the strength of the A's superior pitching: "If the best team wins, the Athletics will be the champions. Their pitchers, with the lowest earned run average in their own league, and lower than those of the Cub pitchers, are much better than the Chicago curving corps." Predictably, the Philadelphia press echoed his reasoning. "The Cubs may have hammered National League southpaws with enthusiasm, but there are no portsiders in the older circuit with the skill and cunning of Grove and Walberg," wrote Myron Huff of the *Public Ledger.* "And as for right-handers— well, there isn't a better pitcher in either league than Earnshaw and it happens he is with the A's." James Isaminger of the *Inquirer* went even further: "In my opinion, the Athletics have the batting power, pitching and defensive strength to beat any team in America. They have swept everything before them and in September were as irresistible as they were at any time during the race. I'm not saying there will be any four-game mop-up, but I do believe the A's will triumph in six."

Of course, there were still others in Philadelphia and Chicago who picked the hometown team out of self-defense. "Never having qualified as a baseball expert," wrote Joe Cunningham of the *Philadelphia Record,* "it doesn't matter who I pick so long as I say the A's will win. About the only reason I give is that I know most of the Athletics personally and do not know the Cubs, but do chew Mr. Wrigley's gum." Harry Neily of the *Chicago American* was even more forthright. "Who do I pick in the Series?" he asked rhetorically. "Naturally—one guess. I live within a mile of the Cubs' park and don't want to sneak home nights up back alleys if I should dare to suggest the A's would take the Series." If nothing else, both Cunningham and Neily deserved to be admired for their candor.[1]

Charlie Root received the starting assignment for the opening game at Chicago on October 8. Mack purposely refused to announce his starting pitcher until moments before the game, but the sellout crowd of 50,740 fans who jammed into Wrigley Field on that cold, rainy day assumed it would be one of his three star hurlers, Grove, Earnshaw, or Walberg.[2] To everyone's great surprise, the Tall Tactician gave the nod to his 35-year-old right-hander, Howard Ehmke. It was the most daring ploy in World Series history.

Ehmke had only pitched 62 innings and two complete games during the 1929 campaign. He had compiled a record of seven wins and two losses, hardly the kind of numbers one would expect to see from the starting hurler in a Series opener. What's more, Ehmke hadn't pitched for nearly a month before the Series.[3] But a heart-to-heart conversation between Mack and his veteran pitcher resulted in the decision.

Shortly before the A's left on their last western trip, Mack called Ehmke to his office in the tower at Shibe. "Howard, there comes a time in everyone's life when there has to be a change," he began, "and I think we've reached the point where we must soon part company."

Ehmke regretfully admitted that his manager was correct. "All right Mr. Mack," he said. "I haven't helped you much this year, and its lucky you didn't need me. But I've always wanted to pitch in a World Series, and I'd like to get the opportunity, if only for a few innings.

Flexing his arm, Ehmke added: "I honestly believe that I've got one more good game left in this arm. I know I'm not as fast as I used to be, but I'm a lot smarter."

Impressed by the veteran pitcher's confidence, Mack, to Ehmke's amazement, agreed. "All right, Howard," he said. "You govern yourself accordingly. Stay at home during this last road trip. Train yourself as you see fit. Keep the arm nice and loose. Go to the Phillies' ballpark and watch them play the Cubs when they come to town. Spend time studying those big hitters. Find out what they like to hit, their weaknesses, and see how we can stop them." Enthusiastic about the prospect of baffling the baseball world at the height of its glory, Mack offered his hand to seal the agreement. "And Howard," he added, "let's not talk to anyone about this. It's between us."[4]

Mack knew exactly what he was doing. The Cubs were intimidated by Grove, Earnshaw, and Walberg because of their masterful pitching during the last month of the season. He realized that if the Cubs, playing on their home field, defeated one of these star hurlers, they might break the A's powerful spell, giving them a decided advantage when the Series moved to Philadelphia. A major surprise, on the other hand, might break their spirit, rendering them incapable of any comeback.[5] At the same time, however, Mack, was taking a calculated risk. If his strategy didn't work, his detractors would be quick to claim that he was slipping in his old age and that it was time to retire.

The night before the Series was to open in Chicago, Jimmie Foxx, who was rooming with Ehmke at the Edgewater Beach Hotel, confided, "I have an idea that the old gentleman is going to pitch you tomorrow!"

The remark took Ehmke by complete surprise. He hadn't said a word about the ploy to anyone, not even his wife. He also knew that Mack was as good as his word. Choosing to ignore Foxx, he replied, "Go to bed and forget about it." But Foxx persisted, "Well, if he does pitch you, I'll hit one out, for you."[6]

The next day, shortly before game time, Ehmke approached Mack and asked, "Is it still me?"

"Yes, Howard, it's still you," he replied.

When Ehmke pulled off his jacket to warm up, the sportswriters, the spectators, and the Cubs' players couldn't believe it. The shock carried as far as Philadelphia where hundreds of A's fans gathered on the streets outside the *Bulletin* newspaper building to watch an electronic scoreboard and listen to an announcer with a direct wire to Wrigley. Even the A's players themselves were dumbfounded. Al Simmons, who was sitting next to Mack on the bench, managed to ask, "Are you going to pitch him?"

Keeping a straight face, Mack turned, stared at his star outfielder, and replied, "Yes I am Al. Is that all right with you?"

Simmons retreated. "Yes, Mr. Mack. If you think he can win," he said rather sheepishly, "it's all right with me."[7]

Ehmke performed magnificently. Pitching off his right hip, close to his shirt, his submarine delivery baffled Cubs' hitters like Wilson, Cuyler, and Hornsby who liked to take hefty cuts. They never could

Pitching with a submarine delivery, Howard Ehmke baffled the Cubs' hitters in Game 1 of the 1929 World Series, setting a new Series record by striking out 13 hitters in a single game. (Courtesy of the National Baseball Hall of Fame.)

get a good look at the ball and by the time they did see the pitch, it was obscured by the white shirts in the center field bleachers.

The Cubs failed to capitalize on a third inning scoring opportunity, when, with one out, McMillan singled and English doubled. But Ehmke struck out both Hornsby and Wilson on a total of seven pitches to retire the side. Ehmke seemed to get stronger as the game unfolded. In the sixth inning, he single-handedly retired the side, striking out English on three pitches and getting Hornsby and Wilson for the second time each.

With the score deadlocked at 0–0 in the top of the seventh, Jimmie Foxx delivered on his promise. The Beast caught hold of a Charlie Root fastball, sending it into the center field bleachers for the first run of the game and a 1–0 A's lead. In the bottom of the inning, the Cubs threatened again. Cuyler singled up the middle, and Stephenson collected another base hit. Charlie Grimm laid down a sacrifice bunt, advancing both runners while accounting for the first out. Pinch hitter Cliff Heathcotte followed with a towering fly to left center field, but Simmons caught it, wielded and threw to the plate to hold Cuyler at third. When Gabby Hartnett struck out on three straight curveballs, Ehmke had pitched himself out of the inning.

The A's added two more runs in the ninth. They loaded the bases for Dykes who singled in Cochrane. Ehmke then helped himself by knocking home Foxx for the third run. With the score 3–0 in favor of the Athletics, Chicago was down to its last three outs.

Again, the Cubs threatened. Wilson led off and smacked a vicious line drive back to the pitcher. The blow knocked Ehmke off the mound, but he recovered and threw the center fielder out at first. Cuyler followed with a hard-hit grounder to third base. Dykes fielded it cleanly but threw wildly to first, allowing Cuyler to race to second. Stephenson's base hit to center scored the speedy Cuyler. Grimm followed with another single, advancing Stephenson to second. Footsie Blair came in to pinch hit. He grounded to Dykes who threw to second to get Grimm. With two outs and runners on first and third, McCarthy sent Chuck Tolson to the plate to pinch hit for Guy Bush, who had replaced Root in relief. Ehmke worked a full count on him. Having already lost his shutout, the veteran hurler faced the possibility of losing the game. He called time and motioned for his catcher, Mickey Cochrane, to come to the mound.

"When you get back there delay as much as you can," he ordered his backstop. "The longer he stands in the box the more nervous he's going to get. With $60,000 on the line I can't afford to fool around."

Umpire Bill Klem got tired of waiting and ordered an end to the conference. Cochrane returned behind the plate and gave his pitcher a sign. Ehmke shook him off. Cochrane gave another sign, and again Ehmke shook it off. They continued the ritual for five minutes in an attempt to frazzle Tollson. It worked. Ehmke took the sign for one last time, shook it off, and quick-pitched a strike right down the middle of the plate. As he released the ball, Cochrane yelled at the top of his lungs, "Hit it!" Tollson took the cue and whiffed. The game was over. The A's had won their first World Series game in 16 years. And Ehmke had established a new Series record by striking out 13 hitters in a single game. Mack, largely because of his risk in pitching the veteran right hander, called the game his "greatest thrill in baseball."[8]

The A's duplicated their success in Game 2. This time, however, there was no secret as to who would start. Earnshaw pitched for the Mackmen and Malone for the Cubs. Another huge crowd of 49,987 packed Wrigley to watch the contest. Foxx began the A's attack in the third when he blasted a three-run homer, scoring Cochrane and Simmons ahead of him. The A's doubled their score in the fourth when Dykes singled, Haas walked, and Boley advanced the runners on a sacrifice bunt. Earnshaw walked to load the bases and Bishop singled in Dykes with the A's fourth run of the game. Cochrane followed with another walk to load the bases again, and Al Simmons singled to center, scoring Earnshaw and Haas. Malone was finished for the afternoon.

With a 6–0 lead, Earnshaw became careless. With one out in the fifth, Hornsby and Wilson broke out of their hitless streaks with singles. After Earnshaw fanned Cuyler for the second out of the inning, Stephenson singled to right, scoring Hornsby. Wilson advanced to second and later scored on Grimm's single to left. Stephenson, who had advanced to third on the hit, scored on Taylor's single through the box. When the dust had settled, the A's lead was cut by half, 6–3. Grove replaced Earnshaw, limiting the Cubs to three scattered hits for the remainder of the game. The A's padded their lead in the seventh when Foxx singled to right, Miller sacrificed him to second, and

Dykes singled him home. Simmons added two more in the eighth when he hit his first home run of the Series, scoring Cochrane ahead of him.

The Series moved to Philadelphia on Friday, October 11. The Athletic's faithful were ready and waiting. "Fans lined up two and three deep outside of Shibe, waiting for the ticket windows to open," recalled Bill Brendley. "To be eligible for a World Series ticket, you had to show 50 rainchecks from regular season games. During the season when each game was over, I used to go around and pick up all the rainchecks I could find. Most people just threw them away. I'd collect 10 to 15 rainchecks a game and pray that the A's would clinch the pennant."[9] Those fans who weren't lucky enough to get a ticket found other, more enterprising ways to enjoy the Series. Residents along North 20th Street hired barkers to advertise their wild-cat bleachers, overlooking the diamond from right field. Because the right field fence was only 12 feet high, residents could see the entire park from their front bedroom. During the 1929 World Series, many not only constructed portable bleachers on their rooftops, but also removed all four windows from their front bedroom and packed another dozen spectators there as well. Mothers made lemonade and sent their children to buy hot dogs from the local street vendors. The kids would purchase a dozen at a nickel each and return home to sell them for a dime. John Rooney, another resident of the Shibe Park neighborhood, found another way to turn a profit. "I would simply sit out on my front porch step well before game time and wait for a car to park in my territory," he said. "Then I'd wave the motorist into the space and ask, 'Want me to watch your car, Mister?' Usually, I'd get a nickel or a dime when the game was over."[10]

When the A's clinched the pennant, the neighborhood residents planned to make a killing. Soon, however, word spread that the tax collectors planned to close down their makeshift bleachers unless they paid $50.00 per house. After negotiating the price down to $30.00, they were permitted to continue their operations. Rooney's father somehow coaxed the officials down to $20.00. "That money was quickly recouped threefold from our paying customers," mused the son. "We got even more income when one of the cameramen from the Pathé Newsreel Service asked what we would charge to let him film the home games of the World Series from our roof. 'Twenty

Rooftop squatters along North Twentieth Street, opposite right field, during the 1929 World Series. (Courtesy of Temple University Urban Archives.)

dollars,' was Dad's quick reply. We soon made similar arrangements with Fox Movietone News and Universal News."[11]

Meanwhile, Connie Mack was making plans of his own. On the train ride east, the Spindly Strategist, acting on a hunch, summoned Earnshaw to his car. "George, I'm going to pitch you again in Philadelphia," he told his big right hander. "You were working too fast yesterday when they knocked you out of the box. I want you to take more time between pitches tomorrow. Step off the mound, look around at your outfielders, rub the ball, pick up some dirt. Just slow down your rhythm and you'll beat those Cubs."[12]

Earnshaw followed Mack's instructions and pitched brilliantly, allowing the Cubs just six hits and striking out ten. Cochrane scored the A's only run of the game in the fifth, but Chicago struck back in the sixth. Earnshaw's free pass to Cub pitcher Guy Bush and Dykes'

George "Mule" Haas played a shallow outfield, loping back to make an over-the-shoulder catch or sprinting in for a shoestring grab. (Courtesy of Jerome Romanowski.)

error on a hard ground ball by English began the rally. Hornsby followed with a single, driving in Bush with the tying run. A single by Cuyler added two more. When all was said and done, the Cubs had won, 3–1, to snap a ten-game National League losing streak in the fall classic.

Game 4 was played on a perfect autumn day. A warm sun and gentle southerly breeze greeted the nearly 30,000 fans who packed Shibe Park to witness a game that has no parallel in World Series competition, producing the most spectacular rally in the annals of baseball history. Mack sent Jack Quinn to the mound against Charley Root, the hard-luck loser of the first game. Again, Root delivered a masterpiece through the first six innings, holding the A's to just three scattered hits. The Cub hitters, on the other hand, gave the fans their greatest power display of the Series. Chicago scored twice in the fourth on Grimm's homer. Quinn was knocked out of the game in the sixth after serving up successive singles by Hornsby, Wilson, Cuyler, and Stephenson. Rommel, who replaced him, fared no better. By the time he fanned Root and McMillan for the final outs, the Cubbies had added another five runs to their lead. Rommel surrendered yet another run in the top of the seventh. To add insult to injury, every time Chicago scored, pitcher Guy Bush placed a blanket over his head and did a mock Indian war dance.[13]

With Philadelphia down by a score of 8–0 going into the bottom half of the seventh, Mack planned to give his regulars one last chance to put the A's on the board.[14] They did more than that. Simmons opened the inning with a towering home run onto the roof in left field. Foxx and Miller followed with singles. Then Dykes drove in Foxx with a base hit to left, adding a second run. Boley continued the rally by bringing home Miller on a fly ball to center field that Hack Wilson lost in the sun. Rommel was lifted for pinch hitter George Burns, who popped up for the first out. But the A's would not be denied. Max Bishop singled to left, scoring Dykes and cutting the Cubs' lead in half, 8-4. Though the A's had made the game respectable, no one really expected the rally to continue, least of all Cub manager Joe McCarthy.

Determined to squelch the A's momentum, McCarthy pulled his starter and brought in his southpaw Art Nehf. Mule Haas, the powerful, free-swinging center fielder, was the first to face him. Jumping on Nehf's first pitch, Haas hit a screeching liner into dead center field. Wilson started in for the ball, but then, seemingly blinded by the sun, he hesitated and the ball shot past him into deep center field. The A's bench came to life. Players jumped to their feet and began cheering on the base runners as Boley crossed the plate, then Bishop. Wilson finally retrieved the ball as Haas was rounding third and heading home. But the throw was late and the Mule had himself an inside-the-park home run. The fans went berserk. Dykes, who was standing at the top of the dugout steps, was so overcome with excitement that he slapped the man next to him across the back, knocking him clear out onto the field. "We're back in the game boys!" he screamed. Horrified to learn that the person he decked wasn't a player at all, but his manager Connie Mack, Dykes jumped out of the dugout and helped the Tall Tactician to his feet. As he apologized profusely for his indiscretion, Mack simply smiled, dusted himself off, and in his own quiet way replied, "That's all right Jimmy. Anything you do right now is all right. Wasn't that wonderful?"[15]

The score now stood at 8–7, but the A's rally wasn't over yet. Noticeably shaken, Nehf walked Cochrane before he was replaced by right-hander Fred "Sheriff" Blake. Simmons and Foxx were not to be denied though, knocking out singles to tie the score. McCarthy was infuriated. He called in big Pat Malone who promptly hit Bing Miller with his first pitch, again loading the bases. Up stepped Jimmy Dykes, who nailed a high line drive to left. Stephenson overran the ball and it flew past him for a double. Simmons and Foxx scored to give the A's a 10–8 lead. Malone somehow managed to regroup, striking out Boley and Burns to retire the side, but the damage had already been done. Mack brought in Grove, who proceeded to snuff out the Cubs in order in the eighth and ninth, fanning four of the six batters he faced.

Not only had the Mackmen taken a commanding lead in the Series, but they had staged the greatest rally in World Series history. In earning the victory, the A's established a new World Series record for runs scored in a single inning, scoring 10 in the seventh. They also broke the previous record for hits in one inning, with 10, as well as the record for at bats, with 15.[16]

Though the Cubs' Hack Wilson proved to be the goat of the game, he still managed to retain his sense of humor. That evening,

Connie Mack greeting President Herbert Hoover before game five of the 1929 World Series at Shibe Park. The A's fans were less welcoming, registering their disapproval of Prohibition with the chant "Beer! Beer! We want beer!" (Courtesy of the National Baseball Hall of Fame.)

as news spread of his misplayed fly balls, Wilson entered a Philadelphia restaurant, pulled down the window shades near his table, and sardonically asked the maitre d' to dim the lights so he wouldn't misjudge the soup.[17]

Game 5 had to wait until Monday, October 14, since the Blue Laws prohibited Sunday baseball in Philadelphia. When the Series resumed, the A's snatched yet another victory out of the jaws of defeat. President Herbert Hoover traveled from Washington, D.C., to see the fifth and deciding game. It was one of the greatest occasions Philadelphia had ever witnessed. "People didn't see the President of the United States at all back in those days," recalls Joe Barrett, a lifelong A's fan. "When Hoover attended the final game of the '29 World Series it was a big occasion. Schools were off. People lined Lehigh Avenue. This was the only opportunity the great majority of Philadelphians would ever have to see the President."[18] Thirteen-year-old Wayne Ambler, who would later go on to play for the Athletics, witnessed the event from the left field bleachers. "That World Series was exciting and colorful," he said. "The bad baseball in it—the way the Cubs lost the eight-run lead in the fourth game— made it exciting. The good baseball—the way the A's came from behind to win the fourth and fifth games—proved how great baseball can be. I don't believe that Philadelphia has produced as great a ball club as those A's since."[19]

Hoover's presence unquestionably added to the pomp and ceremony surrounding the Series. If nothing else, it provided a forum for the public expression against the government's restrictive policy on alcohol distribution and consumption. As the President made his way to his box seat, the fans began chanting: "Beer! Beer! We Want Beer!"[20] It wasn't that Prohibition stopped the sale and consumption of alcohol in the Irish-dominated North Penn District where Shibe was located, but rather that the fans couldn't legally consume beer at the ballpark. In fact, illegal distilleries, warehouses, and speakeasies flourished in the neighborhood. Even the local kids participated, roaming the streets for empty paint bottles for the illegal brew. Worse, some residents were directly engaged in the gangsterism associated with the bootleg industry. But the seriousness of the problem didn't hit home until 1928 when bootleggers gunned down Hughie McLoon near his speakeasy at Tenth and Chestnut streets. McLoon, a gnome-like figure with a hunched back, lived at Twenty-fifth and Lehigh and had been the A's mascot for years before becoming involved in the bootleg industry. His was the first of 20 murders associated with Prohibition, generating a grand jury investigation which exposed the links between Philadelphia politics, corrupt police, and the manufacturing and distribution of alcohol.[21]

Philadelphia's problems were mild compared to Chicago, however, where Prohibition made murder synonymous with the Windy City. Chicago was home to a crime syndicate that grossed $100 million a year and deployed an army of nearly 700 thugs and gunmen. Among them were such gangsters as the infamous Johnny Torrio, Jack "Legs" Banion, "Machine Gun" Kelley, and, of course, public enemy number one, Al Capone.[22] Thus, between Philadelphia and Chicago, the 1929 Fall Classic might have just as well been called the "Bootleggers' Series." Though no game fixing was ever uncovered, America's greatest annual sporting event seemed to invite the bribery, gambling, and gangsterism associated with the illegal industry.

Aside from the crime and violence that Prohibition threatened to cast on the Series, Mack was greatly disturbed by the fans' treatment of the President. "It was a most regrettable occurrence," he stated after the game, "and I am sorry any of our Philadelphia fans were guilty of it. I never have been a party man. I vote for the man, not the party; and in my day I have voted for good men of both parties. But every good citizen should show proper respect for the President and his office."[23] Though he stopped short of saying it, Mack also felt the fans' behavior reflected poorly on the Athletics' organization at a time when it claimed the national spotlight—something that was of great embarrassment to him. True to form, however, the players from both clubs did their fair share to embarrass each other.

The bench jockeying was so severe that Commissioner Judge Kenesaw Mountain Landis, who was seated between the two dugouts and was caught in the crossfire, issued a warning to "cease and shut up." Fearing that the ladies in attendance might be offended by the earthy language, Landis summoned both managers to his box. "If the vulgarities continue," he told them, "the culprits will be fined their full World Series share."[24] When Mack passed the warning on to his players, Cochrane, who had been the ringleader, sarcastically cried out, "After the game, we'll serve tea in the clubhouse!" Landis, clearly within earshot, was not amused by the remark. But rather than to acknowledge it, he stared straight ahead as if he had heard nothing.[25]

Mack apparently chose to turn a deaf ear to the sultry banter of his players. It wasn't his style to allow such profanity. Instead, he insisted that "there is room for gentlemen in baseball." To that end he would "not permit" his players "to indulge in rough jockeying." "There always is an exchange of joshing before and during a game," he admitted. "The average player is a good-natured chap and a practical joker. But I have told our boys that there never can be anything personal or malicious shouted at our opponents."[26] But the Tall Tactician suspended his policy that day. Game 5 would be a hard-fought grudge match between the two teams. McCarthy and his Cubs were smarting from their 10-run collapse of the fourth game and the Mack-men certainly did not appreciate the way Guy Bush and his fellow bench jockeys had ridden them or the eight-run barrage Chicago's "Murderer's Row" unleashed against them in their own ballpark.

Howard Ehmke started the game, but lost his earlier magic and was knocked out in the fourth. With two out, he surrendered a double to Cuyler, a walk to Stephenson, and singles to Grimm and Taylor. The A's were down 2–0 and Mack replaced the veteran righthander with southpaw Walberg. The Rube retired the side by fanning Malone and held the Cubs to only two more hits for the remainder of the game.

Pat Malone, who started for the Cubs, was impressive through the eight innings, giving up only two hits to the 26 batters he faced. Going into the A's ninth, it seemed as though the Series would return to Chicago for a sixth game. With the A's down 2–0, French came in to pinch hit for Walberg and struck out. Bishop followed with a single and Haas, the hero of game four, smashed a line-drive home run over the right-field fence, tying the score at 2–2. Everyone in the park was on their feet as Cochrane came to the plate. But the rally would have to wait, as Black Mike was retired on a ground ball to second base for the second out of the inning. Al Simmons brought the fans back to life with a towering shot that just missed clearing the center-field scoreboard, falling instead for a double. McCarthy, feeling the lead slip away once again, ordered Malone to walk the always dangerous Jimmie Foxx. But Bing Miller didn't disappoint the fans, knocking a 2–2 curveball off the scoreboard for another double. Simmons bounced home with the winning run, giving the A's their first world championship since 1913.

The crowd went berserk. Philadelphia Mayor Mackey leaped from the field box where he had been hosting President Hoover and hugged every A's player he could lay his hands on. When he finally returned to the presidential box, Mackey was reprimanded by a secret service agent for leaving the chief executive. "Don't be silly, man," replied the mayor. "A Philadelphian does as he pleases on a day like this."[27] Meanwhile, in the Athletics' clubhouse, Landis offered his congratulations to all but Cochrane. Just before he was ready to leave though, he elbowed his way to the A's backstop and, with a straight face, said, "Hello Sweetheart, I came in after my tea. Will you pour?"[28]

As all of Philadelphia celebrated, Connie Mack quietly retreated to his private office in the Shibe Park Tower. When they saw him entering, three secretaries rushed towards the 66-year-old manager, fighting to plant a kiss on him. But graciously refusing them the privilege, he closed the door, lay down on his battered couch, and fell sound asleep.[29] The Tall Tactician could now rest peacefully. He had just captured his fourth world championship, a record at the time, and one that placed him head and shoulders above all other managers in the history of the game. It also vindicated his judgment, proving that his advanced age did not blunt his reasoning or his ability to win. It also proved that the so-called advanced ideas ushered in by the lively ball era did not belong solely to younger men.

Chapter 7

REPEATING, 1930

Philadelphia's celebration of the World Champion Athletics was short-lived. Just two weeks after the A's had clinched the Series, the stock market crash ended the golden era of prosperity. Soon the nation slid into a major depression. Because no one industry dominated Philadelphia's economy, the crisis hurt the city less than it did other regions of the country. Philadelphians took economic refuge in the fact that their city was the largest producer of knit goods, refined sugar, cigars, carpets and rugs, cardboard products, dental supplies, and streamlined trains. It also boasted a significant petroleum refining industry. Nevertheless, the Depression hurt.

No other event in the 20th century had a more profound impact on Philadelphia than the Great Depression of the 1930s. The progressive collapse of the city's banks, building and loan associations, and other financial institutions created chaos in the lives of many people. Even before the stock market crashed in October of 1929, more than 10 percent of the city's wage earners were unemployed. By April 1930 the number had climbed to 15 percent. Apple sellers were a common sight on the corners of busy intersections across the city. Quite apart from the growing unemployment and fragile foundation of credit, the Depression took a devastating emotional and psychological toll on many Philadelphians who experienced the

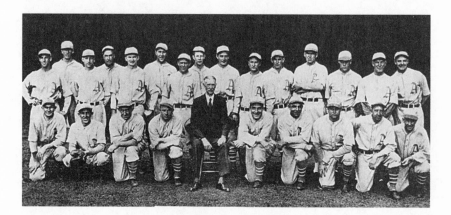

The 1930 Athletics. Standing (left to right)—McNair, Grove, Bishop, Haas, Boley, Walberg, Schang, C. Perkins, Moore, Summa, Williams, Earnshaw, Mahaffey, Quinn and Rommel. Seated—Higgins, Perkins, Cochrane, Dykes, Manager Connie Mack, Simmons, Miller, Foxx, and Eddie Collins and Kid Gleason, coaches.

shame and guilt of being unemployed, the despair that came from losing a business, or being evicted from a home.[1]

In the neighborhoods surrounding Shibe Park, unemployment rose to 30 percent. Mack, realizing his responsibility to the community, employed many of the old Irish residents to run the concession stands. Even the local priests would encourage their jobless parishioners to find work with the A's. Neighborhood kids were hired as sweepers or scorecard sellers for $2.50 a day.[2] For one especially desperate family, Mack proved to be a godsend. After the father's death, Mack hired the mother to clean his offices and gave her four boys jobs as well.[3] According to one neighborhood resident, Maje McDonnell, "After every game, Mr. Mack would send the leftovers that were still fresh from the concession stands to St. Joseph's Home for Boys at 16th and Allegheny."[4] Mack's humanitarianism, coupled with his remarkable success on the diamond, endeared him to Philadelphians. So grateful was the city that he received the Philadelphia Award for Outstanding Citizenship, which had been traditionally given to scientists, artists, and educators.[5] On the other hand, Mack was just as well known for his thriftiness in negotiating player salaries.

Mack could be downright intimidating when it came to those

negotiations. Seated in a big leather chair in his sedate, but hand-somely furnished, tower office, he controlled his payroll with a skill that demanded a certain degree of reverence. "He was pretty rough," admitted Mickey Cochrane. "I tried to hold out once. I walked into that tower office like a lion and a few minutes later came out like a lamb."[6]

Jimmy Dykes was similarly humbled. In 1929, Dykes earned $7,000 plus the $5,231 players were given as their World Series shares. He felt he deserved more for 1930. "After hitting .327, I felt I deserved a raise," he said. "I went up to the tower office and Mr. Mack let me talk for a half hour straight. Then he said to me, 'Is that all, Jimmy?' I told him, 'Yes, Mr. Mack.' Then, he starts talking to me for a half hour. He's going on and on and then he winds up with: 'Jimmy, you're lucky you're in the big leagues.' You know some-thing? I believed him. I simply said, 'Yes sir, Mr. Mack. Thanks for the opportunity." Then the embarrassed infielder got up, opened the door and left without a raise.[7]

"Baseball is just like any other profession," Mack reasoned. "There are very few individuals who can start at the top. Usually you have to go through a period of apprenticeship. To the young fel-low who has a chance to get a contract from a major league team and who thinks he ought to hold out for more money than is being offered him, I say, 'Forget it.' The big idea is not to make a million dollars your first few years in the big leagues, but rather to prove that you belong there."[8]

Predictably, Mack was known to offer one-year contracts only, regardless of a player's performance. But in 1930 his top two slug-gers forced him to reconsider that approach. Jimmie Foxx, who had compiled 46 home runs, 196 RBIs, and a .341 batting average over the previous two seasons, had not only proven to be an exception-ally talented player, but one who quickly endeared himself to the Tall Tactician. Mack signed the 22-year-old to a three-year, $50,000 con-tract. Nevertheless, the $16,666 Foxx earned for each of the next three seasons was still modest compared to the salaries of other mar-quee players like Ruth and Gehrig, who were being paid $30,000 or more a season.[9]

Signing Al Simmons would prove to be more difficult. Simmons refused to waiver on his demand for a three-year contract totaling

$100,000. He sat out all of spring training in order to deliver his message, and he registered it loud and clear. Without Simmon's bat in the lineup, the A's couldn't beat anyone, not even the bearded, long-haired House of David team that barnstormed across the country.[10] Mack was so exasperated by his team's poor performance that he labelled them the "worst-looking ball club I've managed in years."[11] He also began to realize Simmons' importance to the team. Minutes before the opening game against New York, Mack begrudgingly conceded to his star slugger's demand and signed him to the multi-year contract. True to form, Simmons emerged from the home team dugout in the first inning to ram a George Pipgras fastball over the right field wall for a home run. The blast ignited a tumultuous reception from the crowd of 34,000 who packed Shibe Park to see Lefty Grove and the A's go on to defeat the Yankees, 6–2. It was the opening salvo of a season in which the A's would capture their second straight pennant.

The A's were heavy favorites to repeat in 1930 because of their powerful blend of hitting, pitching, and defense. Mack had expected the Yankees to be the A's strongest competition, but New York got off to a poor start, losing its first five games. Clubhouse tensions also existed. Ruth, just signed to a record $80,000 contract, considered himself the rightful successor as Yankee manager after Huggins' death. When owner Jacob Ruppert hired Bob Shawkey, Ruth saw the new manager as an intruder who prevented him from claiming a job that rightfully belonged to him. Predictably, the Sultan of Swat spent more time complaining about management than winning ball games.[12] By May the Yankees were struggling to climb out of last place, and Shawkey began rebuilding the team. Mark Koenig and Waite Hoyt were traded to the Detroit Tigers for younger talent and those veteran Yankees who failed to produce were benched, including Ruth.[13]

Instead, of the Yankees, it was Walter Johnson's Washington Senators that gave the A's a stiff challenge. After Walberg shut out the Senators, 9–0, in their first meeting, Washington went on to win the next seven contests between the two teams. Although the A's won 21 of 30 games in May, they still trailed Washington by 4½ when the Senators came to Shibe for a Memorial Day doubleheader. In the opener, Grove was losing by a score of 6–3 going into the ninth. With two men on and two outs, Simmons came to bat. Having failed to reach base on three previous occasions, the crowd booed him unmercifully. It worked. Simmons became so angry he hit the ball out of the park to tie the game. Then, in the thirteenth, he hit a one-out double and later scored the winning run, despite injuring his right knee on the basepaths.[14]

Between games, team physician Dr. Carnett examined Simmons and discovered that he had broken a blood vessel in the knee. Noticing that the knee had swollen to twice its normal size, Mack asked the doctor: "Do you want to take him to the hospital?"

"Maybe later, but not now," he replied. "I want to watch the second game. Al shouldn't play, but let him sit on the bench. If the spot to pinch hit should come up, use him. In fact, I order it! I'll tend to the knee later."

Simmons got his chance in the fourth inning. With Washington leading 7–4, the A's loaded the bases. Mack called on his star slugger, telling him to "walk around the bases if you can." Simmons limped to the plate to face Bump Hadley. The Washington hurler threw the first pitch outside for a ball. His second offering was in the same spot. Then he threw a change-up that Simmons launched into the left field bleachers for an 8–7 Philadelphia lead. As he hobbled around the bases, pandemonium broke loose. The A's went on to win the contest 14–11, with Simmons' grand slam being the margin of victory.[15] The sweep broke the Washington jinx and the Mackmen followed it up with a 10-game winning streak.

By the end of July, the A's pushed Washington out of first place for good, winning 17 out of 24 on the road. At Boston they won three and lost one, at New York won two and lost two, at St. Louis won four straight, at Chicago won three out of four, at Detroit won two and lost two, and at Cleveland won three and lost one. At the same time, Washington was losing 14 games on their western swing. Things got so bad that Manager Walter Johnson seriously considered returning to the mound as a relief pitcher.[16]

It didn't seem to matter where they played in 1930. The A's won and they had fun doing it, on and off the field. Rudy Baizley often accompanied the A's on those summer road trips with his best friend, Connie Mack, Jr. He recalled that the players "behaved like young kids." On one occasion when the team was in St. Louis, Baizley tagged along with Bing Miller and Walter French, who were going to the movies. "On our way, they asked the cab driver to stop at a hardware store and told me to wait outside," he said. "They returned with two small bags, one filled with rubber bands, the other with staples. I asked, 'What are you going to do with those at a movie theater?' With a mischievous look on their faces, they replied, 'Just wait and see!' When we got inside the theater and the lights went down, they opened up the bags and began shooting the staples up into the air. They had one heck of a time for themselves, and, as you can imagine, turned a lot of heads when those staples met their intended mark! They weren't trying to hurt anyone. They were young men, just having fun."

Even the train rides could be adventuresome. Baizley recalls that cardplaying was a common pastime, only to be interrupted when a female passenger walked by. The young, attractive ones would be greeted with a kind word and a smile, the less attractive ones would elicit a less dignified response. "I remember one female who was rather homely-looking," he said. "As she passed through our car, she smiled at the players and almost immediately three of them jumped up on their seat, grabbed the luggage rack above, and began swinging back and forth in imitation of large apes."

Baizley's most vivid memories, though, involved his favorite players, Lefty Grove—who tossed him into the shower as a prank— and Mickey Cochrane. "I liked Cochrane the most because he was a real competitor," he recalled. "Mr. Mack knew that and always had me assigned to the upper berth on those train rides, right above Cochrane. Whenever I could, I'd also sit by him in the pullman car. He'd often bring along a saxophone on those road trips, though I really don't know why. He certainly couldn't play the thing. Whenever he'd try, he would only get frustrated with it and hand it to me, saying, 'Here kid, you try it!' I guess that's where I picked up a love for the saxophone. I played that instrument for the next twenty years of my life, thanks to Mickey Cochrane!"[17]

The A's clinched the pennant on September 18, with a 14–10 victory over the Chicago White Sox at Comiskey Park. Yielding to superstition, Mack started George Earnshaw, who had pitched the deciding game of the 1929 pennant race, against the White Sox, but Chicago tagged him for five runs in the first. The A's tied the game in the third and went ahead by two in the fourth. The Sox tied it again at 9–9 in the bottom of that inning when Simmons, slow in retrieving a screaming line drive that went into the left field corner, allowed the runner to score from second. After the side was retired and the A's returned to their dugout, Dykes gave the outfielder a nasty glare.

"Well say it!" Simmons snapped.

"If you're the left fielder, play like one," he shot back. "You could have thrown him out if you tried!"

The bickering continued until Mack intervened. "Shut up, you two!"

But Dykes and Simmons were too heated to hear the order and the feud continued. Finally, Mack made his way to the hot-headed third baseman and staring him in the eye commanded: "Dykes, shut your goddamned mouth!"

Both players were so stunned by the profanity they nearly fell off the bench. Neither had ever heard Mack curse before.

When the inning ended, Dykes and Simmons trotted onto the field together.

"We sure got the old man riled, didn't we?" said Simmons with a chuckle.

"Yeah, did you hear that 'goddamn'?" asked Dykes.

As the two players took their positions, Mack turned to one of the benchwarmers and chuckled. "You know what those two are saying?" he asked. "They're gloating over getting the 'old man' mad."[18]

Earnshaw was yanked for Roy Mahaffey, a quiet right-hander Mack had acquired from the Pirates earlier that year. Mahaffey kept Chicago in check until the sixth when he surrendered a triple to Carl Reynolds. Mack then replaced him with Walberg, who retired the side. In the seventh the A's scored five runs on homers by Foxx and Simmons and never looked back.

It was the second straight pennant for the Mackmen, who outdistanced Washington by eight games and third-place New York by 16. Individual honors were enjoyed by Al Simmons, who nosed out Lou Gehrig for the batting crown on the last day of the season, and Lefty Grove, who led the league in three categories with a 28–5 record, 209 strikeouts, and a 2.54 ERA.

Before the A's train pulled out of Chicago, the players came onto the platform and stole Connie Mack's straw skimmer. Before he could retrieve it, two of the ringleaders set it aflame. Even the Tall Tactician couldn't resist and joined in the laughter. It became a traditional prank among the players at the end of the final road trip, one they continued for the next ten seasons.[19]

Upon his return to Philadelphia, Mack was showered with praise by the press for his second straight flag. "We've proven that we are a fine ball club," he modestly replied. "But I have always maintained that no team is entitled to call itself 'great' unless it repeats. By that I mean we won a pennant and a World Series last year. We've won the flag again and if we take the Series, then my boys deserve to be ranked as a great team."[20] To ensure that his A's would repeat, Mack spent hours each day with his assistant coach, Eddie Collins, reviewing the lineup of the St. Louis Cardinals who would be their National League opponents in the Fall Classic.[21]

Collins, who was being groomed as Mack's successor, played his last few games that season. At the age of 43, his best years were behind him. According to his son, Eddie Collins, Jr., "Mr. Mack planned to have my father succeed him as manager of the A's. He was very close to Dad. It was very difficult for him to tell my father that he wanted him to go on the inactive roster. So he chose his words carefully. 'Eddie, you're more valuable to the team as a third base coach than a player.' My father took the hint and replied, 'That's all right, Mr. Mack, I understand your position and I agree with you.' There was such great mutual respect between the two men. Of course, Mr. Mack didn't want to lose him either. Other clubs had already expressed interest in my father as a manager."

Having been considered the smartest man in the game during his playing days, Collins quickly became a superb third base coach and trusted lieutenant to his former manager. He knew the opposing pitchers and their idiosyncrasies, what pitch they were going to throw and when they were going to throw it. "My father was very skilled at reading the pitcher," recalled Collins, Jr. "He would relay the next pitch to the hitter through a series of verbal signals. It wasn't always easy either. The A's were pretty particular. Simmons, for example, didn't want to take any signals at all. Dykes only wanted to know the signals when he was in a slump. And Cochrane only wanted to know when the fastball was coming. I guess you had to be something of a psychologist to coach for that team."[22] The elder Collins also knew the strengths and weaknesses of other teams' infields, as well as the vulnerabilities of opposing hitters. His knowledge was so extensive that it would be instrumental if the A's were to repeat.

The 1930 St. Louis Cardinals were a red-hot team, with many colorful players. Their pennant was almost wholly unexpected, as they enjoyed a late-season surge to win 39 of their last 49 games. In the process, they nosed out the Chicago Cubs by a two-game margin. Their manager was a rookie skipper named Gabby Street, whose greatest claim to fame was snaring a baseball dropped from the top of the Washington Monument during his playing days as a light-hitting catcher with the Senators. The pitching staff included 15-game winner "Wild Bill" Hallahan, who led the National League in both strikeouts as well as bases on balls; spitballer Burleigh Grimes, who posted a 13–6 record after being obtained in midseason from the Boston Braves; Flint Rhem, who managed to compile a 12–8 record despite being a legendary imbiber of Prohibition booze; and right-handers Jesse Haines (13–8) and Sylvester Johnson (12–10). The Cardinal lineup was even more prodigious, having scored 1,004 runs and batting .314 in one of the most remarkable team efforts in baseball history.

All eight starters hit over .300, led by 28-year-old rookie outfielder George Watkins' .373 average. Behind Watkins were second baseman Frankie Frisch (.346), outfielder Chick Hafey (.336), catcher Jimmie Wilson (.318), third baseman Sparky Adams (.314), first baseman Jim Bottomly (.304), shortstop Charlie Gelbert (.304), and outfielder Taylor Douthit (.303). Additionally, the Cards could boast of three reserves who hit .366 or better: Showboat Fisher (.374), Gus Mancuso (.366) and Ray Blades (.396). Ironically, the Cards had been outhit by two other National League clubs, the third-place Giants with a .319 average and the last-place Phillies with a .315 average.

The Series opened in Philadelphia on Wednesday, October 1. Wildcat bleachers lined the rooftops of North Twentieth Street. About 3,000 fans gathered on those rooftops and paid between $7 and $25 for the opportunity to watch the opener and boo Burleigh Grimes, the St. Louis pitcher who was slated to start. Grimes had earned the

George Earnshaw had a Quaker education from the George School and Swarth-more College, as well as a hard breaking curve ball. (Courtesy of Swarthmore College.)

wrath of the A's faithful by calling their team "a bunch of American League bushers" in the local press.[23] Fortunately, the fans were more respectful of President Hoover, who traveled up from Washington to see the opening game. Mack, who quickly spotted the president in a box behind the Philadelphia dugout, overcame his superstition of not going onto the field before the game and shook Hoover's hand. Apologizing once again for the fans' rude behavior during the previous October, Mack said, "It's a pleasure to have you with us again, Mr. President. You know you brought us luck when we beat Pat Malone and the Cubs in the fifth game last year."[24]

Lefty Grove faced Grimes in the opener and was tagged for nine base hits. Although the A's were only able to get five hits off of Grimes, each one went for extra bases. Cochrane and Simmons blasted home runs, Foxx and Haas tripled, and Dykes doubled. The A's won by a 5–2 margin in a game that lasted only one hour and forty-eight minutes, one of the shortest games in World Series history.

George Earnshaw was masterful in Game 2. Aside from Watkins' solo homer in the second inning, the Cardinals could only manage six scattered hits. The A's scored their runs in pairs, in the first, third, and fourth innings, coasting to an almost effortless 6–1 victory. But the Series was far from over.

The Cardinals battled back to tie the Series at Sportsman's Park in St. Louis. Wild Bill Hallahan hurled a 5–0 shutout in Game 3, holding the A's to seven base hits. Walberg pitched brilliantly for four innings before being tagged for two runs on a Douthit homer and consecutive singles by Blades, Wilson, and Gelbert. Mack relieved him with Bill Shores, who lasted until the seventh when he was hit hard for two more runs. The Cards added a fifth and final run in the eighth.

Game 4 was played on Sunday, October 5, before a wildly enthusiastic crowd of some 40,000 spectators. The Cards sent 37-year-old Jesse Haines to the mound against Lefty Grove. It was a magnificent pitcher's duel that was spoiled by a fourth inning miscue that ultimately cost the A's the game. With two outs and the score tied at 1–1 in the bottom of the fourth, Chick Hafey doubled. Ray Blades followed with a high bouncer to third. Although Dykes could have reached out to tag Hafey, who was charging from second, he elected to throw to first base. His throw was low, pulling Foxx off the bag, and the ball got away. Hafey scored and Blades was safe on the error. He would later score on back-to-back singles. The two runs proved to be decisive as Haines held the A's to four hits and the Cardinals won their second game by a score of 3-1. Dykes felt terrible and blamed himself for the loss. The Philadelphia press showed no mercy, calling him a "numbskull" for not tagging Hafey. But Mack, ever the optimist and mentor, consoled his third baseman, telling him, "You went for the right play, Jimmy."[25]

The A's knew that Game 5 would determine the Series. "The fifth game is the big one," insisted Foxx. If you win it, you're over the hump and coasting. If you lose it—well, that's not good at all." For seven innings the game was a brilliant pitching duel between Burleigh Grimes and George Earnshaw. Each hurler had only allowed two base hits and there was no score. In the eighth, Grimes loaded the bases with one out, but managed to retire Dykes and Bishop to end the inning. The A's would not be denied though. In the ninth, Cochrane, the first batter, walked. Simmons popped up, bringing Foxx to the plate. Double X had been held to a single in three previous at bats and was still smarting from game one when Grimes made him look foolish by throwing his spitter and curveball alternately.

"I was nervous," admitted Foxx. "Mr. Mack had already warned me to watch out for his curveball and not to let him fool me with that spitter motion of his. Grimes, of course, was cool as ice. He was deliberately slow in getting ready to pitch, so I stepped out of the box. I got some dirt on my hands and stepped in again. Then he threw the first pitch. I knew in a flash second it wasn't a spitter, for it was coming in close. It was a curve and I swung. Well, that was it. Some fan reached up and pulled it down when it hit the left field bleachers for a home run." Foxx's dramatic blast capped a 2–0 victory for the A's, who were now up by a game and heading back to Philadelphia.[26]

Game 6 was anticlimactic. Earnshaw pitched the A's to an easy 7–1 victory, holding the Cardinals to only five scratch hits. Cochrane and Bing Miller tagged Wild Bill Hallahan for run-scoring doubles in the first and Al Simmons hit a homer in the third. Dykes finished the scoring in the fourth when he nailed reliever Sy Johnson for a two-run homer. The A's had repeated, giving Mack his fifth World Series championship, a new all-time record for managers.

After the Series, many of the A's added to their $5,785 bonus by barnstorming across the Midwest or the South. "It was a big thing back in those days," said Simmons who was a regular barnstormer during his seasons with the A's. You didn't have television or even much radio. People out in the West, up in Canada, or in the South had heard about major league ballplayers, but they had never seen them. So barnstorming gave the fans a chance to enjoy us big leaguers. It was quite a treat for the players too. The money was good. It got to be like a minor World Series."[27] Players received between $3,000 and $5,000 a piece for a two to three week trip, visiting towns across the nation that didn't have a major league club. Sometimes players would divide into two teams by American and National league affiliations. On other occasions, squads would be composed of players from both leagues. On still other occasions, a major league team might play a talented local club or a Negro league team. Whatever the case might have been, barnstorming promoted the national pastime and endeared the players to fans across the country.

After their barnstorming had ended, Foxx would invite his teammates for a week of duck hunting on Maryland's Eastern Shore. Grove, Cochrane, Boley, and Haas often accepted the invitation before heading back to their respective homes for the winter.[28] The off-season found team members engaged in a variety of occupations. Perhaps the most interesting of all was Cochrane's. He was coerced by his friends into doing vaudeville in Brooklyn, New York, Philadelphia, and other eastern cities. "I feel like a fool sitting up there and playing the saxophone," he admitted. "Maybe if I were good at it, I wouldn't mind it." Once, when appearing in Brooklyn, his saxophone fell on the floor and the keys were damaged. He tried to play the first stanza of "Take Me Out to the Ball Game," but it sounded so terrible that the audience couldn't help laughing. The more he played, the worse it sounded. Finally, Cochrane threw down the sax and, leaving the stage, yelled, "Well, I never could play the damned thing anyhow!" The crowd roared so loud that he had to return to take a bow.[29]

Although he never amounted to much as a sax player, Cochrane took consolation in the fact that he was named to *The Sporting News*

All-Star team that December, along with teammates Al Simmons and Lefty Grove. Because the squad was composed of players from both leagues, Jimmie Foxx lost out to Bill Terry of the New York Giants at first base. Terry led the National League in hitting during the 1930 campaign with a .401 average. While Foxx's statistics were impressive (37 HR, 156 RBI, .335 avg.), the glut of A's on the squad and the comparative dearth of Giants most likely made the difference.[30] Foxx, ever the gentleman, took it in stride. He remained modest, being almost embarrassed by all the attention he was receiving by 1930. After all, there would be other honors. He was only 22 years old, far from his prime. What's more, the A's had the potential to become a baseball dynasty, with Foxx as their cornerstone. Only time would tell just how bright their future would be.

Chapter 8

ESTABLISHING A DYNASTY, 1931

T he national pastime was tamer and less spirited in 1931 than it had been during the previous few years. The introduction of a less lively ball brought a more sensitive balance between pitchers and hitters. The difference in statistics between 1930 and 1931 alone reflected the subtle change. In one year's time, the total of major league home runs dropped by 500, in part because balls bouncing over a wall or through a fence, which were previously considered homers, were now ground rule doubles. Batting averages declined as well. The National League average dropped from .303 to .277, while the American League went from .288 to .278. Predictably, pitchers threw more shutouts and compiled lower earned run averages.[1] But the A's continued their rivalry with the Yankees.

New York's new manager, Joe McCarthy, inspired a return to winning ways. The Yanks scored a league high 1,067 runs and compiled a .297 team average. Leading the pack was Lou Gehrig, who hit 46 home runs, batted .341, and set an American League RBI record with 184. The Sultan of Swat enjoyed a typically "Ruthian" season: .373 average, 46 home runs, and 163 RBIs. In addition to Ruth and Gehrig, Bill Dickey, Joe Sewell, Ben Chapman, and Earle Combs all hit over .300 for New York. But with the exception of Lefty

Gomez, who went 21–9, Yankee pitchers were far from pennant-winning caliber.[2] The A's, on the other hand, had the same lineup that won the last two World Series. In fact, it was Mack's bench that allowed the A's to capture their third straight pennant.

From the very start of the 1931 campaign, Mack was forced to play reserves. The infield featured different players on a weekly basis. Foxx was out for the first two weeks, and then it was Dykes and Boley. Fortunately, Mack picked up Phil Todt from the Boston Red Sox, who had placed the first baseman on waivers. The move gave the A's more flexibility at the corners. During the late spring when Dykes was injured, Mack was able to move Foxx to the hot corner and play Todt at first. Todt thrilled the fans with his brilliant defensive play and heavy hitting.[3] Shortly after Dykes returned to the lineup, shortstop Joe Boley was injured and Mack was forced to play a make-shift infield of Todt at first, Bishop at second, Dykes at short, and Foxx at third. By June, the combination was playing so effectively that the A's found themselves in first place by a 6½ game margin. By the end of the month, Boley was still on the injured list and Dykes suffered a charley horse that kept him out of the lineup. Dib Williams, a brash, strong-armed 21-year-old whom Mack discovered in the Southern Association, became the A's regular shortstop and surprised everyone by hitting .320. The son of a country doctor who managed a semipro team in Greenbrier, Arkansas, Williams played only one year in the Southern Association before coming to the A's in 1930. That year, in spring training, he announced, "I'm here to stay!" Though Dykes would return to his original third base position in August, Boley became expendable.[4]

Injuries also plagued the outfield. On August 8, Mule Haas was forced out of action with a broken right wrist. Shortly after, Al Simmons, who had slugged his way into the batting lead, suffered an infected left ankle and was out for two weeks. With Simmons and Haas out, Mack inserted rookie Jimmy Moore in left field and Roger Cramer into center. Moore, nicknamed "Hollywood" because of his good looks and snappy dressing, only played parts of two seasons in the majors, but ended up appearing in World Series both years. Cramer fared better. He proved to be a swift, agile flycatcher whose hitting figured prominently in many games for the A's. While Philadelphia sportswriter Jimmy Isaminger dubbed him "Flit," after

Mule Haas and Doc Cramer platooned in the A's outfield in the early 1930s. (Courtesy of Jerome Romanowski.)

the insecticide, because he was death to fly balls, Cramer was better known among the fans as "Doc" for the informal medical knowledge he gained by observing a local doctor before reaching the majors. His talent, as well as his popular appeal, earned him a regular position in the A's outfield for the next five seasons before he was traded to the Boston Red Sox.[5]

It was pitching, however, that allowed the A's to capture their third straight pennant. Mack purchased Waite Hoyt, the mainstay of the great Yankee teams of the 1920s, in 1931. Though his best years were behind him, Hoyt still managed to post a 10–5 record that season and helped to cultivate the younger pitchers on the staff. Earnshaw and Walberg contributed 20 wins apiece. What is more, the A's staff had the American League's lowest ERA at 3.47. But the highlight of the 1931 season was Lefty Grove's performance.

Grove enjoyed the most remarkable season of his major league career. He won 10 straight games to open the season. Then, in early June, Mack sent him in to relieve in a 1–1 tie against the Chicago White Sox. He lost the game on back-to-back singles in the eleventh. Afterwards, Grove became so infuriated that he dressed, climbed into his Pierce Arrow, and drove full speed to his home in Lanaconing, Maryland. There he remained for five days trying to cool off.[6] When he returned, Grove reeled off another winning streak. He compiled 13 victories heading into August, notching his 14th in a lopsided contest against Detroit. There followed a pitching duel against Wes Ferrell of Cleveland, which Grove won, 4–3, for his 15th. His 16th victory, a 4–2 masterpiece against the White Sox, tied him with Smoky Joe Wood and Walter Johnson as the American League pitcher with the most consecutive wins. Then, on August 23, in the first game of a doubleheader against the lowly St. Louis Browns, the streak ended.

Grove pitched a gem. But the Browns' Dick Coffman pitched even better, surrendering only three scratch hits for a 1–0 victory. Unfortunately for Grove, the one run came on an error by young outfielder Jimmy Moore, who was filling in for Al Simmons. With two out in the fourth inning, Grove walked Red Kress. Second baseman Oscar Melillo followed with a line drive into left field. Moore took a few steps in, then started back. In that split second of indecision, the ball sailed over his head and rolled all the way to the fence, scoring Kress.[7]

When Moore returned to the bench, Mack tried to console him: "Don't feel badly James, I've seen Tris Speaker misjudge some and he was a little better than you are." When the game ended in defeat, Mack suggested that Moore remain in the dugout until "things cooled down in the clubhouse." It was sound advice. Grove went berserk after the game. He began by tearing the uniform off his 6'3" frame, sending buttons flying across the clubhouse. He then splintered the clubhouse door and proceeded to throw anything he could get his hands on—chairs, stools, the water cooler.[8] Grove later admitted, "I was mad as a hornet, but not at Jimmy. He wasn't used to playing that sun field. I was furious at Simmons for not being there. I could have strangled him if I could've gotten my hands on him. Instead, I vented my wrath on the dressing room, really tore it apart. Can you blame me? I hated to lose a game any time, anyway, and especially to lose that way."[9]

To add insult to injury, the A's rediscovered their bats in the second game and lashed out 17 hits to give Hoyt a 10–0 victory. Grove went on to win his next three games. Had he won in St. Louis, the lanky hurler would have recorded 20 straight victories, a record that would have been extremely difficult for any pitcher to break. Perhaps the incident taught him to act with a little bit more maturity though. During the last few weeks of the season, Grove began to assume more responsibility for helping the younger pitchers. On one occasion, he watched with great interest as rookie Jimmy Peterson suffered a tough loss. When the young pitcher came into the dugout and hurt his foot kicking a water bucket, Grove advised, "Kid, when you kick a water bucket never kick it with your toes. Always use the side of your foot."[10]

Robert "Lefty" Grove was the ace of the A's pitching staff. (Courtesy of the National Baseball Hall of Fame.)

Grove's 31–4 record, 175 strikeouts, and 2.05 ERA made him the Baseball Writer's unanimous choice for the American League's first ever Most Valuable Player award.[11] Had there been a statistic for "quality appearances," Grove would have captured that as well. Time and again he relieved fellow pitchers and stopped opponents' rallies in games in which he was not the pitcher of record. While Grove's reputation had been based on speed alone then, 1931 proved that he was a much more versatile pitcher, with an effective curveball and pin-point control. In no other way would be have been able to appear in 41 games that season for a total of 289 innings.

The 1931 series was also the year that the American League required all players to wear uniform numbers so the fans could more easily identify them. Mack compromised on the ruling, deciding that the A's would wear numbered uniforms on the road but not at Shibe.

Instead free scorecards would be handed out at the gate, allowing fans to identify their favorite players. Assigning numbers was an easy task since it followed the same system a fan would use to keep score at the game. That is, a player's number would be determined by the position he played. Cochrane, who was the catcher wore #2, Foxx at first base, #3, Bishop at second, #4, Dykes at third, #5, Boley at shortstop, #6, Simmons in left field, #7, Haas in center, #8 and Miller in right, #9. The exception, of course, was #1 which was reserved for Mack in perpetuity. Thus, pitchers rated from #10 up. Although it was assumed that no one would want to wear #13 because of the player superstition about a jinx, pitcher Bill Shores requested and received that number. At it turned out, Shores might have done better to refuse uniform number 13. In 1931 his record fell to 0–3 from 12–4 the previous season. He didn't need to worry about a new number in 1932 because the A's released him.

The 1931 season also witnessed a fair share of humor as well. In a game at Yankee Stadium, for example, second baseman Max Bishop, stroked a hit to deep right-center field. It looked like a sure triple, but Bishop was called out at third, breaking up an A's rally. At breakfast the next morning, Mack saw his infielder eating a huge stack of pancakes and suggested, "Max, if you hit a triple today, I think you had better stop at second."[12] During another game at Shibe, Mack discovered that his scorekeeper, who posted the numbers from inside the large board in right field, had been drinking prohibition beer to quench his thirst. He became so drunk by the sixth inning that he posted an 87–12 score in favor of the A's. When he staggered out onto the field afterward, the fans gave him a standing ovation.[13] The A's clinched the pennant on September 15 in a 14–3 victory against the Cleveland Indians. By season's end, they had compiled 107 victories, a new club record, and distanced second-place New York by 13½ games. By winning their third consecutive pennant, the A's became the first team in major league history to win 100 games in three straight seasons. Their 313 victories over that time period established a new American League record. Mack now had the chance to set another, more personal record—the first major league manager to win three straight world championships.

Once again, the A's would face the St. Louis Cardinals in the Series. The Cards had romped past the New York Giants to win the

National League flag by 13 games. Their record of 101 victories was the best mark of any National League club since 1913. They had an outstanding pitching staff led by Wild Bill Hallahan (19–9, 3.29 ERA), rookie right-hander Paul Derringer (18–8, 3.35 ERA), and Burleigh Grimes (17–9, 3.65 ERA).

They enjoyed exceptional hitting as well. Second baseman Frankie Frisch was the National League MVP, with a .311 average and 96 runs scored. Outfielder Chick Hafey edged out teammate Jim Bottomly and New York's Bill Terry for the batting crown, with a .3489 average, and led St. Louis in home runs with 16. But the Card's secret weapon was a 27-year-old rookie by the name of John Leonard Martin, more commonly known as "Pepper."

Martin had been shuttled between the Cardinals and their farm system for two years until General Manager Branch Rickey traded away centerfielder Taylor Douthit to make room for him in the lineup. Martin didn't disappoint Rickey. In 1931, he compiled a .300 average and proved to be a daring baserunner. His headfirst slides into the bag excited the fans and ignited many a Cardinal rally. In fact, the 1931 Cardinals were such a well-rounded team that Manager Gabby Street boasted, "We will go into the Series with confidence and determination. We have shown that we are the class of our league. I've seen a lot of great ball clubs in my time, but for pitching, hitting, spirit and all-around balance, I'm willing to back my boys against any team."

When reminded that his Cardinals fell to defeat in last year's World Series against the Mackmen, Street replied, "Remember, too, that Hafey and Bottomly were not hitting last fall, whereas this year they have closed the league season with a slugging race for the batting championship. Their hitting inspires confidence in a team that feels it was not outclassed last year by the Athletics and could have won the championship with a break or two in the form of base hits from its best hitters. We intend to win the Series this year and I am supremely confident that we will."[14]

The Athletics knew they were facing a much stronger team than they had in 1930, but they were at full strength as well. All of the regulars who had been injured were recuperated and had been given just enough playing time over the last two weeks of the season to be primed for the Series. The only lineup change was at shortstop where

Dib Williams replaced Joe Boley. With Williams at short during the regular season, the A's turned more double plays than they had during the 1929 and 1930 seasons combined.

The offense was ready too. Foxx, whose numbers dropped from the previous year (.291, 30 HR, 120 RBI), closed out the regular season with an uninterrupted shower of blows. Simmons beat out Babe Ruth for the league batting crown with a .390 average and contributed 22 home runs and 128 RBIs to the A's attack as well. With the A's pitching being unmatched in either league, the Mackmen didn't have a weak link in any department, which is why baseball writers across the nation picked the A's to win their third straight world championship.[15]

The Series opened at St. Louis' Sportsman's Park on October 1. Lefty Grove faced Paul Derringer. The Cardinals jumped on Grove for two runs in the first. Derringer began the game by striking out four of the first six batters to face him. Then, in the third, the A's got to him. Dykes and Williams both singled. Haas followed with a double, scoring Dykes. Derringer walked Cochrane and then surrendered a long single to Foxx that knocked in two more runs for a 4–2 A's lead. Derringer gave up another two runs in the seventh on a single by Cochrane and a homer by Simmons. Grove coasted from there for the 6–2 victory.

Pepper Martin stole the limelight in Game 2. In the second inning, he hit a single to left. Simmons bobbled the ball and Martin took second. On Earnshaw's next pitch, the firebrand Redbird stole third with a headfirst slide. Cochrane almost threw the ball into left field trying to nail him. Martin scored on Jimmie Wilson's sacrifice fly for the first run of the game. In the seventh, Martin singled again, stole second, took third on Wilson's sacrifice bunt, then scored on Gelbert's suicide squeeze for the second Cardinal run. When Earnshaw returned to the dugout, an exasperated Mack asked, "Can't anyone stop that fellow? What's he hitting?"

"Everything I throw him," replied the disillusioned pitcher.

The A's only scoring threat came in the ninth when Hallahan had a period of wildness, walking Foxx and Dykes. He then managed to get Miller on a fly ball and Williams on a strikeout. Mack then called on Jimmy Moore to pinch-hit for Earnshaw. Moore struck out, but catcher Jimmie Wilson picked the third strike out of the dirt and

Philadelphia Athletics, 1931 American League Champions. (Courtesy of the National Baseball Hall of Fame.)

then foolishly threw down to third baseman Jake Flowers. Thinking the game was over, Flowers began to trot off the field. Mack began screaming at Moore, who was still standing at home plate, to run to first. But because of the noise level, the young pinch hitter could not hear his manager. Collins, coaching at third base, was going through all kinds of gestures and finally prevailed upon him to run down to first. The Cards made no play on him, and Dick Nallin, the home plate umpire, called Moore safe. Unfortunately for the A's, Hallahan found his control and retired the next hitter, Max Bishop, on a foul fly ball to end the game. The Cards had evened the Series at one game apiece with their 2–0 victory.[16]

The Series moved to Philadelphia for Game 3 on October 5. Thirty-eight-year-old Burleigh Grimes faced Lefty Grove. Pitching in his own ball park, Grove was feeling exceptionally cocky. In the second inning, when he faced Pepper Martin, the lanky southpaw shouted, "You country son of a bitch! I'm going to throw this pitch right through your head."

Stepping into the batter's box, Martin replied, "You country son of a bitch! You just try to do that and see what happens!"[17]

Martin singled Grove's first pitch into right field, sending Jim Bottomly, who had walked, to third. Jimmie Wilson followed with a single, scoring Bottomly and advancing Martin to third. Martin then scored on a long fly ball. In the fourth, Grove was tagged for two more runs when Chick Hafey singled, Frisch walked, and Martin doubled off the center field wall.

Grimes, on the other hand, was coasting through a no-hitter through seven innings, and a one-hitter until the bottom of the ninth when Al Simmons hit a two-run homer. But the runs proved to be meaningless as the A's went down to a 5–2 defeat.

Earnshaw faced Syl Johnson in Game 4. The A's big righthander dominated the game, throwing a two-hit shutout. Only Pepper Martin could break through Earnshaw's brilliant effort for a double and a single. Simmons doubled home Bishop in the first and Foxx hit a two-run blast in the sixth to give the A's a 3–0 victory.

Game 5 saw Waite Hoyt against Bill Hallahan. Street decided to move Martin to the cleanup slot, up from his customary fifth place in the batting order, because of his hot bat. Between his baserunning and hitting, the rookie firebrand did not disappoint him either. In the first, he slashed a long fly ball to deep center field that knocked in the first Cardinal run. In the fourth, he caught Hoyt napping when he laid down a surprise bunt and reached first safely. In the sixth, with Frisch on second base, Martin drove one of Hoyt's fastballs into the left field bleachers for a two-run homer.

"I think Hoyt got a little careless with me or maybe he figured I'd try to get Frisch to third by laying one down," said the Cardinal rookie, "because he put a pitch right down the middle and took a couple of steps in as if to field the ball. It looked so good I couldn't help swinging and the ball went into the left field stands for a homer, my first of the World Series. Frisch waited for me at the plate. Shaking my hand he said, 'If you'd a bunted that ball and made me run, I'd a died between third and home. I can't keep up with you!' " As he crossed the plate, A's fans broke with tradition and burst into frenzied cheering. The applause lasted a full five minutes, most likely the first time in Philadelphia baseball history that a partisan crowd cheered for an opposing player. The Cards added two more runs in the eighth to seal the 5-1 victory, sending the Series back to St. Louis.[18]

The A's romped to an 8–1 victory in Game 6, giving Lefty Grove all the runs he needed in a four-run fourth. The Philadelphia victory set the stage for a seventh and deciding game on October 10.

George Earnshaw faced Burleigh Grimes in the final game. The A's had the momentum now and were 8-to-5 favorites to win. Fearing the worst, Cardinal attendance dropped from 39,041 in game six to just 20,805 for game seven. Aside from a wild pitch that resulted in a Cardinal run in the first and Watkins' two-run homer in the third, Earnshaw pitched brilliantly. In fact, after the home run he retired the next 15 batters before being relieved in the eighth. By that time St. Louis had already posted a 4–0 lead. The A's last chance came in the top of the ninth.

Simmons led off with a walk, and then Foxx fouled out. Miller grounded into a fielder's choice. Dykes walked and Dib Williams followed with a single to right that loaded the bases. Mack sent Cramer in to pinch hit for Walberg, who had relieved Earnshaw in the eighth. Cramer singled to center field, scoring Miller and Dykes. Two runs were in, with two outs, and the tying runs were on base. Street pulled Grimes and put in Hallahan. Max Bishop was the first batter to face him. After working a 2–2 count, the A's second baseman lashed a line drive into left-center field. It looked like it was going to fall for a base hit, but Pepper Martin, who took off with the crack of the bat, snared the ball with a spectacular one-handed catch, ending the game and the World Series.

"Much more than a World Series ended with Martin's catch," Jimmy Dykes would recall years later.

> The Athletics' domination of the baseball world came to an end as well. Never again would an independent owner like Connie Mack be able to put together a great ball club without financial support and a nationwide organization.
>
> In a sense, the twenties also ended that day, though the calendar said that it was 1931. We were a team of the twenties, put together in that decade when the sky was still the limit for any American with ambition. Baseball reached its height during the twenties. We outhit the modern players by a big margin. We outran them, outpitched them, outplayed them. We played with dash, with spirit, with high morale. Although we played for pay, mere money was not our major consideration either. We played for sport, for the sake of the game, for the thrill of it. Call us naive. Maybe we were. But we had fun playing.[19]

Chapter 9

MACK THE KNIFE, 1932–35

S hortly after the Athletics lost the 1931 World Series to the Cardinals, many sportswriters began to speculate that Mack would break up the team. When asked about his plans, the Grand Old Man of Baseball insisted that he was "contemplating no upheaval." "If our club was composed largely of aged players who were past their primes and were on the downgrade, the situation would be different," he added. "But with only one or two exceptions, we have a comparatively young team that ought to have a lot more years left in it."[1] Indeed, Mack had reason to be optimistic. The average age of his team was 28 years old. Dykes, at age 35, was the oldest regular on the roster. The pitching trio of Grove, Earnshaw, and Walberg, was coming off a splendid season and, being in their early thirties, still had plenty of good years ahead of them. What's more, Jimmie Foxx, the boy wonder of the team, had become one of the most prodigious power hitters in the game, and he was only 24 years old, not even close to his prime.

The 1932 season would be another career year for Foxx. He went on a home run tear, nearly breaking Babe Ruth's single season record of 60 set in 1927. So extraordinary was his hitting that he carried a .400 average throughout the spring and, by May 1, had already

Jimmie Foxx poses with his Yankee counterpart, Babe Ruth (right) and another premier power hitter of Baseball's Golden Era, Lou Gehrig (left). (Courtesy of Shawn M. Murray, the Bruce Murray Collection.)

collected 19 homers. His power production continued throughout the summer. July was an especially productive month as the Beast knocked out 12 more homers. One of the most remarkable performances came in Cleveland on July 10 when he slugged three homers and scored eight runs in an 18–17 A's victory. A week later in New

York, Foxx hit a Lefty Gomez fastball into the corner of the left field upper deck, shattering a seat three rows from the top. Had the ball carried 20 feet further, Double X would have been the first player ever to hit a fair ball out of Yankee Stadium. In a postgame interview, Gomez admitted that "Foxx can hit me with the lights out. He's so strong, he's got muscles in his hair!"[2] Despite suffering a sprained wrist in early August, Foxx continued to produce. On August 20, he hit a 500-foot shot against Ted Lyons of the Chicago White Sox at Shibe Park. The ball sailed over the center field wall and carried well past 20th Street over a neighboring factory building.[3] By that time, Foxx's power hitting had already cost Mack and the front office $110 to pay for broken windows in homes across the street from Shibe Park.[4]

Comparisons between Foxx and Babe Ruth became inevitable, and yet there were few similarities between the two sluggers. Foxx's home runs were mostly long drives, rather than the towering fly balls launched by Ruth. Foxx also looked the part of a power hitter. He had huge, powerful biceps that he would flaunt by cutting away the sleeves of his uniform. When he dug in at the plate and raised his bat, those muscles would bulge, intimidating many of the league's best hurlers. He had quick wrists and held the bat low, his trigger being a quick hitch that dropped the bat even lower before his swing. Ruth's most distinguishing feature, on the other hand, was a protruding belly. Ironically, he was still able to generate his power from the waist, his swing resembling that of a golfer's. When asked to compare himself to the Yankee's Sultan of Swat, Foxx said, "I'm not as large as Ruth, but I have the proper timing and thorough coordination of hands, wrists, shoulders, and eyes. My fingers and wrists are very strong and I use a thinner handled bat than him, with more weight at the end. The lighter the bat, the faster you can swing it."[5]

The Sporting News kept pace with Foxx throughout the 1932 campaign to see if he would break Ruth's record. Of course, that never happened, and Foxx ended the season with 58. He might have succeeded had St. Louis, Detroit, and Cleveland not erected screens above their outfield fences. Double X hit the screen in St. Louis alone on five separate occasions in 1932, whereas Ruth had a clear shot in those same ball parks when he set the record five years earlier. New ground rules also hindered Foxx's ability to break the record. In 1927, any ball that bounced into the stands was considered a home run. By that measure, Foxx might have set a still existing record of 70 home runs. But a new rule change in 1930 eliminated the "one-hop-homer," making it a ground rule double.[6] Nor had Foxx made such a challenge his top priority. According to Doc Cramer, "[Foxx] wanted to become a more disciplined hitter and take more pitches. If he had been free swinging that year, like he had been in the past, Ruth's record would have gone out the window."[7]

Foxx's hitting allowed the A's to keep pace with the Yankees until late June, then they slowly began to drift behind in the standings. Frequent changes in the lineup also hampered the team's consistency. Shortstop Joe Boley, who had injured his shoulder during the previous season, continued to press in the field. He was replaced by Dib Williams, who played so well that Boley was given his unconditional release in May.[8] Then, in June, when Max Bishop injured himself, Williams was moved to second base and Eric McNair was inserted at short. Mack also experimented with hard-hitting Doc Cramer in center field and moved Haas to right, to replace an aging Bing Miller. Nor was the pitching as effective as it had been over the previous three seasons. While Grove posted 25 wins, Earnshaw, 19, and Walberg, 17, the relievers suffered from an inflated ERA of 7.70. That meant that the starting trio had to complete their games or risk losing them to their own bullpen. Even Eddie Rommel, the most dependable reliever and the designated closer of the staff, was experiencing difficulty. On July 10, for example, in the second inning of a game against the Cleveland Indians, Rommel was brought in to relieve starter Lew Krausse. He threw the next 17 innings, giving up 29 hits and 14 runs. While he managed to pull out an 18–17 victory in one of the most unusual pitching feats in baseball history, his performance only underscored the weakness of the bullpen.

The batting order also lacked the power it had demonstrated in the previous two seasons. Aside from Foxx, who hit .364 with 58 homers and 169 RBI, and Haas, who compiled a .305 average, the A's hitters suffered significant drops in their production. Simmons' average slipped from .390 in 1931 to .322 in 1932 and Cochrane's, from .349 to .293. All the other regulars hit significantly below the .300 mark.

Not surprisingly, the A's were relegated to runner-ups, finishing

13 games behind the Yankees. Again, the naysayers began to question whether the 70-year-old Mack had the physical stamina and mental ability to manage anymore. When confronted with the issue, the Tall Tactician insisted that his "mental outlook is the same that it was ten or twenty years ago and I was never in better health than at present. How long will I manage ball clubs? I don't know, but I expect to be at the head of one as long as I feel that I have the vigor and mind to address myself to the racking problems of a pennant campaign."[9]

On the train ride home from their final road trip, Dykes questioned Mack about a recent story he had read in the Philadelphia press that suggested his manager's intention to break up the team. "Don't worry about what the papers say, Jimmy," reassured Mack. "You'll be with me next year." But a few days later when Dykes was in New York to attend the opening game of the World Series, he was handed a tabloid headline which read: "Simmons, Haas and Dykes Sold to White Sox." When Mack confirmed the report, Dykes was furious. "I've spent my baseball life in Philadelphia," he fumed. "It is my hometown. The Athletics are my home team. Every game I've played has been for the home folks." So bitter was he that rather than play for another team, Dykes contemplated retirement, resolving to "never speak to Mack again."[10]

Almost immediately, rumors began to circulate about the dismantling of the team. The Philadelphia press predicted that Earnshaw and Bishop, "being in the high salaried group" are "certain to be wearing a different uniform next season." Speculation ran high that nobody was safe.[11] According to Doc Cramer, "All the ballplayers knew that the breaking up of the A's was coming because Mr. Mack was broke. He had to do it."[12]

To be sure, Mack was in a financial bind. Before the stock market crashed, he had borrowed $750,000 to enlarge Shibe Park. Now that the renovations had been completed, the loan had to be repaid. At the same time, he also shouldered the highest payroll in major league baseball, every one of his players earning at least $10,000.[13] Even with the Great Depression in full swing, Mack might have weathered the storm if the 1932 A's drew at the gate. But they didn't. Therefore, the only way he could meet the disastrous interplay of high costs and declining profits was to deal the only equity he had.

That meant selling his star players to make up the debt. And the White Sox were willing to buy.

Chicago hadn't finished in the first division since the Black Sox scandal destroyed the franchise in 1920. Their new owner, Louis Comiskey, wanted to build a contender and approached Mack for a deal. After several weeks of negotiation, Mack agreed to sell Simmons, Haas, and Dykes to the White Sox for $150,000. The deal, closed on September 28, was a wise move. Simmons and Haas, were 29 years old, and Dykes was 35. All three were aging veterans who had already seen their best days. Besides, Mack believed that he could field younger talent in their places. Cramer had already proven himself as a center fielder and hit .336. Lou Finney, the Most Valuable Player of the Pacific Coast League, looked as if he could pick up some of Simmons' production. And Pinky Higgins, a scrappy, young infielder, would replace Dykes at third.[14] By adding some new, young talent to a nucleus of proven winners, Mack was not only unloading some of the highest salaries on his payroll, but reconfiguring the team in a way that would still allow them to be competitive and build for the future.

Jimmie Foxx became the centerpiece of the team in 1933, though he agreed to take a $366 salary cut.[15] With the departure of Simmons, Double X moved from the fifth slot in the batting order to cleanup. Throughout the spring he hit at a .360 clip and vowed to "drive in at least 150 runs."[16] Adored by many a youngster, Foxx, in late May, made a Ruthian promise to try and hit a home run for an adolescent fan stricken with infantile paralysis. Though he never boasted about the pledge, the Philadelphia newspapers learned of it and made the promise a matter of public record.[17] One of the 48 homers he hit that season probably did fulfill his obligation to the young fan. Unfortunately, the A's were much less successful.

By the end of July, they were out of the A.L. race. The Mackmen finished third, 19½ games out, while Washington and New York battled it out for the pennant. There were some bright spots to the season though. Baseball's first All-Star game was played on July 6 at Chicago's Comiskey Park. Mack was honored by being named the manager of the American League team. Not only was he accompanied by his ace, Lefty Grove, and slugger Jimmie Foxx, but he was thrilled to be reunited with his former players, Al Simmons and

Jimmie Foxx was a favorite of the youngsters. He was known to speak to large school groups, encouraging them to "do their very best at learning" and for promising to hit a home run for one young fan stricken with infantile paralysis. (Courtesy of the *Baltimore Sun*.)

Jimmie Dykes. The 49,000 fans were treated to a 4–2 American League victory over John McGraw's National League All-Stars. The 1933 season witnessed some individual highlights for the A's as well. Grove had another outstanding season, posting a 24–8 record and a 3.21 ERA. In one of his greatest achievements, the A's southpaw blanked the Yankees, 7–0, on August 3, marking the first time New

York had been shut out in over two years.[18] Bob Johnson, a young Native American, showed great promise in the outfield, hitting .290 and collecting 21 homers and 93 RBIs. Mickey Cochrane regained his form at the plate, hitting .322. And Foxx captured his second MVP Award, as well as the American League's Triple Crown, with a .356 average, 48 homers, and 163 RBIs. There were also disappointments.

Eddie Collins, who had refused an earlier offer to become vice president and general manager of the Yankees, asked for and received Mack's permission to accept an offer as the general manager of the Boston Red Sox. Mack—like most Philadelphians—had assumed that Collins would succeed him as the A's manager at some future date. But realizing that Boston's offer was a great opportunity for his coach and knowing that he was not ready to step aside as the A's skipper, Mack gave Collins his blessing to accept the position.[19]

On the field, there were increasing concerns about the quality of the A's pitching. Aside from Grove, the next highest victory total was 13, held jointly by Roy Mahaffy and Sugar Cain. Earnshaw dropped to 5–10 and lost his fastball. Walberg suffered control problems and ended the season with a 9–13 record. By season's end, the rumor mill had these two hurlers pitching for other clubs.[20] Mack denied all rumors until December when he began dealing his players away.

The first to go was Mickey Cochrane. Mack agreed to accept $100,000 from the Detroit Tigers for his star catcher, as well as a young backstop by the name of John Pasek. Frank Navin, the owner of the Tigers, intended to make Cochrane his player-manager after the Yankees denied Navin's overtures for Babe Ruth.[21] Shortly after the Cochrane deal, Mack negotiated another one with former coach Eddie Collins of the Red Sox, selling Grove, Bishop, and Walberg to the Red Sox for $125,000.[22] Finally, Mack dealt Earnshaw to the Chicago White Sox for $20,000 after a salary dispute with the disgruntled pitcher.[23]

When asked to explain why he sold off such talented players, Mack engaged in double talk. At a December 18 press conference, he insisted that he "did not adopt a policy of selling star players because of poor attendance," and, in the next breath, he admitted that "attendance at home games was dropping down and our club had to act in accordance with that fact."[24] To be sure, Mack continued to campaign for the repeal of the Sunday ban as a way to raise attendance. He got his wish in 1934 when the law permitted Sunday baseball between the hours of 2:00 p.m. and 6:00 p.m.[25] Unfortunately, the lavish gate receipts Mack anticipated never materialized. In his attempt to attract more fans, he even reduced box seat prices from $2.20 to $1.65 and kept the .55¢ admission for bleacher seats and $1.10 for grandstand seats while other owners were raising their admission fees.[26] Nothing seemed to help. The A's attendance, as well as per-

Mickey Cochrane, the uncontested field general of Mack's second championship dynasty. (Courtesy of the National Baseball Hall of Fame.)

formance, continued to plummet, and they finished fifth in 1934 with a 68–82 record. There were some indications that Mack was considering retirement as well.

During the off-season, Mack accompanied a team of American League All-Stars to the Orient to promote the game there. The Tall Tactician served as Commissioner Landis' representative, while Babe Ruth actually managed the squad. The team played 17 games in Japan and five others in Honolulu, Shanghai, and Manila. Impressed by Ruth's remarkable appeal abroad, Mack, who was approaching his 75th birthday, was seriously considering the Bambino as his successor. After all, Mack had always had a special fondness for Ruth, and the Babe's presence would easily help at the gate. But a personal rift between Ruth and Lou Gehrig colored the entire trip, dividing the team into two almost antagonistic cliques.[27] Upon his return to Philadelphia, Mack was asked about the possibility of his stepping aside for Ruth as the A's new manager. "I couldn't make Babe my manager," he replied. "His wife would be running the club in one month."[28] Undaunted by the critics, Mack continued to manage the A's and things only seemed to get worse.

As the Depression lingered on, Mack tried to find other ways to increase revenue. He added a 38-foot-high corrugated metal extension to the 12-foot-high fence that already existed in right field during the spring of 1935. Called the "spite fence," by the residents of North Twentieth Street, the structure completely obstructed their view of the ballfield, preventing them from realizing any profits from the wildcat bleachers they once built atop their roofs. Although Mack built the fence in order to increase attendance, it seemed to have the opposite effect. The locals actively boycotted the games, some telling their children that "Connie Mack is so cheap that he built that spite fence so you couldn't see the games from across the street."[29] Mack also trimmed his payroll, and no one was exempt.

When Jimmie Foxx, the only bona fide star remaining on the team, asked for a salary increase to $25,000—not an unreasonable request given his remarkable hitting and the fact that Ruth was earning $35,000 from the Yankees at the time for even less production—Mack promptly refused. Instead, he tried to reduce Foxx's salary from $16,300 to $11,000. Foxx countered with a request for $20,000, at which point Mack increased his offer to $15,000 and agreed to a bonus clause if the A's drew 900,000 or more. Foxx refused to sign, suggesting that he "might sit out the 1935 season."[30] But two days before spring training began, Double X relented and agreed to $18,000, taking Mack at his word that he "simply couldn't afford to pay him any more than that."[31] Despite their differences over salary, Foxx remained a good soldier. Now that Cochrane was gone, he agreed to move behind the plate, knowing that the rigors of catching might have an adverse effect on his hitting, as well as increase his chances of being injured. Still, he expressed his hope that Mack would eventually "find a catcher" and that until he did he would "do his best for Connie and the club."[32] The experiment lasted until June when Foxx returned to first base and Charlie Berry became the team's backstop. By that time, the A's were buried in last place where they finished the season 34 games behind the first-place Detroit Tigers.

On December 10, 1935, Mack, pleading poverty, traded Foxx to the Boston Red Sox for journeyman pitcher Gorden Rhodes, minor league catcher George Savino, and $150,000 in cash.[33] The last member of the 1929 A's was now gone. The dynasty had been dismantled.

Precisely why Connie Mack dismantled the 1929–31 dynasty continues to be a subject of much speculation. The common assumption is that a combination of factors led him to do so, including the poor economic condition of the country during the Depression, a personal obsession with balancing his budget, and the club's faltering attendance. But at least one member of that championship dynasty took issue with that thinking. Jimmy Dykes insisted that Mack was "not the hard-fisted employer that some have called him." In fact, his payroll was "roughly equal to that of other clubs, except the Yankees." Like any good businessman, Mack "depended on current income to meet his expenses. After 1932 when the Athletics played to slim crowds, he had to readjust his expenses to match his income."[34] But Dykes doesn't attribute the breakup solely to financial motives. When asked pointedly why Mack dismantled the team, he replied, "The bitter truth was that we no longer had it. We no longer believed we were invincible. Our faith in ourselves was no longer there and he knew it too."[35]

To be sure, Connie Mack was a unique baseball businessman who anticipated many of the game's market trends, as well as the fiscal practices of contemporary owners. In general, he operated on a small financial scale, being more concerned about balancing his books than taking the risks that would otherwise be necessary to purchase a championship. After all, his first dynasty was crafted inexpensively out of young collegians and dim-witted roustabouts who would play for little more than food money. During the 1920s, however, he departed from this strategy. Like many of the owners in this era of excess, Mack spent thousands on proven stars like Cobb, Speaker, and Wheat, just as freely as he did on prospects like Grove and Cochrane. Only after the stock market crashed in October of 1929 did he return to his more conservative spending habits.

When attendance began to drop in 1930 and 1931, he realized that there was a correlation between a budding contender and fan appeal, or, as he put it, "Once you win the championship the fans lose interest. Expenses increase and attendance decreases. I can make more money then, if the team finishes in second place because Philadelphians love to follow a contender."[36] Predictably, the trading away of Dykes, Haas, and Simmons after the 1932 season weakened the A's just enough to make the pennant race exciting and the A's finished in second. After the 1933 campaign, Mack weakened the team even more by selling Cochrane to Detroit, Grove, Bishop and Walberg to Boston, and Earnshaw to Chicago, and the A's finished third. By the time he dealt Jimmie Foxx to Boston, the A's were a last-place team. Essentially then, Mack had sold or traded away his stars incrementally to teams that were in the rebuilding process. By doing so, he hoped not only to create greater parity in the American League by redistributing his former talent, but also to unload some of his highest salaries. Ironically, this strategy backfired, and, by 1935, Mack weakened the Athletics so severely that they would never again enjoy the glory of a championship dynasty.[37] "Another great era had come and gone," admitted Mack in the closing years of the decade. "The Athletics operate in an industrial city, where the Depression has hit especially hard. I do not enjoy managing a tail-end club, but in these troublesome years our club is confronted with a situation which is beyond our control."[38]

Conclusion

WHAT HAPPENED
TO THE '29 A'S

N ear the completion of my research on this book, I was
reminded that the Pulitzer Prize–winning novelist James
Michener was a devoted A's fan. Many summer afternoons
of his boyhood were spent riding the trolley from his Bucks County
home to Shibe Park, where he would watch his beloved A's perform
their magic from the bleacher seats. By the age of ten, he could recite
the entire roster along with batting averages. By the age of 20, he
was comparing his own admittedly "drab accomplishments" with
those of his hero, Jimmie Foxx. By the age of 50, he was calling the
1929 A's the "greatest team in the history of the game." The Philadelphia Athletics had provided a benchmark for his own life. I was curious to know why he never anticipated my efforts and wrote a book
of his own on the team. So, I contacted Michener the summer before
he passed away.

He seemed to delight in reminiscing about the 1929 A's, but
claimed that he "never really knew enough about them to do a novel."
When I suggested that his own experience as a young fan could have
easily carried the story, especially if he based it on his boyhood hero,
he replied, "The Jimmie Foxx story would make an excellent book.
But if I wrote it, I would only disappoint the reader. While the drama

171

of Foxx's life was so compelling, its denouement was just as tragic for he entered the decline in his mid-thirties when there is still so much of a person's life remaining. Nor was he the only member of that great dynasty who would never again enjoy the glory of their playing days"[1]

I did not truly appreciate Michener's remark until I began sifting through the newspaper accounts of what had happened to the 1929 Athletics after their major league careers had ended. What I discovered was that several of the A's struggled with adversity in their personal lives.

Mickey Cochrane, the field general of the team, completed his major league career as player-manager of the Detroit Tigers, helping to lead the team to two pennants and a World Championship in 1935. Faced with the prospect of rebuilding in 1936, Cochrane became increasingly intolerant of his players and too impatient with his young pitching staff to give them the opportunity they needed to prove themselves. His intensity led to a nervous breakdown.[2] Matters became worse the following season when he was struck by a pitch from the Yankees' Bump Hadley and suffered a fractured skull.[3] The incident ended his playing career, but he continued as manager until August 7, 1938, when he was dismissed by the Tigers.

When World War II broke out, Cochrane served as coach of the Great Lakes Naval Base baseball team. In 1944 the team won 33 consecutive games, finishing their season with a remarkable 48–2 record. When the season ended, Cochrane, who earned the rank of lieutenant commander, was assigned to the Pacific Theater.[4] After the war, Cochrane returned to Philadelphia, first as a coach and later as general manager of the A's. He was elected to the Hall of Fame, along with his old batterymate Lefty Grove, in 1947. Sadly, he continued to suffer from the head injury he sustained and fell on hard times later in life. His close friend, Ty Cobb, helped to support him financially until he passed away at the age of 59 on June 28, 1962.[5]

Lefty Grove continued to enjoy success with the Red Sox after Mack sold him to Boston in 1934. He was among the league leaders in ERA and strikeouts for the next five years, completing his storied 17-year career in 1941 with a 300–140 record, 2,266 strikeouts, and a career ERA of 3.06. That December he was given his unconditional release from the Red Sox. When 15 other clubs waived on the 40-year-old veteran, Grove, bitterly disillusioned, retired. He returned to his hometown of Lonaconig, Maryland, where he opened a bowling alley. Though he was a familiar figure at old-timers' games, Grove never really grew accustomed to his celebrity status and tended to avoid the fans after his election to the Hall of Fame in 1947.[6] In 1962, he moved to Norwalk, Ohio, to live with his son. He died of a heart attack at age 75 on May 23, 1975.

Al Simmons managed to extend his baseball career longer than any of his Hall of Fame teammates. After being sold to the Chicago White Sox in 1933, Bucketfoot Al played for 12 more years, though his short temper made for a brief stay wherever he went. Among the stops were Detroit (1936), Washington (1937–38), Boston (1939), Cincinnati (1939) and back to Philadelphia (1940–44). His inability to control his temper resulted in numerous fines and, ultimately, a costly divorce. After he retired, Simmons briefly coached for the Cleveland Indians. He died of a heart attack at the age of 54 in 1956.

Jimmie Foxx, the last of the great 1929 A's to leave Philadelphia, spent the twilight of his career with the Boston Red Sox. Double X's last good season came in 1938 when he hit 50 homers and drove in a career-high 175 runs to win his third and final MVP Award. Alcohol caught up with him after that. Injuries also plagued him, and in 1942 he was waived to the Chicago Cubs. He retired from baseball at the end of that season, only to return three years later with the Philadelphia Phillies. With many of the game's star players still off at war, the 38-year-old slugger came out of retirement to play for the hapless Phils, who were more interested in his drawing power than his baseball ability. He embarrassed himself, hitting a lowly .268 with only seven home runs.

Another public relations ploy came in 1952 when Foxx, recently inducted into Baseball's Hall of Fame, agreed to manage the Fort Wayne (IN) Daisies of the All-American Girls Professional Baseball League. Several other jobs followed—salesman, public speaker, baseball coach at the University of Miami—none of which Foxx seemed to hold for very long. Whenever he needed money, though, someone was always there to write him a check or give him a loan because of who he once was. But eventually, they, too, forgot about him. A year shy of eligibility for baseball's pension system, by 1958, Foxx found himself living in poverty on the eastern shore of Maryland.

He relied on his three adolescent children for income, his only personal assets being a tarnished MVP trophy from 1932, a friend's personal check for $400, and another one for $100.[7] When asked about his financial circumstances, he admitted that he "earned more than $275,000 playing baseball" but "blew most of it." "Suddenly you're 50 years old," he added, "and nobody wants you."[8] Foxx spent the last ten years of his life in a losing battle with alcoholism. He died July 21, 1967, at the relatively young age of 59.[8]

Of course, there were other members of that championship dynasty who managed to adjust to life after their playing days were over. Many remained in the game. Jimmy Dykes, for example, proved to be a capable big league manager with the Athletics, White Sox, Tigers, and Indians. Mule Haas and Bing Miller experienced lengthy careers in the American League coaching ranks. Joe Boley and Rube Walberg rejoined the A's as fairly successful scouts. Max Bishop became a highly regarded baseball coach at Navy, where he posted an impressive 306–143 record over a 24-year tenure. And Eddie Rommel became a respected umpire in the International League.

Still others discovered success outside the game. George Earnshaw, for example, distinguished himself during World War II as a chief gunnery officer on the aircraft carrier *USS Yorktown*, earning a bronze star for bravery. After the war, he returned to baseball briefly as a coach for the Phillies. But by 1951, his interest in the game had waned and he retired to Hot Springs, Arkansas, where he became a gentleman farmer.

Howard Ehmke remained in Philadelphia and opened his own business at 15th and Lehigh making canvass tarpaulin. He parlayed the business into a small fortune among major league clubs, which used the tarp to cover their dirt infields during inclement weather.[9]

For Connie Mack, however, the waning years of his managerial career were bittersweet. Elected to baseball's Hall of Fame in 1937, Mack's glory days were clearly behind him. His teams performed more like a "gentle comedy," to use the phrase of novelist John Updike, than a legitimate contender. Outfielders ran into walls—or worse, into each other—in pursuit of fly balls; quality players were constantly traded away for unknowns; the team continued to lose and nobody seemed to mind. Through it all, the Tall Tactician remained optimistic, undaunted by the critics or the A's lack of success. The

A rift over the management of the A's occurred within the Mack family in 1950, resulting in the eventual sale of the team to Kansas City. Pictured here are (left to right): Connie Jr., Connie Sr., Roy, and Earle Mack. (Courtesy of the National Baseball Hall of Fame.)

only reprieve from those dismal seasons came in 1948 when the A's contended for the pennant. But even then, injuries and poor relief pitching cost the A's first place in the last weeks of the season, and they fell to fourth, finishing 12 games behind the Cleveland Indians. At the same time, contention for ownership of the club was building within the Mack family.

Control and ownership of the Athletics was divided equally between Mack and his three sons, Roy, Earle, and Connie Jr. But Roy and Earle's desire to implement their own plans led to tensions between them and their father. The feud became so severe that the elder Mack and his second wife separated for a few months.[10] Faced with a weak and unprofitable team, a deteriorating and inaccessible stadium, and poor health, Mack, in 1950, issued his eldest sons an ultimatum—buy him out or sell out to him and Connie Jr. When Roy

Elected to the Baseball Hall of Fame in 1937, Connie Mack joined other baseball immortals: back row, left to right—Honus Wagner, Grover Alexander, Tris Speaker, Nap Lajoie, George Sisler, and Walter Johnson. Front row—Eddie Collins, Babe Ruth, Mack, and Cy Young. (Courtesy of National Baseball Hall of Fame.)

and Earle chose the former alternative, they ended their 87-year-old father's baseball career, forcing him to retire.[11] On October 18, 1950, Connie Mack retired from baseball, saying, "I'm not quitting because I'm getting old, I'm quitting because I think people want me to."[12]

After an unsuccessful effort to revive the A's, Roy and Earle Mack began to consider selling the franchise. They were encouraged by other American League franchises who had become resentful of having to visit Shibe, with its deteriorating facilities and poor gate receipts. Chief among the advocates were the New York Yankees who proposed a sale to Arnold Johnson, a primary owner of their farm team in Kansas City. Plans called for Johnson to sell the minor league club's existing ballpark to the city of Kansas City, which would renovate it and lease it back to him. He would then use the gate receipts to liquidate the Macks' debts, which Johnson would assume in purchasing the A's, and would move the A's to Kansas City. When a last-ditch "Save the A's" campaign in the summer of 1954 failed to generate much fan interest, American League owners met and approved the sale, despite a personal plea from Connie Mack himself.[13] Two years later, Mack died, brokenhearted.

Ironically, the Yankees, who had been the A's greatest rival during the Roaring Twenties, had now won at the bargaining table, becoming the major beneficiary of the sale. For the next 13 years—until they relocated to Oakland, California—the Kansas City Athletics regularly sold or traded outstanding players to the Yankees, the most notable of whom was Roger Maris.

Today, baseball seems to have forgotten about the 1929 Athletics. Even in Philadelphia almost nothing remains of the greatest sports franchise in the city's history. Not even the ballpark where they performed their magic exists. After the A's moved to Kansas City, Shibe Park, renamed "Connie Mack Stadium," became the home of the Philadelphia Phillies. It hosted its final baseball season in 1970. A year later, when the Phillies moved to the brand new multisport Veterans Stadium, the old park became a breeding ground of crime and waste. Neighborhood residents used it as a dumping ground. Police routinely checked it for missing persons. Drug addicts used it as a shooting gallery, and juvenile delinquents set it on fire. Finally, in 1976, the city put the old stadium out of its misery, demolishing it.[14] Today, all that remains of the Philadelphia A's is a statue of Connie Mack, outside of Veterans Stadium. The Tall Tactician is waving his trademark scorecard, a poignant reminder of a manager and a baseball team that were among the greatest of all time.

AFTERWORD

The Athletics made Philadelphia their home for 54 years. During that span, they played in 8,064 major league games, won nine American League pennants, and garnered five world championships. They produced a Hall of Fame manager in Connie Mack and nurtured the careers of nine players who were later enshrined in Cooperstown: Frank "Home Run" Baker, Albert "Chief" Bender, Mickey Cochrane, Eddie Collins, Jimmie "Double X" Foxx, Robert "Lefty" Grove, "Gettysburg Eddie" Plank, "Bucketfoot Al" Simmons, and George "Rube" Waddell. For at least a brief period, six other Hall of Famers played for the A's: Ty Cobb, Stan Coveleski, George Kell, Nap Lajoie, Tris Speaker, and Zach Wheat. With that kind of talent, it is not surprising that the team drew over 25 million fans to Shibe Park and attracted countless others who listened to the players' heroics on the radio or read about them in the newspapers. In short, the A's were a team whose fabric is intimately woven into Philadelphia's sports history, the most successful franchise ever to grace the city.

As Bill Kashatus points out, time certainly has not been kind to the Athletics. The 1929–31 A's, arguably the best team in the history of major league baseball, has been overlooked time and again by sportswriters and baseball historians. Even here in Philadelphia, it is difficult to pay homage to that remarkable team when one would have to be well into their eighties today to have enjoyed their feats. Thus, Kashatus, by giving us *Connie Mack's '29 Triumph*, has performed an invaluable service for baseball fans not only in Philadelphia, but across the nation as well.

However, the A's of more recent vintage, the teams that played in the post–World War II era, have also struggled with a distorted myth that they were "a bunch of losers who played in a bad ballpark." While those teams were not as successful as the earlier championship dynasty of 1929–31, they still were exciting to follow, being stocked with a mix of pedestrian players, stars, near-stars, and two future Hall of Famers. During that span, the A's produced a two-time batting champion (Ferris Fain), a Most Valuable Player (Bobby Shantz in 1952), a Rookie of the Year (Harry Byrd, also in 1952), and an infield combination (Joost-to-Suder-to-Fain) that set the American League record for double plays in 1949, and one that still stands today.

One cannot help but wonder if the A's might have enjoyed one more dynasty had Mack not traded away George Kell and Nelson Fox, allowing their Hall-of-Fame careers to unfold elsewhere. Perhaps the team might have even remained in Philadelphia.

Many of us who were youngsters at the time felt betrayed when the A's were sold to Kansas City. It was almost as if the Liberty Bell had been sold to Boston. Some reluctantly became Phillies fans, others continued to follow the American League, rooting for the A's from afar. But it was never the same.

As an adult, I became involved in the baseball card and sports memorabilia hobby. My passion was collecting items related to the Philadelphia Athletics. Over the years, I noticed that there were others of my age who were competing with me for some of the more rare items. In the summer of 1996, I made an appeal in my *Philadelphia Daily News* column, inquiring whether those readers who still loved and missed Connie Mack's A's would be interested in forming an A's Fan Club. A close friend told me that I was crazy and that I would be lucky to interest two dozen "old guys" in such a club.

Fours days after the column appeared, my post office box was so full of mail that I had to collect the overwhelming number of responses from the post office counter. It was mind-boggling. Either those two dozen "old guys" sure wrote a lot of letters, or there were many others who felt just as I did about my childhood team. Fortunately, the latter proved to be the case and, later that year, the Philadelphia Athletics Historical Society had its coming-out party at the Philadelphia Baseball Card and Sports Memorabilia Show in Fort Washington, Pennsylvania. It has been nonstop ever since.

Like similar organizations which honor and help preserve the memories of the Boston Braves, Brooklyn Dodgers, St. Louis Browns, and Washington Senators, the Philadelphia Athletics Historical Society was established by myself and Ernie Montella, another long-time memorabilia collector and devoted A's fan, to preserve the memory of Connie Mack's teams. Currently, there are over 600 members in the organization representing 40 states, the District of Columbia, Puerto Rico and Canada. We regularly produce a lengthy newsletter, called *Along the Elephant Trail*, and hold two reunions each year attended by former A's players. The proceeds from these reunions are given to those former A's who are in financial need. Over the last year, members have participated in the Jimmie Foxx statue project in Sudlersville, Maryland, and the erection of an historical marker by the Pennsylvania Historical and Museum Commission at the former site of Shibe Park. Within the next year, the A's Historical Society plans to acquire and archive oral histories from former players and team officials as well as establish a permanent home for our growing collection of A's artifacts and a facility to house our day-to-day operation.

Nearly a half-century after the A's left Philadelphia, there are those of us who have found that they never really left at all. Hank Majeski, Ferris Fain, Elmer Valo, Bobby Shantz, Lefty Grove, Jimmie Foxx, Mickey Cochrane, Connie Mack, and all the men who wore the A's colors continue to live on in our hearts and our memories. There is a great deal of comfort in that. After all, a defunct team can never disappoint its fans. Our A's will always win nine pennants and five world championships. Connie Mack will always be the Tall Tactician. Lefty Grove, the ace of the second dynasty. And Bobby Shantz, the 1952 MVP. What baseball, for us, has become is really a celebration of what baseball has been.

> Ted Taylor, President
> Philadelphia A's Historical Society
> Summer 1998

NOTE: Anyone interested in joining the organization can request a membership application or other information by writing to: Philadelphia Athletics Historical Society, P.O. Box 273, Abington PA 19001.

Appendix A

PHILADELPHIA ATHLETICS TEAM STATISTICS, 1929–31

1929

Pitching:

Name	T	AGE	W	L	PCT.	SV	G	GS	CG	IP	H	BB	SO	ShO	ERA
Earnshaw	R	29	24	8	.750	1	44	33	13	255	233	125	149	2	3.28
Grove	L	29	20	6	.769	4	42	37	21	275	278	81	170	2	2.82
Walberg	L	29	18	11	.621	4	40	33	20	268	256	99	94	3	3.59
Rommel	R	31	12	2	.875	4	32	6	4	114	135	34	25	0	2.84
Quinn	R	45	11	9	.550	2	35	18	7	161	182	39	41	0	3.97
Shores	R	25	11	6	.647	7	39	13	5	153	150	59	49	1	3.59
Ehmke	R	35	7	2	.778	0	11	8	2	55	48	15	20	0	3.27
Yerkes	L	26	1	0	1.000	1	19	2	0	37	47	13	11	0	4.62
Breckinridge	R	23	0	0	.000	0	3	1	0	10	10	16	2	0	8.10
Orwoll	L	28	0	2	.000	1	12	0	0	30	32	6	12	0	4.80
Totals		31	104	46	.693	24	151	151	72	1357	1371	487	573	8	3.44

Hitting (Regulars):

Name	B	AGE	G	AB	R	H	2B	3B	HR	RBI	BB	SO	SB	BA	SA
Foxx	R	21	149	517	123	183	23	9	33	117	103	70	9	.354	.625
Bishop	L	29	129	475	102	110	19	6	3	36	128	44	1	.232	.316
Boley	R	32	91	303	36	76	17	6	2	47	24	16	1	.251	.366
Hale	R	32	101	379	51	105	14	3	1	40	12	18	6	.277	.338
Miller	R	34	147	556	84	186	32	16	8	93	40	25	24	.335	.493
Haas	L	25	139	578	115	181	41	9	16	82	34	38	0	.313	.498

Name	B	AGE	G	AB	R	H	2B	3B	HR	RBI	BB	SO	SB	BA	SA
Simmons	R	27	143	581	114	212	41	9	34	157	31	38	4	.365	.642
Cochrane	L	26	135	514	113	170	37	8	7	95	69	8	7	.331	.475
Dykes	R	32	119	401	76	131	34	6	13	79	51	25	8	.327	.539
Totals:		29			814	1,354	258	72	117	746	492	282	60	.309	.477

Fielding (Regulars):

Name	Pos.	PO	A	E	DP	TC/G	FA
Foxx	1B	1226	74	6	98	9.2	.995
Bishop	2B	301	371	21	58	5.4	.970
Boley	SS	161	229	15	50	4.6	.963
Hale	3B	90	171	12	13	2.8	.956
Miller	RF	311	10	10	4	2.3	.970
Haas	CF	373	10	7	2	2.8	.982
Simmons	LF	349	19	4	2	2.6	.989
Cochrane	C	659	77	13	9	5.5	.983
Dykes	UT	203	273	33	41		.953
Totals:		3,673	1,234	121	277		.975

1930

Pitching:

Name	T	AGE	W	L	PCT.	SV	G	GS	CG	IP	H	BB	SO	ShO	ERA
Grove	L	30	28	5	.848	9	50	32	22	291	273	60	209	2	2.54
Earnshaw	R	30	22	13	.629	2	49	39	20	296	299	139	193	3	4.44
Walberg	L	30	13	12	.520	1	38	30	12	205	207	85	100	2	4.70
Shores	R	26	12	4	.750	0	31	19	7	159	169	70	48	1	4.19
Rommel	R	32	9	4	.692	3	35	9	5	130	142	27	35	0	4.29
Mahaffey	R	27	9	5	.643	0	33	16	6	153	186	53	38	0	5.00
Quinn	R	46	9	7	.563	6	35	7	0	90	109	22	28	0	4.40
Liebhardt	R	19	0	1	.000	0	5	0	0	9	14	8	2	0	11.00
Ehmke	R	36	0	1	.000	0	3	1	0	10	22	2	4	0	11.70
Perkins	L	24	0	0	.000	0	8	1	0	24	25	15	15	0	6.37
Mahon	L	19	0	0	.000	0	3	0	0	4	11	7	0	0	24.75
Totals		32	102	52	.662	21	154	154	72	1371	1457	488	672	8	4.28

Hitting (Regulars):

Name	B	AGE	G	AB	R	H	2B	3B	HR	RBI	BB	SO	SB	BA	SA
Foxx	R	22	153	562	127	188	33	13	37	156	93	66	7	.335	.637
Bishop	L	30	130	441	117	111	27	6	10	38	128	60	3	.252	.408
Boley	R	33	121	420	41	116	22	2	4	55	32	26	0	.276	.367
Dykes	R	33	125	435	69	131	28	4	6	73	74	53	3	.301	.425
Miller	R	35	154	585	89	177	38	7	9	100	47	22	13	.303	.438
Haas	L	26	132	532	91	159	33	7	2	68	43	33	2	.299	.398
Simmons	R	28	138	554	152	211	41	16	36	165	39	34	9	.381	.708
Cochrane	L	27	130	487	110	174	42	5	10	85	55	18	5	.357	.526
Totals:		30			796	1,267	264	60	114	740	511	295	42	.313	.488

Fielding (Regulars):

Name	Pos.	PO	A	E	DP	TC/G	FA
Foxx	1B	1362	79	14	101	9.5	.990
Bishop	2B	267	418	17	61	5.5	.976
Boley	SS	221	296	16	62	4.4	.970
Dykes	3B	124	191	13	18	2.7	.960
Miller	RF	309	10	8	3	2.1	.976
Haas	CF	360	11	9	5	2.9	.976
Simmons	LF	275	10	3	1	2.1	.990
Cochrane	C	654	69	5	11	5.6	.993
Totals:		3,572	1,084	85	262		.979

1931

Pitching:

Name	T	AGE	W	L	PCT.	SV	G	GS	CG	IP	H	BB	SO	ShO	ERA
Grove	L	31	31	4	.886	5	41	30	27	289	249	62	175	3	2.05
Earnshaw	R	31	21	7	.750	6	43	30	23	282	255	75	152	3	3.67
Walberg	L	31	20	12	.625	3	44	35	19	291	298	109	106	0	3.74
Mahaffey	R	28	15	4	.789	2	30	20	8	162	161	82	59	0	4.22
Hoyt	R	31	10	5	.667	0	16	14	9	111	130	37	30	2	4.22
Rommel	R	33	7	5	.583	0	25	10	8	118	136	27	18	1	2.97
McDonald	R	20	2	4	.333	0	19	10	1	70	62	41	23	1	3.73
Krausse	R	19	1	0	1.000	0	3	1	1	11	6	6	1	0	4.09
Peterson	R	22	0	1	.000	0	6	1	1	13	18	4	7	0	6.23
Shores	R	27	0	3	.000	0	6	2	0	16	26	10	2	0	5.06
Carter	R	22	0	0	.000	0	2	0	0	2	1	4	1	0	22.50
Totals		29	107	45	.704	16	153	153	97	1366	1342	457	574	12	3.47

Hitting (Regulars):

Name	B	AGE	G	AB	R	H	2B	3B	HR	RBI	BB	SO	SB	BA	SA
Foxx	R	23	139	515	93	150	32	10	30	120	73	84	4	.291	.567
Bishop	L	31	130	497	115	146	30	4	5	37	112	51	3	.294	.400
Williams	R	21	86	294	41	79	12	2	6	40	19	21	2	.269	.384
Dykes	R	34	101	355	48	97	28	2	3	46	49	47	1	.273	.389
Miller	R	36	137	534	75	150	43	5	8	77	36	16	5	.281	.425
Haas	L	27	102	440	82	142	29	7	8	56	30	29	0	.323	.475
Simmons	R	29	128	513	105	200	37	13	22	128	47	45	3	.390	.641
Cochrane	L	28	122	459	87	160	31	6	17	89	56	21	2	.349	.553
Totals:		29			646	1,124	242	49	99	593	422	314	20	.309	.479

Fielding (Regulars):

Name	Pos.	PO	A	E	DP	TC/G	FA
Foxx	1B	964	49	7	89	9.1	.993
Bishop	2B	314	414	12	84	5.7	.984
Williams	SS	152	214	27	59	5.5	.931
Dykes	3B	105	153	7	19	3.0	.974
Miller	RF	305	7	4	1	2.3	.987

Name	Pos.	PO	A	E	DP	TC/G	FA
Haas	CF	272	6	3	4	2.8	.989
Simmons	LF	287	10	4	0	2.4	.987
Cochrane	C	560	63	9	9	5.4	.986
Totals:		2,959	916	73	265		.979

WORLD SERIES STATISTICS, 1929–31

1929
Philadelphia Athletics defeat
Chicago Cubs (4 games to 1)

Line Scores								*Pitchers (innings pitched)*	*Home Runs (men on)*
Game 1—October 8									
PHI	A	000	000	102	3	6	1	Ehmke (9)	Foxx
CHI	N	000	000	001	1	8	2	Root (7), Bush (2)	
Game 2—October 9									
PHI	A	003	300	120	9	12	0	Earnshaw (4.2),	Foxx (2), Simmons (1)
								Grove (4.1) SV	
CHI	N	000	030	000	3	10	1	Malone (3.2), Blake (1.1),	
								Carlson (3), Nehf (1)	
Game 3—October 11									
CHI	N	000	003	000	3	6	1	Bush (9)	
PHI	A	000	010	000	1	9	1	Earnshaw (9)	
Game 4—October 12									
CHI	N	000	205	100	8	10	2	Root (6.1), Nehf (0),	Grimm (1)
								Blake (0), Malone (0.2),	
								Carlson (1)	
PHI	A	000	000	(10)0x	10	15	2	Quinn (5), Walberg (1),	Simmons, Haas (2)
								Rommel (1),	
								Grove (2) SV	

Line Scores   *Pitchers (innings pitched) Home Runs (men on)*

Game 5—October 14
CHI	N	000	200	000	2	8	0	Malone (8.2)	
PHI	A	000	000	003	3	6	0	Ehmke (3.2),	Haas (1)
								Walberg (5.1)	

Team Totals:	W	AB	H	2B	3B	HR	R	RBI	BA	BB	SO	ERA
PHILADELPHIA	4	171	48	5	0	6	26	26	.281	13	27	2.40
CHICAGO	1	173	43	6	2	1	17	15	.249	13	50	4.33

Individual Batting:

PHILADELPHIA (American League)   CHICAGO (National League)

	AB	H	2B	3B	HR	R	RBI	BA		AB	H	2B	3B	HR	R	RBI	BA
Bishop, 2b	21	4	0	0	0	2	1	.190	English, ss	21	4	2	0	0	1	0	.190
Haas, of	21	5	0	0	2	3	6	.238	Hornsby, 2b	21	5	1	1	0	4	1	.238
Simmons, of	20	6	1	0	2	6	5	.300	McMillan, 3b	20	2	0	0	0	0	0	.100
Foxx, 1b	20	7	1	0	2	5	5	.350	Cuyler, of	20	6	1	0	0	4	4	.300
Dykes, 3b	19	8	1	0	0	2	4	.421	Stephenson. of	19	6	1	0	0	3	3	.316
Miller, of	19	7	1	0	0	1	4	.368	Grimm, 1b	18	7	0	0	1	2	4	.389
Boley, ss	17	4	0	0	0	1	1	.235	Taylor, c	17	3	0	0	0	0	3	.176
Cochrane, c	15	6	1	0	0	5	0	.400	Wilson, of	17	8	0	1	0	2	0	.471
Earnshaw, p	5	0	0	0	0	1	0	.000	Root, p	5	0	0	0	0	0	0	.000
Ehmke, p	5	1	0	0	0	0	0	.200	Malone, p	4	1	1	0	0	0	0	.250
Burns, p	2	0	0	0	0	0	0	.000	Hartnett, p	3	0	0	0	0	0	0	.000
Quinn, p	2	0	0	0	0	0	0	.000	Bush, p	3	0	0	0	0	1	0	.000
Grove, p	2	0	0	0	0	0	0	.000	Blair	1	0	0	0	0	0	0	.000
Summa	1	0	0	0	0	0	0	.000	Blake, p	1	1	0	0	0	0	0	1.000
Walberg. p	1	0	0	0	0	0	0	.000	Gonzalez, c	1	0	0	0	0	0	0	.000
French	1	0	0	0	0	0	0	.000	Heathcote	1	0	0	0	0	0	0	.000
									Tolson	1	0	0	0	0	0	0	.000

Errors: Dykes (2), Miller, Walberg

Errors: English (4), Hornsby, Wilson, Cuyler
Stolen Bases: McMillan

Individual Pitching:

PHILADELPHIA (American League)   CHICAGO (National League)

	W	L	ERA	IP	H	BB	SO	SV		W	L	ERA	IP	H	BB	SO	SV
Earnshaw	1	1	2.63	13.2	14	6	17	0	Root	0	1	4.73	13.1	12	2	8	0
Ehmke	1	0	1.42	12.2	14	3	13	0	Malone	0	2	4.15	13	12	7	11	0
Grove	0	0	0.00	6.1	3	1	10	2	Bush	1	0	0.82	11	12	2	4	0
Walberg	1	0	0.00	6.1	3	0	8	0	Carlson	0	0	6.75	4	7	1	3	0
Quinn	0	0	9.00	5	7	2	2	0	Blake	0	1	13.50	1.1	4	0	1	0
Rommel	1	0	9.00	1	2	1	0	0	Nehf	0	0	18.00	1	1	1	0	0

1930
Philadelphia Athletics defeat
St. Louis Cardinals (4 games to 2)

Line Scores								*Pitchers (innings pitched)*	*Home Runs (men on)*

Game 1—October 1

STL N 002 000 000   2   9   0   Grimes (8)

PHI A 010 101 11x   5   5   0   Grove (9)   Simmons, Cochrane

Game 2—October 2

STL N 010 000 000   1   6   2   Rhem (3.1), Lindsey (2.2), Watkins
                               Johnson (2)

PHI A 202 200 00x   6   7   2   Earnshaw (9)   Cochrane

Game 3—October 4

PHI A 000 000 000   0   7   0   Walberg (4.2),
                               Shores (1.1), Quinn (2)

STL N 000 110 21x   5   10   0   Hallahan (9)

Game 4—October 5

PHI A 100 000 000   1   4   1   Grove (8)

STL N 001 200 00x   3   5   1   Haines (9)

Game 5—October 6

PHI A 000 000 002   2   5   0   Earnshaw (7), Grove (2)   Foxx (1)

STL N 000 000 000   0   3   1   Grimes (9)

Game 6 —October 8

STL N 000 000 001   1   5   1   Hallahan (2), Johnson (3),
                               Lindsey (2), Bell (1)

PHI A 201 211 00x   7   7   0   Earnshaw (9)   Simmons, Dykes (1)

Team Totals:	W	AB	H	2B	3B	HR	R	RBI	BA	BB	SO	ERA
PHILADELPHIA	4	178	35	10	2	6	21	20	.197	24	32	1.73
ST. LOUIS	2	190	38	10	1	2	12	11	.200	11	33	3.35

Individual Batting:

PHILADELPHIA (American League)   ST. LOUIS (National League)

	AB	H	2B	3B	HR	R	RBI	BA		AB	H	2B	3B	HR	R	RBI	BA
Simmons, of	22	8	2	0	2	4	4	.364	Frisch, 2b	24	5	2	0	0	0	0	.208
Miller, of	21	3	2	0	0	0	3	.143	Douthit, of	24	2	0	0	1	1	2	.083
Boley, ss	21	2	0	0	0	1	1	.095	Bottomley, 1b	22	1	1	0	0	1	0	.045
Foxx, 1b	21	7	2	1	1	3	3	.333	Hafey, of	22	6	5	0	0	2	2	.273
Haas, of	18	2	0	1	0	1	1	.111	Adams, 3b	21	3	0	0	0	0	1	.143
Cochrane, c	18	4	1	0	2	5	3	.222	Gelbert, ss	17	6	0	1	0	2	2	.353
Dykes, 3b	18	4	3	0	1	2	5	.222	Wilson, c	15	4	1	0	0	0	2	.267
Bishop, 2b	18	4	0	0	0	5	0	.222	Watkins, of	12	2	0	0	1	2	1	.167
Earnshaw, p	9	0	0	0	0	0	0	.000	Blades, of	9	1	0	0	0	2	0	.111
Grove, p	6	0	0	0	0	0	0	.000	Mancuso, c	7	2	0	0	0	1	0	.286
Moore, of	3	1	0	0	0	0	0	.333	Grimes, p	5	2	0	0	0	0	0	.400
Walberg, p	2	0	0	0	0	0	0	.000	Fisher	2	1	1	0	0	0	0	.500
McNair	1	0	0	0	0	0	0	.000	Haines, p	2	1	0	0	0	0	1	.500

	AB	H	2B	3B	HR	R	RBI	BA
Hallahan, p	2	0	0	0	0	0	0	.000
High, 3b	2	1	0	0	0	1	0	.500
Lindsey, p	1	1	0	0	0	0	0	1.000
Orsatti	1	0	0	0	0	0	0	.000
Puccinelli	1	0	0	0	0	0	0	.000
Rhem, p	1	0	0	0	0	0	0	.000

Errors: Boley, Cochrane, Dykes

Errors: Frisch (3), Rhem, Watkins
Stolen Bases: Frisch

Individual Pitching:

PHILADELPHIA (American League)

	W	L	ERA	IP	H	BB	SO	SV
Earnshaw	2	0	0.72	25	13	7	19	0
Grove	2	1	1.42	19	15	3	10	0
Walberg	0	1	3.86	4.2	4	1	3	0
Quinn	0	0	4.50	2	3	0	1	0
Shores	0	0	13.50	1.1	3	0	0	0

ST. LOUIS (National League)

	W	L	ERA	IP	H	BB	SO	SV
Grimes	0	2	3.71	17	10	6	13	0
Hallahan	1	1	1.64	11	9	8	8	0
Haines	1	0	1.00	9	4	4	2	0
Johnson	0	0	7.20	5	4	3	4	0
Lindsey	0	0	1.93	4.2	1	1	2	0
Rhem	0	1	10.80	3.1	7	2	3	0
Bell	0	0	0.00	1	0	0	0	0

1931
St. Louis Cardinals defeat
Philadelphia Athletics (4 games to 3)

Line Scores									*Pitchers (innings pitched)*	*Home Runs (men on)*

Game 1—October 1

PHI A   004 000 200   6   11   0   Grove (9)   Simmons (1)
STL N   200 000 000   2   12   0   Derringer (7), Johnson (2)

Game 2—October 2

PHI A   000 000 000   0   3   0   Earnshaw (8)
STL N   010 000 01x   2   6   1   Hallahan (9)

Game 3—October 5

STL N   020 200 001   5   12   0   Grimes (9)
PHI A   000 000 002   2   2   0   Grove (8), Mahaffey (1)   Simmons (1)

Game 4—October 6

STL N   000 000 000   0   2   1   Johnson (5.2),
                             Lindsey (1.1),
                             Derringer (1)
PHI A   100 002 000x   3   10   0   Earnshaw (9)   Foxx

Game 5—October 7

STL N   100 002 011   5   12   0   Hallahan (9)   Martin (1)
PHI A   000 000 100   1   9   0   Hoyt (6), Walberg (2),
                             Rommel (1)

Game 6—October 9

PHI A   000 040 400   8   8   1   Grove (9)
STL N   000 001 000   1   5   2   Derringer (4.2),

Line Scores   *Pitchers (innings pitched) Home Runs (men on)*

Game 6—October 9

Johnson (1.1),
Lindsey (2), Rhem (1)

Game 7—October 10

PHI	A	000	000	002	2	7	1
STL	N	202	000	00x	4	5	0

Earnshaw (7), Walberg (1)
Grimes (8.2),   Watkins (1)
Hallahan (0.1) SV

Team Totals:	*W*	*AB*	*H*	*2B*	*3B*	*HR*	*R*	*RBI*	*BA*	*BB*	*SO*	*ERA*
ST. LOUIS	4	229	54	11	0	2	19	17	.236	9	41	2.32
PHILADELPHIA	3	227	50	5	0	3	22	20	.220	28	46	2.66

Individual Batting:

ST. LOUIS (National League)   PHILADELPHIA (American League)

	AB	H	2B	3B	HR	R	RBI	BA		AB	H	2B	3B	HR	R	RBI	BA
Frisch, 2b	27	7	2	0	0	2	1	.259	Bishop, 2b	27	4	0	0	0	4	0	.148
Bottomley,1b	25	4	1	0	0	2	2	.160	Simmons, of	27	9	2	0	2	4	8	.333
Hafey, of	24	4	0	0	0	1	0	.167	Miller, of	26	7	1	0	0	3	1	.269
Martin, of	24	12	4	0	1	5	5	.500	Williams, ss	25	8	1	0	0	2	1	.320
Wilson, c	23	5	0	0	0	0	2	.217	Cochrane, c	25	4	0	0	0	2	1	.160
Gelbert, ss	23	6	1	0	0	0	3	.261	Foxx, 1b	23	8	0	0	1	3	3	.348
High, 3b	15	4	0	0	0	3	0	.267	Haas, of	23	3	1	0	0	1	2	.130
Roettger, of	14	4	1	0	1	4	2	.286	Dykes, 3b	22	5	0	0	0	2	2	.227
Watkins, of	14	4	1	0	1	4	2	.286	Grove, p	10	0	0	0	0	0	0	.000
Flowers, 3b	11	1	1	0	0	1	0	.091	Earnshaw, p	8	0	0	0	0	0	0	.000
Grimes, p	7	2	0	0	0	0	2	.286	Moore, of	3	1	0	0	0	0	0	.333
Hallahan, p	6	0	0	0	0	0	0	.000	McNair, 2b	2	0	0	0	0	0	0	.000
Adams, 3b	4	1	0	0	0	0	0	.250	Hoyt, p	2	0	0	0	0	0	0	.000
Orsatti, of	3	0	0	0	0	0	0	.000	Cramer	2	1	0	0	0	0	2	.500
Johnson, p	2	0	0	0	0	0	0	.000	Boley	1	0	0	0	0	0	0	.000
Blades	2	0	0	0	0	0	0	.000	Heving	1	0	0	0	0	0	0	.000
Collins	2	0	0	0	0	0	0	.000	Todt	0	0	0	0	0	0	0	—
Derringer, p	2	0	0	0	0	0	0	.000									
Mancuso, c	1	0	0	0	0	0	0	.000	**Errors:** Cochrane, Foxx								

Errors: Wilson, Bottomley, Flowers, Hafey
Stolen Bases: Martin (5), Frisch, Hafey, Watkins

Individual Pitching:

ST. LOUIS (National League)   PHILADELPHIA (American League)

	W	L	ERA	IP	H	BB	SO	SV		W	L	ERA	IP	H	BB	SO	SV
Hallahan	2	0	0.49	18.1	12	8	12	1	Grove	2	1	2.42	26	28	2	16	0
Grimes	2	0	2.04	17.2	9	9	11	0	Earnshaw	1	2	1.88	24	12	4	20	0
Derringer	0	2	4.26	12.2	14	7	14	0	Hoyt	0	1	4.50	6	7	0	1	0
Johnson	0	1	3.00	9	10	1	6	0	Walberg	0	0	3.00	3	3	2	4	0
Lindsey	0	0	5.40	3.1	4	3	2	0	Mahaffey	0	0	9.00	1	1	1	0	0
Rhem	0	0	0.00	1	1	0	1	0	Rommel	0	0	9.00	1	3	0	0	0

Appendix C

PHILADELPHIA ATHLETICS, 1929–31, VS. NEW YORK YANKEES, 1926–28: A STATISTICAL COMPARISON

A s I have already argued in the introduction to this book, trying to single out one team as the greatest of all time might be an enjoyable exercise, but it is ultimately futile. To bestow that honor on the 1927 New York Yankees, as generations of sportswriters have done, is to ignore the achievements of the 1929 Philadelphia Athletics, a team that was comparable in many respects.

Overall Records

One of the truly distinguishing characteristics that made both of these teams great was their consistency, or their mutual ability to capture the American League pennant for three straight years. The Yankees accomplished that feat in 1926, 1927, and 1928. They were succeeded by the A's who had a monopoly on the AL flag from 1929 to 1931. In fact, when the overall records of those two dynasties are compared, the Athletics emerge as the superior team, having compiled 11 more victories, 17 fewer losses, and a higher winning percentage than the Yankees.

PHILADELPHIA A'S, 1929-31   NEW YORK YANKEES, 1926-28

	W	L	Pct.		W	L	Pct.
1929	104	46	.693	1926	91	63	.591
1930	102	52	.662	1927	110	44	.714
1931	107	45	.704	1928	101	53	.656
1929-31	313	143	.686	1926-28	302	160	.654

When the hitting, pitching, and fielding statistics of these two dynasties are compared, the Yankees rightfully deserve to be called a better hitting team than the A's, but Philadelphia had stronger pitching and defense.

Hitting

The 1926–28 New York Yankees have earned the title "Murderer's Row" largely on the prodigious power hitting of Babe Ruth and Lou Gehrig. Although the team compiled 412 home runs during that three-year period, Ruth and Gehrig, together, accounted for more than 60 percent of them as well as for nearly 30 percent of all the Yankee runs scored. It should also be noted that Ruth and Gehrig hit for high averages as well. Ruth averaged .350 over the course of the Yankee dynasty and Gehrig, .353. Aside from outfielders Earle Combs and Bob Meusel, who averaged better than .300 during that same period, several of the regulars hit below that mark. Consequently, many of the league-leading hitting statistics the Yankees compiled during their dynasty were compliments of Ruth and Gehrig.

The Philadelphia Athletics of 1929–31 were comparable in that they relied on the power hitting of Jimmie Foxx and Al Simmons. Of the 365 home runs the A's hit during that three-year span, Foxx and Simmons accounted for more than 50 percent of them. Like their Yankee counterparts, Foxx and Simmons hit for fairly high averages. Foxx averaged .326 over the course of the dynasty and Simmons, .378. The A's could also rely on the hitting of their catcher Mickey Cochrane, who compiled a .346 average during the 1929–31 period, and Bing Miller, who hit .306.

Although the A's team production at the plate (365 HR, .292 BA, .452 SA) was comparable to the Yankees (412 HR, .297 BA, .458 SA) during their respective dynasties, New York was a better hitting club.

PHILADELPHIA A'S, 1929-31   NEW YORK YANKEES, 1926-28

	R	HR	BA	SA		R	HR	BA	SA
1929	901	122	.296	.451	1926	847	121	.289	.437
1930	951	125	.294	.452	1927	975	158	.307	.489
1931	858	118	.287	.453	1928	894	133	.296	.450
1929-31	2,710	365	.292	.452	1926-28	2,716	412	.297	.458

Pitching

Both teams enjoyed exceptional pitching staffs. Lefty Grove, George Earnshaw, and Rube Walberg anchored the A's rotation during the 1929–31 period. Not only did Grove compile an astounding .840 winning percentage during that time, but he also led the major leagues in earned run average and strikeouts as well. The A's could also boast of experience in the bullpen with knuckleballer Eddie Rommel and Jack Quinn, who was still permitted to throw the spitter.

The Yankees, on the other hand, had Herb Pennock, Waite Hoyt, and Urban Shocker in 1926 and 1927. George Pipgras assumed Shocker's place in the rotation in 1928. During that three-year period, New York posted an earned run average of 3.60, second in the American league to the A's 3.44 during the same period. Although the 1929–31 A's posted an earned run average of 3.73, it should be noted that earned run averages were up in both leagues during that period.

Over all, the 1929–31 A's pitched 12 more complete games, recorded 93 more strikeouts and compiled a better record (313–143, .686) than the 1926-28 Yankees, who were 302–160 with a winning percentage of .654. For pitching, the A's were the superior team.

PHILADELPHIA A'S, 1929-31

	CG	BB	SO	ShO	SV	ERA	W	L	Pct.
1929	72	487	573	8	24	3.44	104	46	.693
1930	72	488	672	8	21	4.28	102	52	.662
1931	97	457	574	12	16	3.47	107	45	.704
1929-31	241	1,432	1,819	28	61	3.73	313	143	.686

NEW YORK YANKEES, 1926-28

	CG	BB	SO	ShO	SV	ERA	W	L	Pct.
1926	64	478	486	4	20	3.86	91	63	.591
1927	82	409	431	11	20	3.20	110	44	.714
1928	83	452	487	13	21	3.74	101	53	.656
1926-28	229	1,339	1,404	28	61	3.60	302	160	.654

Fielding

The 1929–31 Philadelphia Athletics were a better fielding team than the 1926–28 New York Yankees, and in 1929 and 1930, they were the best fielding team in baseball. The A's outfield of Miller, Haas, and Simmons posted a .984 fielding average, compared to the .970 average of Meusel, Combs, and Ruth. During the 1929–31 span, the A's replaced shortstop Joe Boley with Dib Williams and third baseman Sammy Hale with Jimmy Dykes, but still managed to field a scrappy defense. Together with first baseman Jimmie Foxx and second baseman Max Bishop, these four players posted a combined .972 fielding average that was superior to the .958 average compiled by the Yankee infield of Gehrig, Lazzeri, Koenig and Dugan. The A's defense topped the Yankee's behind the plate as well, with Cochrane's average of .987 being better than the Yankee trio of Collins, Grabowski, and Bengough, who combined for a fielding average of .980. Thus, Philadelphia's cumulative fielding average of .975 was higher than New York's .968, and the A's committed 167 fewer errors than the Yankees.

PHILADELPHIA A'S, 1929-31   NEW YORK YANKEES, 1926-28

	E	DP	FA			E	DP	FA
1929	146	117	.975		1926	210	117	.966
1930	145	121	.975		1927	195	123	.969
1931	141	151	.976		1928	194	136	.968
1929-31	432	389	.975		1926-28	599	376	.968

NOTES

Introduction

    1. For complete statistics on Connie Mack's managerial record see Major League Baseball, *The Baseball Encyclopedia* (8th edition, New York: Macmillan, 1990), 595–96.

    2. Lieb, *Connie Mack*, 3–11.

    3. Lee Allen, *The American League Story* (New York: Hill & Wang, 1965), 7.

    4. *Philadelphia City Item*: August 7, 1866.

    5. Irving A Leitner, *Baseball: Diamond in the Rough* (New York: 1972), 29.

    6. Allen, *American League*, 7.

    7. John M. Rosenburg, *The Story of Baseball* (New York: 1970), 39–40.

    8. *Ibid.*

    9. Sheed, "Manager," 106.

    10. Allen Lewis, *The Philadelphia Phillies* (Virginia Beach, VA: JCP Corporation, 1981), 25.

    11. Sheed, "Manager: Mack & the Main Chance," 108.

    12. Harvey Frommer, *Shoeless Joe and Ragtime Baseball* (Dallas, TX: Taylor Publishers, 1992), 13.

    13. Eliot Asinof, *Eight Men Out: The Black Sox Scandal and the 1919 World Series* (New York: Henry Holt and Company, 1988, paperback edition), 56.

    14. Wallop, *Informal History of Baseball*, 119–120.

    15. Frommer, *Shoeless Joe*, 20; and Asinof, *Eight Men Out*, 56–57.

    16. Mack, *My 66 Years in Big Leagues*, 30.

    17. Mack, *My 66 Years in Big Leagues*, 92; and Lieb, *Grand Old Man of Baseball*, 89.

    18. Wallop, *Informal History of Baseball*, 121.

    19. Mack, *My 66 Years in Big Leagues*, 93.

20. Literary Digest (April 1914) quoted in Wallop, *Informal History of Baseball*, 120.

21. Mack, *My 66 Years in Big Leagues*, 196.

22. Sheed, "Manager," 108.

23. Romanowski, *Mackmen*, 30–31.

24. Lieb, *Connie Mack*, 184–87.

25. Allen, *American League*, 80–81; and Wallop, *Informal History of Baseball*, 148–49.

26. Mack, *My 66 Years in Big Leagues*, 35–36; and Lieb, *Grand Old Man of Baseball*, 181–82.

27. Mack, *My 66 Years in Big Leagues*, 36.

28. Mack, *My 66 Years in Big Leagues*, 187–90; and George Kochanowicz, "Why Connie Mack's Hair Turned White," *The National Pastime* (1991): 17–18.

29. Yagoda, "Legend of Mack," 53.

30. *Sporting News*: October 21, 1926; Jimmy Powers, "Cochrane, Foxx on Mack's All-Timers," *Sunday News* (Lake Charles, Louisiana): March 5, 1939.

31. Romanowski, *Mackmen*, 77–79.

32. *Ibid.*, 80–81.

33. *Ibid.*, 75–76, 82–83.

34. David S. Neft, et al. "Return from Exile," *The Sports Encyclopedia: Baseball* (New York: Grosset & Dunlap, 1974), 170.

35. See James R. Harrison, *New York Times*: October 9, 1927; and H.I. Phillips. *New York Sun*: October 10, 1927.

36. Lowell Reidenbaugh, *Baseball's 25 Greatest Teams* (St. Louis: The Sporting News, 1988), 6–7; see also Fleming, *Murderer's Row*, 7.

Chapter 1

1. Sam Bass Warner, *The Private City: Philadelphia in Three Periods of its Growth* (Philadelphia: University of Pennsylvania Press, 1987, revised paperback edition), 161, 178.

2. *Ibid.*, xx–xxi.

3. *Ibid.*, 178–83.

4. *Ibid.*, 183–85; and Russell F. Weigley, *Philadelphia: A 300 Year History* (New York: W.W. Norton, 1982), 587–89.

5. Warner, *Private City*, 185–94.

6. Weigley, *Philadelphia*, 588.

7. Warner, *Private City*, 194–97.

8. *Ibid.*, 197–99.

9. Bruce Kuklick, *To Everything a Season: Shibe Park and Urban Philadelphia, 1909–1976* (Princeton: Princeton University Press, 1991), 67.

10. Joseph P. Barrett, "The Life and Death of an Irish Neighborhood," *Philadelphia Magazine* (March 1970): 85–87, 128–33. Swampoodle took its name from the Cohocksink creek which once weaved its way through its low-lying environs only to be channeled into a sewer and paved over with streets in the mid–nineteenth century.

11. Edwin Wolf II, *Philadelphia: Portrait of an American City* (Philadelphia: Library Company of Philadelphia, 1990), 272.

12. Weigley, *Philadelphia*, 581; and J.T. Salter, *The People's Choice: Philadelphia's William S. Vare* (New York: Exposition Press, 1971), 66–68.

13. Salter, *People's Choice*, 32, 42–43.

14. Wolf, *Philadelphia*, 266; and Weigley, *Philadelphia*, 567–71.

15. See "How Wet Is Pennsylvania?" *Literary Digest* (November 10, 1923): 38–44; and O.H.P. Garrett, "Why They Cleaned Up Philadelphia," *New Republic* (February 27, 1924): 11–14.

16. Weigley, *Philadelphia*, 578–80.

17. Wolf, *Philadelphia*, 267, 281.

18. Rich Westcott, *Philadelphia's Old Ballparks* (Philadelphia: Temple University Press, 1996), 106; and Lawrence S. Ritter, *Lost Ballparks: A Celebration of Baseball's Legendary Fields* (New York: Penguin Books, 1992), 178.

19. Kuklick, *To Everything a Season*, 53; and Ritter, *Lost Ballparks*, 178.

20. Westcott, *Philadelphia's Old Ballparks*, 113.

21. Westcott, *Philadelphia's Old Ballparks*, 113; and Kuklick, *To Everything a Season*, 178.

22. Connie Mack quoted in *New York Times*: August 11, 1926.

23. Kuklick, *To Everything a Season*, 70–71.

24. Interview with Eddie Collins, Jr., July 12, 1995, Kennett Square, PA; and interview with Joseph Barrett, January 20, 1996, Havertown, PA.

25. Kuklick, *To Everything a Season*, 56.

26. Barret interview, January 20, 1996.

27. *Ibid.*

28. Westcott, *Philadelphia's Lost Ballparks*, 161; Kuklick, *To Everything a Season*, 55; interview with James McAndrews, January 14, 1996, East Falls, Philadelphia, PA.

29. Barrett interview, January 20, 1996.

30. Westcott, *Philadelphia's Lost Ballparks*, 163.

Chapter 2

1. Frederick Lieb, *Connie Mack*, 195.

2. *Ibid.*, 196.

3. Mike Sowell, *The Pitch That Killed: Carl Mays, Ray Chapman and the Pennant Race of 1920* (New York: Macmillan, 1991, revised paperback).

4. Asinof, *Eight Men Out*.

5. Seymour, *Baseball's Golden Age*, 330.

6. Interview with Frank Cunningham (son-in-law of Connie Mack), July 20, 1995, Ambler, PA.

7. Connie Mack, *Connie Mack's Baseball Book* (New York: Alfred A. Knopf, 1950), 32–33.

8. Red Smith interviewed by Lindsey Nelson in "The Connie Mack Story," National Baseball Hall of Fame Library, Cooperstown, NY (hereafter "NBHOFL").

9. Mack, *My 66 Years in the Big Leagues*, 35–36; Mack quoted in Allen, *The American League Story*, 80–81. In fact, Mack didn't make much of a profit at all. He ended up giving away star pitchers Chief Bender and Eddie Plank as well as Jack Barry to Boston. The only real money he made was on the sale of Eddie Collins to the Chicago White Sox for $50,000. Desperate to balance his books, Mack, in

1916, proposed to his players a profit-sharing system whereby their salaries would be based on a percentage of the gate receipts. But because the A's were floundering in last place with no hope of getting out in the near future, the players wisely opted for salaries that were guaranteed by contracts.

10. Lieb, *Connie Mack*, 38.

11. Mack, *Baseball Book*, 34–35.

12. Lieb, *Connie Mack*, 199. The presidency of the A's was assumed by Shibe's son Thomas who, in turn, deferred to Mack on most administrative matters.

13. Mack, *Baseball Book*, 187.

14. *Ibid.*, 54–55.

15. Paul Dickson, *Baseball's Greatest Quotations* (New York: HarperCollins, 1991), 261.

16. Jimmy Dykes and Charles O. Dexter, *You Can't Steal First Base* (Philadelphia: J.B. Lippincott, 1967), 16.

17. Interview with Joe Hauser, January 19, 1997, Sheboygan, WI; also see John Pierce, "Joe Hauser: Home Run King of the Minors," *Baseball Digest* (February 1974): 70–76; and Michael Knuth, "Still Swinging After All These Years," *Sheboygan (Wisconsin) Press*: September 19, 1993.

18. Macht, "Sammy Hale," in Shatzkin, *Ball Players*, 434; Dykes, *You Can't Steal First*, 35; and Reidenbaugh, *Baseball's Greatest Teams*, 32–34; and Interview with Rudolph Baizley: December 9, 1997, Philadelphia, PA.

19. Lieb, *Connie Mack*, 203.

20. Philadelphia sportswriters quoted in Jimmy Powers, "Cochrane, Foxx on Mack's All Timers," *Sunday News* (Lake Charles, Louisiana): March 5, 1939.

21. Lieb, *Connie Mack*, 205.

22. Gerald Astor, "Second Dynasties," in *The Baseball Hall of Fame 50th Anniversary Book* (New York: Prentice Hall Press, 1988), 159.

23. Lieb, *Connie Mack*, 203; and Astor, "Second Dynasties," 160.

24. Dykes, *You Can't Steal First*, 27.

25. Astor, "Second Dynasties," 159.

26. Mack, *Baseball Book*, 75.

27. Neil J. Sullivan, *The Minors* (New York: St. Martin's Press, 1990), 71–78.

28. *Ibid.*, 97

29. *Ibid.*, 74

30. Mack quoted in *The Sporting News*: December 23, 1943.

31. Babe Ruth and Bob Considine, *The Babe Ruth Story* (New York: Penguin, 1922, revised paperback edition), 20–21.

32. Astor, "Second Dynasties," 157–58.

33. Seymour, *Baseball's Golden Age*, 441; Lieb, *Connie Mack*, 206; and Astor, "Second Dynasties," 158.

34. Mack, *Baseball Book*, 49–50; Lieb, *Connie Mack*, 205; Reidenbaugh, *Baseball's Greatest Teams*, 35.

35. Ed Walton, "Jimmie Foxx," in Shatzkin, *Ball Players*, 356–57.

36. Bob Gorman, *Double X: Jimmie Foxx—Baseball's Forgotten Slugger* (New York: Bill Goff Inc., 1990), 13; Frank Baker to Bill Werber as retold by Brent Kelley, "What If Jimmie Foxx Had Played for the Yankees?" *Baseball Digest* (April 1995): 58–59; and Norman Macht, "Hall of Famer Jimmie Foxx Was a Phenom at a Young Age," *Baseball Digest* (April 1990): 86–89.

37. Mack, *Baseball Book*, 38–39, 55.

38. *Ibid.*

39. *Ibid.*, 32–33.

40. John W. Evans, "Jack Quinn: Stitching a Baseball Legend" (unpublished paper delivered at the American Catholic Historical Association meeting, Charlottesville, VA, April 1994), 16.

41. *Ibid.*

42. *Ibid,* 16–17.

43. *Ibid.*, 17.

44. *Ibid.*, 12.

45. Mack, *Baseball Book*, 40–41.

46. Swindell, "1929 Athletics," 22.

47. *Sporting News*: March 19, 1925.

48. *Sporting News*: March 5, 1925.

49. Astor, "Second Dynasties," 157.

50. Harrison Daniel, *Jimmie Foxx: Baseball Hall of Famer, 1907–1967* (Jefferson, NC: McFarland, 1996), 21.

51. John P. Carmichael, *My Greatest Day in Baseball* (New York: Grosset & Dunlap, 1951), 78; and Foxx interviewed by Nelson, "Connie Mack Story," NBHOFL.

52. See Cox, *Lively Ball*, 122–23; Lieb, *Connie Mack*, 209; and Westcott, *Philadelphia's Old Ballparks*, 177.

53. Cox, *Lively Ball*, 119–29.

54. *Sporting News*: June 10, 1926.

55. *Sporting News*: June 24, 1926.

56. *Sporting News*: July 8, 15, 1926.

57. *Sporting News*: August 5, 1926.

58. *Sporting News*: October 21, 1926.

Chapter 3

1. Cox, *Lively Ball* , 38 & 68; and Al Stump, *Cobb: A Biography* (Chapel Hill, NC: Algonquin Books, 1994), 380–83.

2. Ty Cobb with Al Stump, *My Life in Baseball: The True Record.* (New York: Double Day, 1961), 248–49.

3. *Philadelphia Record*: February 5, 1927.

4. *Philadelphia Record*: February 9, 1927; also see *New York Times*: February 9, 1927.

5. Stump, *Cobb*, 168–169, 385.

6. Cobb quoted in *Sporting News*: March 31, 1927.

7. *Sporting News*: March 31, 1927; and Mack, *Baseball Book* , 59–60, 202.

8. Cobb, *My Life in Baseball*, 45; Stump, *Cobb*, 389; and interview with Bruce Kulick, June 27, 1995, University of Pennsylvania, Philadelphia, PA.

9. Mack, *Baseball Book*, 202.

10. Interview with Eddie Collins, Jr., July 12, 1995, Kennett Square, PA.

11. Kavanaugh, "Zach Wheat," in Shatzkin, *Ball Players*, 1160–61.

12. Stump, *Cobb*, 387; Mack, *My 66 Years in the Big Leagues*, 55–56; and Cobb, *My Life in Baseball*, 250–51.

13. *Sporting News*: March 31, 1927.

14. *New York Sun*: April 15, 1927.

15. *New York Daily News*: April 15, 1927.

16. *New York American*: April 17, 1927.

17. *New York Times*: April 14, 1927.

18. *Philadelphia Evening Bulletin*: April 21, 1927.

19. *Philadelphia Record*: May 6, 8, 1927; Stump, *Cobb*, 390–91; and Frederick Lieb, *Connie Mack: Grand Old Man of Baseball* (New York: G.P. Putnam's Sons, 1945), 215.

20. *New York Daily Mirror*: May 31, 1927.

21. Fred Stein, "Managers and Coaches," in *Total Baseball*, edited by John Thorn and Peter Palmer (New York: Warner Books, 1989), 460; and Hal Lebovitz, "A Tribute to Lefty Grove, Baseball's Fierce Warrior," *Baseball Digest* (September 1975): 83.

22. *New York Evening Journal*: June 1, 1927.

23. *Sporting News*: June 30, 1927.

24. *New York Graphic*: June 28, 1927. Before joining the *New York Graphic* as a 25-year-old sports editor in 1927, Sullivan wrote for the *Philadelphia Public Ledger* and harbored a personal grudge against Bill Brandt. Sullivan would eventually leave sportswriting and become the Broadway columnist for the New York Daily News and, later, the host of the enormously popular television variety show which bore his name. (See Fleming, *Murderer's Row*, 235–36.)

25. *Detroit Free Press*: July 19, 1927; See also Ernie Harwell, "When Ty Cobb Collected his 4,000 Hit," *Baseball Digest* (May 1977): 59–61.

26. Trachtenberg, *Wonder Team*, 131–52.

27. Dan Shaughnessey, *Curse of the Bambino* (New York: Viking, 1991), 52,139.

28. Geoffrey C. Ward & Ken Burns, *Baseball: An Illustrated History* (New York: Alfred A. Knopf, 1994), 184–85; and Cox, *Lively Ball*, 172.

29. Robert W. Creamer, *Babe: The Legend Comes to Life* (New York: Simon & Schuster, 1974), 309.

30. *Ibid.*, 320–23.

31. Creamer, *Babe*, 149.

32. Ray Robinson, *Iron Horse: Lou Gehrig in His Time* (New York: W.W. Norton, 1990), 149.

33. *New York Daily News*: September 3, 1927.

34. Interview with Shirley Povich, May 12, 1997, Washington DC.

35. Swindell, "1929 Athletics," 25–26.

36. Joseph Lawler, "Joe Dugan," in Shatzkin, *Ball Players*, 296.

37. *Sporting News*: July 7, 1927.

38. *Sporting News*: September 22, 1927. Foxx's home run against the White Sox was the first of many that would be compared to Babe Ruth's prodigious blasts.

39. Lieb, *Connie Mack*, 212–13; and Collins interview.

40. *Philadelphia Evening Bulletin*: September 16, 1927.

41. *Philadelphia Inquirer*: April 21, 1927.

42. *Philadelphia Evening Bulletin*: June 25, 1927.

43. *Sporting News*: July 7, 1927.

44. *Sporting News*: November 10, 1927.

45. *Philadelphia Inquirer*: November 1, 1927; and *Sporting News*: November 10, 1927.

46. Stump, *Cobb*, 393.

Chapter 4

1. Interview with Frank Cunningham (son-in-law of Connie Mack): July 20, 1995, Ambler, PA; interview with Rudolph Baizley (Connie Mack Jr.'s childhood friend): December 9, 1997, Philadelphia, PA; and Paul Gallico, "MaGillicuddy: The Three Decade Pennant Winner of Baseball," *Liberty Magazine:* January 11, 1930 73.

2. Baizley interview.

3. Interview with Ruth Clark: December 26, 1997, Ambler, PA.

4. Cunningham interview.

5. Cunningham interview.

6. Clark interview.

7. Interview with the Reverend Jerome Romanowski, June 24, 1997, Malaga, NJ.

8. Clark Interview.

9. Eddie Collins, "Connie Mack and His Mackmen," *The American Magazine* (no date): 18.

10. Clark interview.

11. *Philadelphia Record*: May 17, 1941.

12. Lieb, *Connie Mack*, 52.

13. Mack, *Baseball Book*, 31.

14. Smith in Nelson, "Connie Mack Story."

15. Mack, *Baseball Book*, 156–57.

16. *Sporting News*: March 8, 1928; and Stump, *Cobb*, 393–95.

17. *Sporting News*: February 9, 1928.

18. *Sporting News*: March 1, 1928.

19. *Sporting News*: April 5, 1928.

20. *Ibid.*; and Daniel, *Jimmie Foxx*, 29.

21. *Sporting News*: April 5, 1928.

22. Reidenbaugh, *Baseball's Greatest Teams*, 36.

23. *New York American*: April 13, 1928; and Stump, *Cobb*, 396.

24. Astor, "Second Dynasties," 160.

25. *Sporting News*: June 7, 14, 1928.

26. *Philadelphia Evening Bulletin*: August 13, 1928; and Jimmie Foxx, "The Secret to Slugging Power," *Baseball Magazine* (August 1934): 394.

27. Interview with Joe Hauser, January 19, 1997, Sheboygan, Wisconsin.

28. John Pierce, "Joe Hauser: Home Run King of the Minors," *Baseball Digest* (Feb. 1974): 70–76.

29. Collins interview.

30. Babe Ruth, *Babe Ruth Story*, 164–65.

31. Leo Durocher, *Nice Guys Finish Last* (New York: Simon & Schuster, 1978), 48–50.

32. Hauser interview.

33. *Philadelphia Inquirer*: September 10, 1928.

34. Collins interview.

35. Durocher, *Nice Guys Finish Last*, 53.

36. *Philadelphia Evening Bulletin*: September 12, 1928.

37. Stump, *Cobb*, 398; Cobb, *My Life in Baseball*, 258.

38. Ruth, *Babe Ruth Story*, 159–60; and Ruth quoted in Creamer, *Babe*, 310.

39. Creamer, *Babe,* 318–19. When the newspaper headlines disclosed Ruth's

rebuff of Hoover, Christy Walsh prepared a statement for Ruth, apologizing for the misunderstanding and later had the Bambino oblige the picture-taking request. Walsh was concerned that Ruth's behavior would damage his credibility with the Republican newspapers that carried his syndicated column.

40. Dykes quoted in *Sporting News*: September 27, 1928; and Dykes, *Can't Steal First*, 32–33.

Chapter 5

1. *Sporting News*: February 28, 1929.
2. *Sporting News*: April 18, 1929.
3. Dykes, *You Can't Steal First Base*, 53.
4. Povich interview.
5. Dykes, *You Can't Steal First Base*, 29–30; Astor, "Second Dynasties," 159.
6. Paul Dickson, *Baseball's Greatest Quotations* (New York: HarperCollins, 1991), 171.
7. Shatzkin, *Ball Players*, 204.
8. Gorman, *Double X*, 28.
9. Cramer quoted in Astor, "Second Dynasties," 157.
10. Reidenbaugh, *Baseball's Greatest Teams*, 35; and Mack, *Baseball Book*, 203.
11. Reidenbaugh, *Baseball's Greatest Teams*, 35.
12. Gorman, *Double X*, 21.
13. Astor, "Second Dynasties," 160.
14. Lieb, *Connie Mack*, 222.
15. *Sporting News*: March 21, April 11, 1929.
16. Gorman, *Double X*, 23.
17. *Sporting News*: May 2, 1929; and *Philadelphia Inquirer*: April 23, 1929.
18. *Sporting News*: May 9, 1929.
19. *Sporting News*: June 6, 1929.
20. *Sporting News*: June 20, 1929
21. *Philadelphia Evening Bulletin*: May 2, 1929.
22. *Sporting News*: June 14, 1929.
23. Terry Bitman, "Mr. Mack & Company," *Philadelphia Inquirer*: June 13, 1997.
24. Lieb, *Connie Mack*, 221.
25. *Sporting News*: March 24, 1938.
26. *Philadelphia Record*: July 25, 1929.
27. Dooley in *Philadelphia Record*: July 25, 1929.
28. *Sporting News*: August 8, 15, 22, September 5, 1929.
29. *New York Times*: September 26, 1929; *Sporting News*: October 3, 1929; and Creamer, *Babe*, 346–47.
30. Ruth, *Babe Ruth Story*, 175.
31. Kuklick, *To Everything a Season*, 57–58.

Chapter 6

1. *Sporting News*: September 26, October 3, 1929.

2. Frederick Lieb, *The 1929 Chicago Cubs World Series Program* (Santa Clara, CA: RDO Publications, 1983), 11.

3. Lieb, Connie Mack, 223.

4. Nelson, "Connie Mack Story"; Connie Mack in John Carmichael, *My Greatest Day in Baseball* (New York: Grosset & Dunlap, 1951), 127–28; *Sporting News*: October 17, 1929; Schoor, *History of the World Series*, 130; and Lieb, *Connie Mack*, 223.

5. Reidenbaugh, *Baseball's Greatest Teams*, 38.

6. Nelson, "Connie Mack Story."

7. Reidenbaugh, *Baseball's Greatest Teams*, 38–39.

8. Mack, *Baseball Book*, 53, 91; Mack quoted in Carmichael, *My Greatest Day in Baseball*, 127.

9. Westcott, *Philadelphia's Old Ballparks*, 136.

10. Michael Gershman, "Steeling Home: Shibe Park and Forbes Field," *Athelon 1996 Baseball Annual*, 56–57.

11. *Ibid.*, 58; and Kuklick, *To Everything a Season*, 73–74.

12. Schoor, *History of the World Series*, 131; and Dykes, *Can't Steal First*, 39.

13. Schoor, *History of the World Series*, 132.

14. Mack, *Baseball Book*, 47–48.

15. Dykes, *You Can't Steal First*, 64–65; and Mack, *Baseball Book*, 48.

16. *Sporting News*: October 17, 1929

17. Cox, *Lively Ball*, 181.

18. Barrett interview.

19. Interview with Wayne Ambler, June 11, 1997, Ponte Vedra Beach, FL.

20. Lieb, *Connie Mack*, 228.

21. Kuklick, *To Everything a Season*, 58–59.

22. Norman H. Clark, *Deliver Us from Evil: An Interpretation of American Prohibition* (New York: W.W. Norton, 1976).

23. *Philadelphia Public Ledger*: October 15, 1929; see also Lieb, *Connie Mack*, 228–29.

24. Dykes, *You Can't Steal First*, 43–44.

25. *Ibid.*

26. Lieb, *Connie Mack*, 38.

27. Dykes, *You Can't Steal First*, 43.

28. *Ibid.*; and Astor, "Second Dynasties, 160–61.

29. Schoor, *History of the World Series*, 133.

Chapter 7

1. Tinkcom, "Depression and War, 1929–46," in *Philadelphia: A 300 Year History*. Edited by Russell F. Weigley (New York: W.W. Norton, 1982), 601–13.

2. Joseph P. Barrett, "The Sweeper," Roman Catholic High School Alumni News (Spring/Summer 1993), 5.

3. Kuklick, *To Everything a Season*, 77; Clark interview; and Barrett interview.

4. Westcott, *Philadelphia's Old Ballparks*, 163.

5. *Sporting News*: February 20, 1930.

6. Nelson, "Connie Mack Story" (audio tape).

7. *Philadelphia Bulletin*: June 2, 1970.

8. Mack, *Baseball Book*, 186-87.
9. *Sporting News*: February 26, 1931.
10. *Philadelphia Bulletin*: March 21, 1930; and Cochrane quoted on Nelson, "Connie Mack Story" (audio tape).
11. Quoted by Cochrane on Nelson, "Connie Mack Story," (audio tape).
12. *Sporting News*: May 8, 1930; and Babe Ruth, *Babe Ruth Story*, 176–77, 183.
13. *Sporting News*: June 5, 1930.
14. *Sporting News*: June 5, 1930.
15. Carmichael, *My Greatest Day in Baseball*, 191–92; and Reidenbaugh, *Baseball's Greatest Teams*, 40.
16. *Sporting News*: July 31, 1930.
17. Baizley interview.
18. Dykes, *You Can't Steal First Base*, 18–19.
19. Baizley interview.
20. *Philadelphia Bulletin*: September 19, 1930.
21. *Philadelphia Bulletin*: September 23, 1930.
22. Collins Jr. interview.
23. Gershman, "Steeling Home," 38; *Philadelphia Bulletin*: October 1, 1930; and *Philadelphia Public Ledger*: September 29, 1930.
24. Lieb, *Connie Mack*, 236.
25. *Philadelphia Bulletin*: October 6, 1930; *Sporting News*: October 16, 1930; and Dykes, *You Can't Steal First Base*, 45.
26. *Philadelphia Bulletin*: October 7, 1930; *Sporting News*: October 16, 1930; and Carmichael, *My Greatest Day in Baseball*, 80–81.
27. Nelson, "Connie Mack Story" (audio tape).
28. Daniel, *Jimmie Foxx*, 31.
29. *Detroit News*: December 24, 1933.
30. *Sporting News*: December 11, 1930, January 1, 1931.

Chapter 8

1. Nemec, *Baseball Encyclopedia*, 146, 149; and Honig, *Baseball in the '30s*, 29.
2. *Sporting News*: April 16, July 23, 1931; and Honig, *Baseball in the '30s*, 32.
3. *Sporting News*: April 16, August 27, 1931.
4. *Sporting News*: July 30, September 24, 1931.
5. *Sporting News*: August 27, September 17, 24, 1931; and Norman L. Macht, "Doc Cramer," in Shatzkin, *The Ball Players*, 231.
6. Dykes, *You Can't Steal First Base*, 31.
7. *Philadelphia Bulletin*: August 24, 1931.
8. Norman L. Macht, "The Day Lefty Grove Ravaged a Clubhouse," *Baseball Digest* (September 1989): 58–60; Kuklick, *To Everything a Season*, 39–40; and Hal Lebovitz, "A Tribute to Lefty Grove, Baseball's Fierce Warrior," *Baseball Digest* (September 1975): 80.
9. Macht, "Day Grove Ravaged Clubhouse," 60.
10. Grove quoted in Paul Dickson, *Baseball's Greatest Quotations* (New York: Edward Burlingame Books, 1991), 171.

11. Daniel, *Jimmie Foxx*, 54–55.

12. Mack quoted in Lieb, *Connie Mack*, 241.

13. Interview with Jim McAndrews: January 14, 1996 at East Falls, Philadelphia, PA; and Barrett interview.

14. *Sporting News*: October 1, 1931.

15. *Sporting News*: October 1, 1931.

16. *Philadelphia Bulletin*: October 3, 1931: and *Sporting News*: October 8, 1931.

17. Gorman, *Double X*, 64.

18. Carmichael, *My Greatest Day in Baseball*, 145–46; *Philadelphia Bulletin*: October 8, 1931: *Sporting News*: October 15, 1931; and Schoor, *History of the World Series*, 141.

19. Dykes, *You Can't Steal First Base*, 51–52.

Chapter 9

1. Reidenbaugh, *Baseball's Greatest Teams*, 42.

2. *New York Times*: July 26, 1932.

3. *Philadelphia Evening Bulletin*: August 21, 1932.

4. *Sporting News*: July 21, 1932.

5. Foxx quoted in Gorman, *Double X*, 73.

6. "The Threat to Babe Ruth's Home Run Record," *Literary Digest* (August 12, 1933): 20.

7. Gorman, *Double X*, 75.

8. *New York Times*: May 10, 1932.

9. Connie Mack, "I'm Not Ready to Quit," *The Rotarian* (July 1932): 16–18.

10. Dykes, *You Can't Steal First*, 61–62.

11. *Philadelphia Evening Bulletin*: October 3, 1932.

12. Gorman, *Double X*, 78.

13. Dykes, *You Can't Steal First*, 77; Lieb, *Connie Mack*, 249, 255.

14. Lieb, *Connie Mack*, 249.

15. Daniel, *Jimmie Foxx*, 61.

16. *Philadelphia Evening Bulletin*: March 27, 1933; *Sporting News*: April 6, 1933.

17. *Philadelphia Evening Bulletin*: May 26, 1933.

18. Emil Rothe, "When Grove Finally Shut Out the Yankees," *Baseball Digest* (November 1973): 88–90.

19. Collins Jr. interview.

20. *Sporting News*: August 24 and November 9, 1933.

21. *Detroit News*: December 18, 24, 1933.

22. *Sporting News*: December 21, 1933.

23. *Sporting News*: December 21, 1933.

24. *Philadelphia Evening Bulletin*: December 18, 1933.

25. *Sporting News*: November 16, 1933.

26. *Sporting News*: April 19, 26, 1934.

27. Lieb, *Connie Mack*, 253; Creamer, *Babe*, 378–80; and Gorman, *Double X*, 92.

28. Creamer, *Babe*, 380.

29. Noel Hynd. "The Wall Went Up and the A's Came Tumbling Down," *Sports Illustrated* (August 17, 1987): 10.

30. *Sporting News*: February 22, 1934.

31. *Sporting News*: March 15, 29, 1934.

32. *Philadelphia Evening Bulletin*: January 15, 1935; *Sporting News*: February 7, 1935.

33. *Philadelphia Inquirer*: December 11, 1935.

34. Dykes, *You Can't Steal First Base*, 52.

35. *Ibid.*, 60–61.

36. Cunningham interview.

37. Kuklick, *To Everything a Season*, 63; and Kulick interview.

38. Mack quoted in Lieb, *Connie Mack*, 255.

Conclusion

1. Interview with James Michener, August 21, 1997, Austin, TX. See also Michener, *Sports in America* (New York, 1971), 253.

2. *New York Times*: May 26, 1937.

3. *Detroit Free Press*: May 27, 1937; *Philadelphia Evening Bulletin*: May 27, 1937.

4. Tom Jozwik, "Mickey Cochrane," in Shatzkin, *Ball Players*, 205.

5. Stump, *Cobb*, 411; *Philadelphia Evening Bulletin*: June 29, 1962.

6. Jack Kavanaugh, "Lefty Grove," in Shatzkin, *Ball Players*, 423.

7. *New York Daily News*: January 17, 1958.

8. Foxx quoted *ibid.*

9. Interview with Louis Verna (owner of Ehmke Manufacturing Co.) July 18, 1995, Philadelphia, PA.

10. Harry Robert, "The Philadelphia Athletics," *Sport Magazine* (February 1951): 28.

11. Cunningham interview.

12. *Philadelphia Evening Bulletin*: October 18, 1950.

13. *Philadelphia Evening Bulletin*: October 18, 1954; Ritter, *Lost Ball parks*, 183; and G. Edward White, *Creating the National Pastime. Baseball Transforms Itself, 1903–1953* (Princeton: Princeton University Press, 1996), 312–13.

14. Kelley, "And There Used to Be a Ballpark Right Here," *Philly Sport* (April 1990): 44–49, 64–66.

SELECTED
BIBLIOGRAPHY

Alexander, Charles C. *Ty Cobb*. New York: Oxford University Press, 1984.

Allen, Lee. *The American League Story*. New York: Hill & Wang, 1965.

Astor, Gerald. "Second Dynasties," in National Baseball Hall of Fame, *The Baseball Hall of Fame 50th Anniversary Book*. New York Prentice Hall, 1988.

Baseball Digest, 1974–1997.

Carmichael, John P. (Editor). *My Greatest Day in Baseball*. New York: Grosset & Dunlap, 1951.

Cobb, Ty, with Al Stump. *My Life in Baseball: The True Record*. New York: Doubleday, 1961.

Cochrane, Gordon S. *Baseball. The Fan's Game:* New York: Funk & Wagnall's, 1939.

Cox, James A. *The Lively Ball: Baseball in the Roaring Twenties*. Alexandria, VA: Redefinition Books, 1989.

Creamer, Robert W. *Babe: The Legend Comes to Life*. New York: Simon & Schuster, 1974.

Daniel, W. Harrison. *Jimmie Foxx: Baseball Hall of Famer, 1907–1967*. Jefferson, NC: McFarland, 1996.

Doyle, Ed. *Yanks '27 vs. A's '31*. Philadelphia: n.p., 1976.

Dykes, Jimmie, and Charles O. Dexter. *You Can't Steal First Base*. Philadelphia: J.B. Lippincott, 1967.

Fleming, G.H. *Murderer's Row: The 1927 New York Yankees*. New York: William Morrow, 1985.

Gershman, Michael. "Steeling Home: Shibe Park and Forbes Field," *Athelon 1996 Baseball Annual*, pp. 52–59.

Gorman, Bob. *Double X: Jimmie Foxx, Baseball's Forgotten Slugger*. New York: Bill Goff, 1990.

Honig, Donald. *Baseball in the '30s: A Decade of Survival*. New York: Crown, 1989.

Hynd, Noel. "The Wall Went Up and the A's Came Tumbling Down," *Sports Illustrated* (August 17, 1987): 10–13.

Kashatus, William C. "Philadelphia's Mr. Baseball and His Amazing Athletics," *Pennsylvania Heritage* (Summer 1990): 10–17.

Kelley, B.G. "And There Used to Be a Ballpark Right Here," *Philly Sport Magazine* (April 1990): 44–49.

Kuklick, Bruce. *To Everything a Season: Shibe Park and Urban Philadelphia, 1909 –1976.* Princeton: Princeton University Press, 1991.

Lieb, Frederick G. *Connie Mack: Grand Old Man of Baseball.* New York: G.P. Putnam's Sons, 1945.

Mack, Connie. *Connie Mack's Baseball Book.* New York: Alfred A. Knopf, 1950.

_____. "I'm Not Ready to Quit," *The Rotarian* (July 1932): 16–18.

_____. *My 66 Years in the Big Leagues.* Philadelphia: John C. Winston Co., 1950.

Nack, William. "The Team that Time Forgot," *Sports Illustrated* (August 19, 1996): 74–85.

Neft, David S. (Editor). *The Sports Encyclopedia: Baseball.* New York: Grosset & Dunlap, 1974.

Nemec, David (Editor). *20th Century Baseball Chronicle.* New York: Beekman House, 1991.

Philadelphia Bulletin, 1922–35.

Philadelphia Inquirer, 1927–35.

Philadelphia Public Ledger, 1927–32.

Philadelphia Record, 1927–35.

Philadelphia Sporting Writers' Association, *Connie Mack's Philadelphia Athletics, American League Champions of 1929.* Philadelphia: Philadelphia Sporting Writers' Association, 1930.

Reidenbaugh, Lowell. *Baseball's 25 Greatest Teams.* St. Louis: The Sporting News, 1988.

Ritter, Lawrence S. *Lost Ballparks: A Celebration of Baseball's Legendary Fields.* New York: Penguin Books, 1992.

Robert, Harry. "The Philadelphia Athletics," *Sport Magazine* (February 1951): 28–32.

Romanowski, Jerome C. *The Mackmen.* Delair, NJ: Baseball Padre, 1979.

Ruth, Babe, and Bob Considine. *The Babe Ruth Story.* New York: Penguin, 1992.

Schoor, Gene. *The History of the World Series.* New York: William Morrow, 1990.

Seymour, Harold. *Baseball: The Golden Age.* New York: Oxford University Press, 1971.

Shatzkin, Mike (Editor). *The Ballplayers: Baseball's Ultimate Biographical Reference.* New York: William Morrow, 1990.

Sheed, Wilfred. "Manager: Mr. Mack and the Main Chance," in *The Ultimate Baseball Book,* edited by Daniel Ikrent & Harris Lewine. Boston: Houghton Mifflin Company, 1981, pp. 105–20.

The Sporting News, 1926–1931.

Stump, Al. *Cobb: A Biography.* Chapel Hill, NC: Algonquin Books, 1994.

Sullivan, Neil J. *The Minors.* New York: St. Martin's Press, 1990.

Swindell, Larry. "The 1929 Athletics: Really the Greatest Ever," *Philadelphia Inquirer Magazine* (Sunday, August 15, 1976): 22–29.

Thorn, John, and Pete Palmer (Editors). *Total Baseball.* New York: Warner Books, 1989.

Trachtenberg, Leo. *The Wonder Team: The True Story of the Incomparable 1927 New York Yankees.* Bowling Green, OH: Bowling Green State University Popular Press, 1995.

Warner, Sam Bass. *The Private City: Philadelphia in Three Periods of Its Growth.* Philadelphia: University of Pennsylvania Press, 1968.

Weigley, Russell F. *Philadelphia: A 300 Year History.* New York: W.W. Norton, 1982.

Westcott, Rich. *Philadelphia's Old Ballparks.* Philadelphia: Temple University Press, 1996.

Wolff, Rick (Editor). *The Baseball Encyclopedia.* 8th edition, New York: Macmillan, 1990.

Yagoda, Ben. "The Legend of Connie Mack," *Philly Sport Magazine* (August 1989); 52–62.

INDEX